Catherine Seymour

The Staircase Girls

*The secret lives, heartaches and joy of the
Cambridge 'bedders'*

PAN BOOKS

First published 2016 by Pan Books
an imprint of Pan Macmillan
20 New Wharf Road, London N1 9RR
Associated companies throughout the world
www.panmacmillan.com

ISBN 978-1-5098-0291-3

Printed and bound by CPI Group (UK) Ltd, Croydon, CR0 4YY

In memory of my family of bedders:
Great-Nana Mizen, Nana Seymour,
Nana Adams and Aunty Shirley

Contents

Introduction 1

Joyce Jones *Cambridge, October 1952*
9

Ann Pilcher *Folkestone to Cambridge, 1937–40*
22

Rose Hobbs *1920s–40s*
40

Joyce *Redhill and Caterham, Surrey, September–October 1940*
56

Ann *Cambridge 1941*
67

Joyce *Redhill to Cambridge, January 1941*
79

Ann *Cambridge 1942–43*
90

Joyce *Cambridge 1941–46*
113

Maud Cooper *Cambridge 1945–50*
123

Ann *Cambridge 1945–47*
139

Contents

Joyce *Cambridge 1946–53*
154

Rose *Cambridge 1954*
165

Maud *Cambridge 1950–55*
175

Audrey Perry *Cambridge 1955–56*
186

Rose *Cambridge 1959–63*
201

Audrey *Cambridge 1960*
209

Ann *Cambridge 1948–62*
218

Joyce *Cambridge 1953–62*
228

Audrey *Cambridge 1962–63*
239

Maud *Cambridge 1960–68*
251

Ann *Cambridge 1962 onwards*
262

Audrey *Cambridge 1965–70s*
273

Rose *Cambridge 1965–66*
286

Contents

Joyce *Cambridge 1962 onwards*
295

Audrey *Cambridge 1974 onwards*
307

Acknowledgements 321

Bibliography 325

Introduction

One of my earliest memories is of being five years old and sitting on a freshly made single bed, in a tiny room at a major Cambridge college, watching my nana, Ann 'Nance' Adams, as she went through her daily cleaning routine. A 'bedder' of some years, she looked smart in her starched tabard and smelled of my early childhood – a mix of lavender and carbolic soap. I sat transfixed by the smooth efficiency of her movements, as she picked up clothes from the floor, which needed vacuuming, emptied the bin ready for the next deposit of scrapped notes and wiped the surface of the desk in preparation for more studying. I always hoped to catch one of my nana's infectious grins in those days, so I'd stare at her when I should have been reading, just in case she gave me one of her smiles. I think she liked my company; I know I liked hers.

It was 1976 and Ann was a mother of four; almost fifty, and looked a lot older. Life had not been easy so far. Her two youngest children suffered with epilepsy. Kenny had contracted meningitis at five years old and was left permanently brain damaged. The second youngest, known to all as 'our Shirl', was struck on the head by a swing while playing at the park when she was eight years old, and was never the same after that. Her eldest (and my mum), Glenis, was Ann's 'rock', but she missed a lot of schooling in order to help look after the youngest two children. Then there was Dorothy, who Ann worried about because she suffered with ill health.

Over the years I watched my nana at work during the school holidays and on days when a persistent ear infection kept me from school. That was when I learned a lot about our family, and saw the great affection she had for her students. She would tell me her fears for the family and the hopes and dreams she once had for herself, before snapping out advice about marriage and children, half-informed by her observation of her students. 'Don't you dare get married early, Catherine!' she'd exclaim. 'You must study and travel the world. You have to have a life before children. Wait until you are at least thirty-five. Keep your hand on your ha'penny, my girl!'

She drummed that into me from an early age, maybe even as early as 1976. A lot of it stuck, perhaps too well. At the age of eighteen I left my family behind in the working-class area of Barnwell in Cambridge, performing with Cambridge Youth Theatre and other theatre companies before becoming the first female in the family to attend university. After graduating from drama school, I stayed in London and worked in television. But I always knew that there'd be a welcome in the homes of my extended family when I returned, and particularly in that of my Aunt Shirley, who followed her mother into the business of being a bedder.

From our Shirl I sometimes heard intriguing tales of the comings and goings, loves, hates and peculiarities of her 'boys', as she called the students on her staircase at college. I enjoyed hearing how one boy had been discovered with a girl in his room, or how another had simply disappeared without trace for a few days, only to return and claim to not remember anything. But I was too busy making my way in London to be really interested in people of Cambridge who were not family or close friends.

Like many of her friends and family before her, Aunt Shirley remained in the same job and worked the same stair-case for decades. She did so because, while the job was hard – until the 1980s bedders were expected to carry buckets of coal up the stairs to set fires in the grate for fellows in their rooms, as well as dust, tidy, take away rubbish and in some colleges, make the students' breakfasts – it came with privileges and offered an experience unlike other jobs available to her class and gender. Some women who became bedders previously worked in shops or as waitresses, cleaners, factory hands or at similarly low-paid, manual work that demanded an 8–4 or 9–5 shift (some took on seasonal work such as picking fruit during the summer months when colleges were closed). Once employed by a college though, they, like Aunt Shirley, appreciated the more family-friendly hours that being a bedder brought. Starting early, but home in time for the midday meal, they could cook dinner for their children, for one thing. Or if their kids had school dinners, they could get on with the housekeeping at home after work, and have tea ready and waiting at the end of the school day. Often bedders with pre-school children would pay a neighbour to mind them while they worked. Many informal pre-school playgroups existed in areas where a number of bedders with similarly aged children lived, usually run by a child minder who had perhaps retired from other work, or for whom childcare was the only way to earn a living.

As well as working hours that suited working mums, bedders enjoyed certain perks that went with their job. For some, getting to know the occupants of the rooms that they cleaned and the beds they made was a perk in itself, allowing as it did a glimpse into a world of which they had little knowledge or experience. A few bedders I met while doing research for this project resented the way that students 'looked down' on them, and as a result were reluctant to engage in anything but necessary communication with students and masters. But for the very many, who not only cleaned but also dispensed advice, physical aid and a reassuring maternal presence, they found a return of affection, and at Christmas, end of term or on graduation there would be small parcels addressed to their bedder left in newly vacated rooms. For the bedders who really got to know their students, graduation was almost like watching their own children leave home.

For most of the twentieth century, in getting to know their students so well, Cambridge University's bedders were the only members of their social class to have close-up, intimate contact with the chosen few who made it into the hallowed halls and quads of the 800-year-old institution. It is true that many of the upper-class students (and masters and fellows) who attended Cambridge in the first half of the twentieth century saw bedders as simply the latest of the 'servant class' to engage with, having grown up with nannies, governesses, butlers and maids. However, for many others, the women who roused them from sleep and instructed them in how to do everything from dressing properly to combing their hair and tying their shoe-laces, and who kept their living quarters habitable, were exotic, strange and the only faintly maternal presence in an otherwise lonely and paternalistic environment.

I knew from hearing the stories that Aunt Shirley, Nana and their friends told that there was a unique relationship between bedders and students that the multitude of 'Town vs Gown' books and articles never even hinted at. I was prompted to begin exploring the intriguing living history of bedders in 2008 when our Shirl – then a fifty-six-year-old mother of two and a recent grandmother – failed to turn up for work one Thursday.

We know that the day started for Aunt Shirley as it usually did: she was woken at 5 a.m. by the sound of the alarm clock that sat on the landing outside her bedroom door – kept there, she always said, so she didn't have to hear the incessant tick-tock that it made throughout the night. It seems that she went about her routine as usual, getting out of bed to turn the alarm clock off before going downstairs to make herself a cup of tea. Then Shirley returned to her bedroom with her tea, because she liked to have a 'leisurely' morning before her journey on the first bus at six o'clock from Arbury to start work at Sidney Sussex College for half past six. She always began with the cleaning of the chapel, the part of her duties which, along with looking after the chaplain's cat, she was most proud of. 'You know Oliver Cromwell's head is buried in my chapel, don't you?' she'd ask me on my frequent visits from London, never forgetting to add, 'You can come in anytime.' But Aunt Shirley never made it into her beloved chapel that day, because she collapsed and died on her bedroom floor. We are still unsure why.

When the news broke, we were helped enormously through the grief we felt by seeing the love that was held for our Shirl and the support given to us by the domestic staff, the students and the chaplain at the college. They all insisted that the flag should be flown at half mast during the beautiful funeral service, which was held for Shirley in the chapel that she so loved. It was made very clear that it wasn't only us, her family, who would miss her but also her 'family' at Sidney Sussex.

Inspired and surprised by the clear bond that existed between my aunt and her employers – something that increasingly few of us ever get to experience, I think – I decided to make a short film that explored and celebrated the life and work of Cambridge's bedders, aiming to finish it in time for the university's 800th anniversary in 2009. So my serious research into the role of the Cambridge bedmaker began, and it wasn't long before I discovered another family tie to the occupation. While searching the nineteenth-century archives of the *Cambridge News* I spotted the eerily familiar features of my paternal great-grandmother in a photograph. She was seated among a group of fellow bedders, and I hadn't known that she too had worked at the colleges until that moment.

After weeks of research I became extremely frustrated, though. While there were a few photographs and passing comments about bedders made by ex-students and masters, I could find very few personal stories told by the bedders. I decided to gather as many first-person stories as I could from the women who play an integral, but largely unseen and unsung, part in the everyday life of the university, even if they couldn't all be included in the film, simply titled *The Bedders*. Beginning with my own family, I was introduced to bedders going back three generations. From them I heard stories that are in turns joyous, heartbreaking, revealing, sometimes gob-smacking and often very funny. There are enough to fill a book, or two, I thought.

In gathering stories from the bedders who worked from after the Second World War to the present day, I have heard tales of personal tragedy, vicarious triumph, small victories and failures, huge generosity, births, deaths and marriages, all taking place against a backdrop of a strangely unchanging society secreted away from what, to them, was often a fluctuating and sometimes bewildering world.

For me, the voices of the bedders of Cambridge that are gathered together in this book add a vital and unique strand to the history of the university. At the same time, they provide an extraordinary glimpse into working-class life in the latter half of the twentieth century. These are personal histories told by families of women who have touched the lives of thousands of men and women with whom they had little in common, but on whom they have left a lasting impression. From John Keats to Prince Charles, world-changing scientists, prize-winning authors and the greatest legal minds of generations have all had reason to bless their luck in having a bedder to help them stay the course of their studies. The bedders know, but they rarely make a fuss about it. After each graduation, they'll have a cup of tea and wonder who will be on their staircase next year. They are remarkable women with remarkable stories to tell. Here are just a few of them.

CATHERINE SEYMOUR, 2016

JOYCE JONES

Joyce Jones leaned her black Triumph bicycle against a wall, and shivered in the foggy, early dawn light. Glancing up at the enormous wooden, carved gate, she hesitated. While it wasn't the first job that she had begun, it was the first to take her into the colleges that were firmly closed to people like her. This was a secret world she was about to enter, as she'd been told by more than one person, her mum included. People inside here had all the rights, while the likes of her had none. Some of the students, she'd heard, had taken advantage of girls from the town and got away with it because of who they were, or who their parents were. They'd get girls merry with gin and beer and, while some of the girls might say no, others might not. The students on the other side of this door had a bad reputation, alright. They also had money and didn't need the ration cards that Joyce and her family were still dependent on, and would remain so until well into next year. Or so people said.

Apprehension filled Joyce with a stiffness that she'd never felt when serving the young gentlemen from behind the counter at Woolies. That counter and her uniform somehow kept her separate and safe from them, even though sometimes a boy would squeeze her hand as she took money from them – one mad boy in his cape and tweed jacket had even quoted poetry at her as she tried to take his thruppence ha'penny. Now she was about to go into their rooms – their bedrooms, too – all alone, maybe even without a uniform to protect her.

It's a shame about that job in Woolies, she thought, her fingers rising to trace the scar on her neck, still raw from the operation. She'd caught septicaemia in an accident at work and nearly died. Her mum was definite that she couldn't go back there after that, and told her that their neighbour Maud knew about an old lady who was retiring from her job as a bedder. As her mum said, 'You're young and fit enough to go up and down them twisty stairs – the old lady can't do them any more, reckons Maudie.' And that was it, as far as Joyce's mum was concerned.

So here she was, hours before anyone else had to go to work, feeling cold and thinking about the job she'd loved, especially meeting customers – or most of them anyway. Joyce had really liked chatting with her friends who worked behind the counter. They'd be having a right laugh on their way to the shop this morning without her, she thought, before realizing that they wouldn't even be getting up for another hour or more. Lucky sods. Her breath left her in plumes, and she felt the cold creep up through the thinning soles of her 'sensible' shoes – which were a half size too big, because they were her mum's and the only ones in the house that her mum said would do for running up and down stairs all day.

Was that what she'd be doing, then, running up and down stairs, wondered Joyce. Hard to imagine that being the case since the old biddy that she was taking over from was well into her eighties, and Maud had said she moved with as much speed as the milkman's old horse. Joyce really had no idea of what being a bedder entailed. She guessed that she had to make beds, that much was obvious, and clean the rooms and lug coal to make fires – but she did that at home anyway, and it didn't seem much like a job that anyone would pay her for. But apparently the colleges would (and a whopping £5 a week, too). Staring at the door in front of her, she wondered, where were the stairs in there? Was this old place built like a house inside, then?

The cold air, deadened by the fog, gathered around Joyce as she stood uncertainly, wondering whether to bang on the stupid big door with her fist, or if there was a bell somewhere.

'Can I help you, miss?'

Joyce almost jumped out of her skin, and turned to see a smartly dressed man in a black overcoat and bowler hat. In his mid-thirties, she thought (old, anyway), he was peering intently at her, his hands behind his back.

'Er, no. I mean yes, that is . . .' Joyce's mind went blank. What was the name of the old woman she was supposed to meet?

'Are you looking for someone, miss?' the man asked in his slightly stuck-up voice. He wasn't posh, Joyce could tell, but he was talking as if he wanted to be.

'Yes!' Joyce rushed her words: 'An old woman, a bedder, I'm here to learn the job, take over from her doing for the young gentlemen, you see.'

The man stood up straight and looked down his nose at her. 'Oh.'

He turned, pulled open a small door cut into the big one, leaned in and shouted, 'Trevor! There's a new bedder here, for old Annie.' He looked over his shoulder at Joyce, jerked his head to motion her inside, and held the door open wider. Inside the little door, under an arch that was as deep as her bedroom at home, Joyce gawped at a big expanse of green grass. Straight paved footpaths cut through it, making squares of lawn.

Surrounding her was a building that looked like a church, with leaded windows, carvings on the walls, and turrets and crows silently perched along the top of the slate roof which loomed high in the air. They're watching me, she thought, and almost blurted out 'Blimey!', but noticed that the man in the bowler hat had opened another door a few feet to her right and was walking through it, so she turned and moved towards him. Joyce got to the door just as it was closing, and pushed her way through, into what looked like a cobbler's shop, with a wooden counter in front of a wall of wooden boxes out of which poked papers and envelopes. Between the boxes and the counter she could see a single bar electric heater that stood in front of a hard chair, which blocked the entrance to another, even smaller room, lined with more wooden shelves and boxes. Joyce could feel her cheeks flushing, her face getting hot. The thin, utility-issue overcoat that she wore started to lose the sheen of water that the dense fog had left on it as it soaked into the material. The man in the bowler hat moved round to the other side of the counter, took off his overcoat – though not his hat – and hung it inside the smaller room behind him. He looked Joyce up and down with a blank expression.

'You're a bit younger than we're used to seeing here,' he told her. 'Quite a bit younger in fact. How old are you anyway?'

Uh-oh, thought Joyce, so it's true that you have to be ancient before they let you work as a university servant. No point in lying, she thought, and said firmly, 'I'm nearly seventeen,' and stood up straight, jutting out her chin, even though she knew that in doing so her scar could be clearly seen. She was properly grown up, she wanted to tell him. She thought of telling him that she remembered serving him when she was a waitress at Lyons two years ago (she hadn't, but he wouldn't remember), or that she thought she knew him from Saturday night dances at the Rex – but then he might think she was one of those girls who went with the Yanks from the air base. Instead, she sniffed, and tried to look haughty. Half a smile disfigured the man's face.

'I'm Percy,' he said. 'Pleased to meet you . . . ?'

'Joyce.'

'Well, pleased to meet you, nearly seventeen Joyce. I'm what the boys here call a bulldog, but don't worry, I only bite them that deserve it. I bark a lot more, and at everyone and anyone who comes into these here grounds. This is my yard, if you like, and I have to patrol it. It's up to me and Bill to keep things running smoothly, and on time. Otherwise we'd be in a right state, wouldn't we?'

Joyce smiled lightly, and didn't think she was expected to answer. He's not as tough as he wants me to think he is, she thought. Percy continued, leaning with both fists on the counter, tipping onto his toes just like she'd seen a police sergeant do at the Regent Street station when she and her mum had gone in to see them about her next-door neighbours' shouting and fighting last Sunday morning.

'Good to see that you're nice and early, Joyce, and if you keep that up you'll be alright with me. As long as you don't get up to anything untoward concerning the boys or masters – or anyone else here, come to that – you and me will get on just fine. Right?' Percy's raised eyebrows made his hat bob up to comical effect. Joyce could only agree, 'Right,' and stopped short of indignantly proclaiming, 'Untoward? How dare you, I'll just be cleaning and making beds!'

Percy moved back around to Joyce's side of the counter and opened the door again, motioning her into the archway. He pointed across the grass to the building opposite, and a doorway that was another arch, although much, much smaller than the one she was stood under now. The quadrangle somehow resisted the fog, which appeared to have stopped at the front gate. It was shut out like the rest of the world, thought Joyce. 'Take this path past the big oak tree to staircase B,' he told her. 'They all have letters on them, keep going left until you reach it, then go in, there's a door on the left and you should find the old woman, tell her who you are and she'll get you started.'

He stood watching Joyce (she knew he would) as she started along the path towards the big tree. Hope his silly hat falls off when he's talking to the next person to come in, she thought, as she walked with a straight back and stiff arms towards the dark entry to staircase B.

Inside the cold, dark corridor she saw a dim light coming through a crack in the door on her left, and knocked on it. An old, tired voice half-whispered, ''Ave yer clocked in?'

Joyce craned her neck through the door and tried to see where the voice was coming from. She half-shouted in reply, 'No, I've just been sent over here to you – I'm the new girl.'

There was a snort and a short, almost square figure shuffled towards Joyce. 'C'mon, this way 'ere.'

Joyce stepped away from the door and the brown-coated figure moved slowly past her towards the staircase on the right. The old woman began a halting, panting, climb up well-worn stone steps, half-hauling herself along by a dull metal rail. Joyce stepped slowly behind her, in no need of the rail, listening to the broken wheeze grow louder above the echoing slap of the old woman's feet as they rose into the dark recesses of the stairwell. At the first proper landing (having gone through one half landing turn), the old woman paused, leaned back slightly and panted, 'Here y'are.' A gnarled finger pointed to a plain wooden door about twenty feet away. Joyce looked at the door and back at the woman, who'd set her eyes on the stone floor at her feet, breathing deeply, getting her breath back. Noticing that Joyce hadn't moved, the old woman impatiently waved at the door again. 'Thas yer gyp room,' she said as if talking to a child. 'Get in there and find a bucket an' fill it up, pick up yer mop and come back 'ere. Might as well get yer begun, we in't got all day.'

'What's a gyp room, missus?' Joyce had never heard the name before.

'Is where the gentlemen's breakfast and tea used to git made by their gyps, back in the old days, when they was proper gents and had money to pay for men to run, fetch and carry for 'em. They reckon gyp is on account of a uniform their servants used to wear with all buttons on the front, what had some French word for 'em. Anyways, nowadays is our tea room and they can use it sometimes if they wants, but they don't seem to know how to do anything for theirselves. We keeps our stuff in there, so in you go.'

Just as Joyce made to enter the room a smiling, middle-aged lady came towards them. Nodding at the old woman, she turned to Joyce.

'Hello dear, I'm Mrs Atkins the housekeeper here. My, you do look young! Maud said you were, but I wasn't expecting you to be a child, practically. Well, never mind, you'll certainly be able to run up and down these stairs, won't you? Now, are you being looked after?' Joyce nodded and noticed that the old woman was making her way into the gyp room.

'Lovely,' continued Mrs Atkins. 'You'll be shown where everything is, which is usually all in there,' she half-turned towards the door through which the old woman had disappeared without another word. 'If you run low on anything, come and find me and I'll make sure that you get new supplies. You'll be cleaning before anything else, and making the beds or stripping them last, when the boys have gone off to lectures for nine o'clock, and when you've done, just get yourself off home. It'll usually take you three hours to do your floors, which are this and the one above – the ground floor will still be done by old Annie.' Mrs Atkins leaned in closer to Joyce and whispered, 'She's slow now, but still a damned good bedder, and she hasn't got anything else in her life – no husband and no pension – so we'll keep her here for as long as she wants and is able. Now . . .' she straightened up and stepped back, folded her arms and appraised Joyce with half-closed eyes. Quickly taking in Joyce's thick brown stockings, dark blue calf-length gabardine skirt, navy school jumper over a white blouse and those flat shoes, Mrs Atkins assessed her size and said, 'I'll find you an overall to wear that you'll have to take home and wash yourself. Come find me when you've finished, and I hope you enjoy it. Ta-ta for now!' With that the housekeeper stepped around Joyce and made her way down to the ground floor.

Joyce walked over to the gyp room and peered in. 'She seems nice,' she said to old Annie's back, which presented an impenetrable wall to her.

'Humph,' the old woman turned with a mop in one hand and a bucket, sloshing soapy water, in the other. 'You working today or in't you? Here, get on wiv it.'

Joyce took them, stepped back and stood quietly, thinking she might not be able to stand much of this job as she was given a quick, brutal run down of what she was expected to do. 'Wash the stairs, then the washing up, tidy the sitting rooms, but be quiet till they wake up. Scrub the floors when yer've swept 'em if they're asleep. Clean the grate and lay a fire, then make sure the gyp room is clean and tidy so's the boys can make their breakfast when they get up.' Boys? Joyce thought, how old are they, then, fifteen, sixteen? 'An' if they're not up in time for their lekchers at nine, you get 'em all up.'

What have I let myself in for? Joyce wondered, as she took the heavy metal pail into the stairwell, and climbed to the next landing to start cleaning from the top down. And not even a cuppa. The old bag.

It was still cold as Joyce began, and she could feel her lungs taking time to warm up. As she moved her mop across each step her breath began to appear in clouds. At the bottom of the stairs the old woman stood, looking up at her through the slowly lifting gloom. No clouds of breath escaped her pursed lips, Joyce noticed as she mopped. The old lady watched in silence for a while, and then called up to her, ''Ow old are yer, then?' Joyce had been warned by Maud that her being so young would make her something of a surprise for not just the students, but especially the masters and staff. Bedders, she was told, were always older women, until recently at least, what with the war and all that.

'Eh? 'Ow old?' Joyce stopped sloshing her mop, straightened up and spoke into the grey-white air, 'I'm sixteen-and-a-half, missus.'

'Humph,' the old woman grunted. 'Don't know what they're thinking lettin' you in 'ere.' She clucked, and went on, her face indistinct to Joyce. 'When I was your age they'd never let me in 'ere, they'd as soon arrest me for standin' around in Petty Cury as they would wave me into one of these places.'

Joyce said nothing, but continued mopping her way down the stairs. Like most people born and raised in Cambridge, she knew very little about the university except that it was powerful and only a very few townspeople ever got through the gates of a college. It was generally believed that there were different rules and even laws for the university, and that normal people like her had to be respectful of university folk or they might end up in trouble without knowing what they'd done wrong. She'd read in a book Maud had lent to her that university men had the right to go into town and arrest people, even as recently as her grandmother's day. Which made her wonder . . . Joyce stopped mopping.

'How old are you then?' she asked.

'Never yer mind, yer cheeky beggar. Let's just say I'm old enough to remember when that Daisy 'opkins gave 'em what for.'

'Daisy who?' Joyce thought the old woman might be a bit mad.

''Opkins!' barked the old girl. She moved away from the foot of the stairs, and said, 'Come and 'ave a cup a tea, yer doing alright.' Joyce picked up her pail and carried it with the mop sticking out up to the gyp room. She stood in the doorway while the old woman put a blackened kettle onto the single gas ring on the side of the stone sink. There was only one chair, so Joyce waited in the doorway.

The old woman was grumbling and mumbling, almost to herself. 'It was a crime the way them bulldogs would run after young girls in them days, chasin' 'em and callin' 'em whores and all. In the day as well as night-times, it got so yer couldn't go out in yer own town back then – they even 'rested the vice chancellor's own daughter! It were when I were a girl, about Daisy's age – yer, I was your age once. There was another one before 'er an all. 'Ow many sugars you want?' The old woman pulled a spoon out of the drawer in the small, well-scrubbed wooden table on which she stood the teapot, and reached to a shelf above the sink to a Kilner jar half-filled with granules of sugar.

'Another what?' Joyce felt herself getting lost. 'Er, two sugars please.' The old woman rustled towards the window, opened it slightly and pulled in a half-empty bottle of milk. 'Another girl put in the Spinning House after being caught by bulldogs in Petty Cury,' she continued. 'Just before Daisy it were. This one – Jane I think her name were – she escaped and ran away back 'ome to Suffolk, but do you know, the silly old bugger sent 'is men after 'er at home and they brought 'er back and put 'er in court for breaking out of jail.'

'What happened to her then?' Joyce was becoming intrigued.

'Well, she dint get off, but 'er lawyer gave the vice chancellor hell, and 'cused 'im of being no better than Russian secret police, so 'e did. I think she got a pardon off the 'ome sec'try an' all. An' she were only seventeen, as well.'

'But why were they being arrested?' asked Joyce.

''Cos they was young and out in Petty Cury – all the old tarts and the young 'uns did used to get blokes there, an' the students was always walking up an' down looking, or doing things with the girls. So them bulldogs in their silly 'ats used to run up and down, 'coosin' any woman of this an' that and sending young gentlemen 'ome with a clip round the ear.'

'Really? In Petty Cury?' Joyce couldn't imagine the narrow street which ran from the entrance of one of the oldest colleges, Christ's, to the market place, with its crumbling old buildings and busy shops, being such a place.

'Yer, and it weren't just the poor girls eiver what got arrested. I 'eard one year the students tried to 'ave a ball in Shelford and asked lots of 'spectable girls – dressmakers, maids and the like – to go to it, an' they sent a bus round to pick 'em up. But the proctor stopped the bus when it were full, got the boys off and drove it to the police station, where they kept all those nice girls in overnight. Well, they was wrong there, and one of the girls who was kept for days in the Spinning House tried to sue 'em for false arrest. After that, if the bulldogs was trying to 'rest a girl in town loads of people would go an' help her – lots of them got away. My own mum said she saw some blokes 'avin' a go at bulldogs in broad daylight once. Well, the proctors stopped looking for 'em for a few years 'cos they was getting beat up, bones broke an' everything by blokes looking to fight 'em in town.'

'So what about Daisy, then?' asked Joyce.

'Ah well, she was a smart girl, dressed all nice they reckon, an' at only seventeen she must have worked 'ard to get her smart dresses. She were well known to the bulldogs, and this one time they give 'er two weeks in the Spinning House, but she got out 'cos they dint write her charge prop'ly or something, and then she only went and sued 'em for wrong arrest! Well, it were all over the papers and everyone knew what the bulldogs were doing was wrong, so they stopped it. By the time I started 'ere after the first war, they couldn't arrest no one no more.'

Well, thought Joyce, plenty of people said that all young girls round town were only after the students for one thing or another. She'd felt the stare of the porters and bulldogs as she walked about town, whatever the time of the day, but especially at night. And she knew that there were some colleges that only let a woman who was a bedder get past the porter – they wouldn't have no girl students, no girls in the rooms, no girls in their colleges.

'So how come young 'uns like me get jobs like this?'

'It were the first war what did it,' Annie sniffed. 'All the married and old women left these jobs to do the men's work on farms, in hospitals an' factories. The colleges 'ad to get young 'uns in as bedders' assistants. That were the start of it, but not many as young as you 'ave been in 'ere, I'd say.'

Joyce felt slightly proud of herself. She was the only one of her friends who'd got a job at college, she thought. Maybe it was true what people were telling her, that Britain was changing at last, and getting better for young people. She knew that not everyone was happy about the likes of her being allowed into the bedrooms of smart and posh young gentlemen, and never would be she reckoned.

'Are yer done with that tea, then?' the old woman moved past her into the hallway, forcing Joyce out of the doorway. 'Yes,' she put the cup in the sink. 'What's next, then?'

''Ass nearly eight in't it? Go and see what them boys doin'

and if they ain't out of bed yet. But you watch 'em, don't let 'em get up to anything with yer.'

Yes, thought Joyce, I know the likes of you – if any of the boys did get up to something with me then everyone round town would soon know about it, wouldn't they? As she walked along the corridor from the gyp room to the first door into a sitting room with two bedrooms off it, Joyce thought to herself, I'm not going in their bedrooms while they're in bed, or even if they're in there at all if I can help it. She opened the door, stood in the doorway and raised her voice, 'Hello? Hello – I'm Joyce, your new bedder!' The bedroom doors were open, and voices called out from each in reply, 'Hello!', 'Who?' Almost at the same time two men – not boys at all – appeared, one wearing striped pyjamas and scratching his head, his hair all over the place, the other in a shirt that hung out over his neatly pressed trousers, his hair flat if not neatly combed. 'Oh . . .' said the half-dressed man, 'Hmmm!' said the other.

Joyce felt a small shock and said, 'I'll come back when you're done dressing,' and she turned sharply to quick-step her way back to the gyp room, outside of which the old woman stood, watching to see how Joyce handled her first meeting with the 'boys'.

Lord, thought a rapidly blushing Joyce, why didn't Maud warn me that they might not be dressed when I got to work! She'd have to ask her when she got the chance, she decided, what was best to do when speaking to the 'boys' and they were in their PJs.

ANN PILCHER

Folkestone to Cambridge, 1937–40

Ann Pilcher, known as Nance to her family, was ten years old in 1937 when her mother told her that she was going to have to spend a long time at the hospital. For the previous two years Ann had made many visits to hospital, but she'd never had to stay in. This time though, her mum Grace said, she'd need to be kept in because, 'They have to do an operation on you, so's you can hear properly and it won't hurt no more.' Since a small child Ann had suffered almost constantly from earaches and fought infections in her ear, and she'd missed lots of school days due to pain and dizziness. Grace didn't know exactly what the problem was, but she just knew it could get to be as bad as her husband's hearing unless the doctors did something drastic for their eldest daughter. Jack Pilcher had been almost completely deafened by the field guns he operated during WWI. One eardrum had burst, and the other was severely lacking in effectiveness. It was just a matter of time before he'd lose his hearing altogether, Grace was always telling him.

Ann felt a mixture of hope and fear at the idea of an operation in hospital. Her bad ear had long prevented her from playing out with her sisters and their friends during the cold months, when the wind swept in off the sea and made her head ache something rotten. If having an operation meant that she'd be able to play just like the others, she'd be happy. On the other hand, the hospital smelled funny and she'd be kept away from her family for ages.

But when, early in 1937, doctors told Grace that they had to remove Ann's mastoid bone deep inside her ear, she'd readily agreed. As it turned out, the procedure couldn't be done in one go and Ann had to have a series of operations, and different stays in hospital over the following year. With each visit she got to like the hospital more, though. 'The nurses are lovely,' she told her sister Bet after the second stay, 'they even make me egg sandwiches if I really want one and no one ever tells me off. Not like Mum does, anyway.' After the final operation in 1938, Grace was told by the surgeons that they'd had to go so deep into her daughter's ear canal to clear the infection, that following it – as Grace later told Ann – 'you could get two fingers down the back, in there'. Which made Ann think of all the things that might get into her head. She determined there and then to keep that ear covered whatever it took, especially when it was windy or raining.

On the Sunday before she was due to be released from the hospital, Ann asked her mother when she'd be able to play outside with her sisters Bet and Rene, and brother Derek. 'It's been horrible only being able to see them and Dad through the window,' she said with feeling. Her siblings used to visit the park across the road from her ward on weekends, while Grace went up to see Ann. The children were lifted onto a bench by her dad who pointed to the window high up in the building, through which Ann would wave madly and they'd wave back at her, smiling madly as they did.

'Now Nance,' her mother said loudly, 'you're going to have to get better at my mum's for a month or more. I can't have you home all day, every day. I've got to go to work and I've got the others to think about, and as you can see I'm getting bigger every day.'

Ann nodded mutely at her pregnant mother. She didn't argue, she knew it was best not to, and instead thought about the train journey to Cambridge, where her mother's family all lived. She liked seeing the countryside fly by out of the train window, and really liked staying at Nana Wolfe's tiny house in Kettle's Yard, but she wouldn't see her sisters and brother at all. Fighting back tears, she tried to smile as her mother fussed about her, tidying her small, metal-framed bed with its two pillows and thick blankets. 'That'll be lovely,' Ann tried to sound brave.

Grace ignored her and pulled the blankets taut across the bed. 'Right then, tomorrow I'll come and collect you and we'll be off on the train. I'll go with you as far as London, then you'll be met at Cambridge by your aunties.'

After a fretful night, Ann got out of bed as dawn broke and dressed, ready for Grace to collect her. She couldn't eat any breakfast and cried a little as she said goodbye to the nurses, but Grace's no-nonsense mood had her daughter 'bucking up' and concentrating on catching the train to London in time. The pair sat silently looking away from each other during the journey, and Grace only muttered 'this way' and 'left' as they found the Tube line to King's Cross station. Once she'd put Ann on the train to Cambridge, Grace gave her a sandwich wrapped in newspaper and then pinned a piece of paper to her lapel with her name and where she was going to stay written in her broad print.

'Bye love, don't forget to ask the conductor to let you know when to get off,' Grace said briskly. Then she simply turned on her heels without kissing her daughter and headed to Waterloo station in order to be back in Folkestone for teatime.

Ann thought perhaps her mother was going to cry and didn't want her to see it. Ann cried, briefly and quietly as the train pulled out of the station, puffing smoke and clanking as it went. Then she settled into the corner of the cigarette-smelling carriage, trying not to rest her face against the prickly criss-crossed fabric of the seat by putting a handkerchief on the side of her head that was covered with her elasticated bandage.

Ann brightened immediately on seeing her Aunty Elsie and Aunt Edie at the tiny Cambridge station. She'd spent summer holidays with one or both of them ever since she could remember (Grace was glad to be free of looking out for her sickly eldest child) and Ann was delighted to be spoiled by her aunts and Nana Wolfe. They wouldn't let her play out much, but were always happy to bake scones for her.

Riding the bus into town, Ann sat quietly next to Edie and looked out of the window. It was her first time in Cambridge during the spring, when the university was mid-term. Five minutes into the journey, she began to giggle. 'What are them men doing wearing dresses?' she asked her aunt, who turned to look at the source of her amusement.

A look of puzzlement gave way to a smile, and Edie laughed. 'Oh, Nance, they're the scholars. That's gowns they're wearing, not dresses. They've come to Cambridge to get a good education, and they have to wear them.'

Ann thought it was strange that they had to wear a gown to get a good education, and Edie continued, 'It's tradition. They still do a lot of things that they did hundreds of years ago at the university.' She paused, pinched her niece's cheek and winked. 'So do us townies, though!'

Ann's gaze returned to the road, just as a scholar on a bicycle passed in the opposite direction. 'Aunty Edie!' she shouted, pointing at the cyclist. 'They'll do themselves an injury! They're going to get their gown caught in the wheel!'

'Goodness, you are a worrier!' Edie teased her. 'They have to wear them, Nance, otherwise the colleges don't know who's a townie and who's a gownie, and they got to know who's their boys!'

Ann noticed more men in gowns walking in and out of the big wooden gates set in castle-like walls that she'd never seen past, although she had daydreamed about them being the home to princes and princesses. Some of the dark grey buildings had statues and carvings on them like churches, and usually they were closed up and silent. Today, she saw that the windows and doors were open, giving tantalizing glimpses of green squares and clean paths as her bus rolled by them. 'Are there butlers and ladies-in-waiting in there, Aunty Edie?' she asked. 'I thought they was castles or churches . . .'

Edie smiled and looked across at her sister. Elsie answered with a laugh in her voice. 'No, luvvy, although there's churches inside them places, but they're all colleges, where the men in dresses . . .'

'Gowns!' shouted a delighted Ann.

'. . . sorry, gowns,' Elsie continued, 'who are students go to learn about important things the likes of which we don't understand.'

Edie snorted a laugh. 'Yeah, right, 'cept old Maggie who works in one of them places says the boys ain't got the sense they was born with!'

'Hush,' Elsie interrupted, 'the girl's got her ideas about the place, haven't you, Nance?'

She certainly had. With every lovely stone arch and old-looking wooden door that she passed, Ann thought the places looked magical. She barely noticed the shops in between each college.

Ann was intrigued by what went on in Cambridge colleges, and her curiosity only grew as the days at her aunt's and nana's house passed. The more she heard about students the more she wanted to know about them. According to her aunts they were from all over the country, wore fancy clothes, ate strange food and talked like the king. She would sometimes sit in the front garden and hope that her aunts would take her into town so she could look at the colleges where the scholars lived, but Grace had told her sisters that Ann had to have peace and quiet to get better, and town would be far too noisy for her. Afraid of the repercussions that disobeying their bossy big sister would bring, Elsie and Edie respected Grace's wishes and kept to their word. Ann didn't even get to see her other aunties and uncles who lived in Cambridge, although she loved talking to them almost as much as she did with her nana and granddad Samuel.

Although Ann was rarely taken into town, that didn't mean that she couldn't go out into the streets around their house and play during that mild season, although she preferred not to go too far from the passage in front of Nana's house. Embarrassed about the fabric strap she had to wear around her head to protect her ear from further infections, Ann explained to the local children, when they asked her to play with them, that she'd had a serious brain surgery and any activity could be dangerous. But Ann really liked adult company, anyway. During her spells in hospital she used to help nurses making beds and spent a large part of her day chatting to nurses about other patients' medical conditions. In Cambridge Ann helped her nana with the cooking or housework, when she wasn't whiling away the hours daydreaming about the colleges and the boys who studied there.

She had missed a lot of school in Folkestone over the years because of her mastoiditis, and being in Cambridge meant that she missed even more. Pretty much everything that Ann knew she had learned at the sink or oven, with her mother, nana and aunts. By the age of eleven she was as capable of cooking for her family and cleaning the house as any grown-up, and she was missed in Kent for that, as much as anything else.

*

Reluctantly, after a few weeks (which felt like only days to her), Ann returned to the south coast in order to have a check-up at the hospital, and to resume her life with the family.

During the few weeks of not seeing her mum, it seemed to Ann that she'd grown much bigger. She hadn't grown jolly though, like big people were supposed to (like Oliver Hardy, thought Ann, or that Two-Ton Tessie she heard on the radio). Grace was quite the opposite, Ann thought one evening, while the children chattered and laughed as they finished the last of their bread pudding.

'Gawd help me, stop making such a racket!' Grace cried, leaning heavily against the table, her left hand on the small of her back. 'What'll I do when there's five of you? Bloody run away and leave yer, that's what I'll do!'

Stunned and frightened, Ann's sisters turned to her as their mother limped out of the kitchen. 'It's alright,' Ann soothed Bet's hair, 'she don't mean it, you know that, when has she ever left us? And I think the nurse is going to bring us another brother or sister in her black bag real soon.'

Not long after, Ann and Bet were on their Dad's smallholding, just up the hill behind the house, playing with the ducks and chickens – they especially loved going 'up top' to watch chicks hatching in the incubator – when Ann told Bet, 'I can't wait to get married and be a mum. My husband is going to be smart, he's going to have studied at Cambridge. He would 'ave been a scholar. I'll iron his gown for him so he can wear it at formal hall where they have them there grand dinners with lots of fish. All our children will go to university, Bet.'

Bet looked at her sister with surprise. 'Where are you going to meet a gentleman, Nance?'

'What do you mean?' Ann asked Bet.

'Nothing, Nance, nothing. Of course you will.'

Barely two months later, Grace went into labour at home.

Luckily Jack was there and he set about rousing a couple of female neighbours, who fetched a midwife and began boiling water on the stove and carrying clean old sheets into the bedroom where Grace lay, moaning. When her moans turned to screams, Ann crept up the stairs towards the closed door and stood impatiently for what seemed like hours and hours, waiting to hear the cries of the baby. When Grace's screams stopped, all Ann could hear were grown-ups' voices, not a baby crying.

The midwife opened the door, looked at Ann and said, 'There's something wrong with your new sister. Go outside and tell your sisters and brother it's a girl, but best not to mention anything else.'

Ann shook her head and asked what was wrong. The midwife sighed and said, 'She's got something wrong with her eyes, I'm afraid. The doctor will need to examine her but it looks like she could be blind in one of them, it's just not opening.'

Confused, Ann thought that her black bag must have had some sort of disease or infection in it, there was no other explanation. With a sinking feeling she turned and walked down the stairs, trying to think of what to tell the others. Maybe she'll only be a little ill, like me with my ears, she thought. Yes, she convinced herself, little Joy (her dad's idea for a name if the baby was a girl) will be alright, she must be.

For the next few months, life at the Pilcher house continued as usual, and baby Joy behaved just like Rene had done when she was so small. Ann took turns with her mother, pushing Joy in the old pram during the day, and rocking her to sleep in her arms at night. Maybe the nurse was wrong, thought Ann, who kept the knowledge of what she'd been told the night Joy was born to herself.

Over the autumn and winter, Ann made a few more trips to

Cambridge in order for her ear to 'heal', and whenever she was there, she would miss Joy more than she did even Bet, Rene and Derek. She loved being a kind of mother to Joy, taking care of her when Grace was working or otherwise too busy.

When Joy was a year old, she began seeing doctors more often, and Grace's mood became darker after every visit. In the summer of 1939, Jack began talking about Hitler, Germans and a war coming, but Ann and her siblings didn't really pay any attention to any of that; they were more concerned with how and when to keep out of their mother's way. When Grace was in a mood, or when her nerves were playing up, they'd all five go down to the beach and play (Ann was in charge of Joy, of course), coming home only when they were hungry, or if a wind got up and the clouds rolled in off the sea.

But just as the summer was coming to a close, and Ann, Bet, Rene and Derek were dreading their return to school, war with Germany was declared. They all sat around the radio one Sunday evening, listening to the prime minister, Mr Chamberlain, as he told them that because Hitler hadn't retreated from Poland, then Britain had to fight them. Jack, who'd had his left ear, the only one with any semblance of hearing left in it, stuck up against the radio's Bakelite casing, slowly sat up straight in his armchair and stared at Grace. She continued to look down at her hands as they furiously knitted. 'Bed, kids!' barked Jack, and they all went quietly.

They couldn't hear what their parents talked about that night, but one evening a few days later, just before bedtime when it was still light outside, Grace told Ann to sit down at the kitchen table. Rene and Bet were taking turns to push their baby sister up and down the street outside, and Ann watched them as they fussed over the pram. 'Nance,' her mother rapped the table to get her attention, 'we're making arrangements to have Joy sent away.'

Ann's eyes instantly filled with tears. 'But why, Mum? We can look after her. There's enough of us at home to help. It's only one eye that's not right.'

'No,' Grace insisted, 'the doctor said she's got a condition called coloboma and they're going to take her right eye out. When she's older they can put a glass one in. They can leave the other one, even though it's funny and egg shaped, they said. But her pupil's really small and she's going to struggle to see out of it. We don't know how long this war is going to go on for this time, and it's going to be hard for us to cope with the four of you. Anyway, I haven't got the first idea of how to look after a handicapped kid.'

Ann knew why she had been told; her mum didn't want to have to explain it to the others. So now she had to think of the best way to break the news to her sisters and brother. They all adored Joy and loved looking after her. She was such an easy baby that Bet had renamed her Sleeping Beauty.

Ann decided to hold off telling them for a while, until she knew more about the home, at least. The following day her dad answered questions about the place that Joy was being sent to as best as he could, but it was clear that he didn't really know. He handed her a pamphlet that had small photos of the place in it.

At breakfast two days after finding out, Ann told Bet, Rene and Derek, 'Joy's going to go to the Sunshine Home for Blind Babies in East Grinstead. Mum and Dad will take her there and she'll learn how to cope with being blind. It's like a board-ing school, there's more than twenty other babies there – look, I've read about it. It looks nice. I'm sure we can visit.' She pulled the pamphlet out of her pocket. 'Here, you can read about it.'

The children sat stunned into silence. Joy was their sister and should stay with them, Bet argued. She was only a year old and that was too young to be sent away. 'It's just not right, Nance,' Bet told her.

Joy was taken by Grace and Jack to East Grinstead one rainy Saturday in late September 1939. Grace refused to say anything about their trip when they returned home hours later except that, 'It's a lovely big house and the nurses seem very nice. Now we'll see her once a year, don't you worry.' Jack looked pale and said nothing. He went upstairs, changed out of his Sunday suit into his work clothes, and headed up top to get what vegetables he could before it became too dark to see anything.

It wasn't long before the Pilchers heard about families who were evacuating from Folkestone and moving to places far away. Lots of children were being sent to a place called Merthyr Tydfil without their mums or dads, which sounded horrible to Ann, Bet and Rene. Plenty of new people began arriving at Folkestone's port too, on boats that braved the Channel from France. The army moved into the town, which became a garrison – this was difficult for Jack because when he was challenged by soldiers for being out after dark, he couldn't hear what they were saying. More than once he was marched off to the police station by suspicious sentries who thought he couldn't speak English. He never complained, though.

When Jack became an air raid warden, he only went out at night wearing his armband and helmet, which meant he was no longer stopped by the army. He didn't complain when the smallholding up top of the hill was commandeered by the Ministry of War for army use. He thought it his patriotic duty to do what he could on the home front, he explained proudly to his children, when he told them they couldn't go up and see the chicks any more. The people of Folkestone who chose to stay in the town prepared for war as they were instructed to by the government. Jack and Grace made blackout curtains for the house. When the children all had to be fitted with gas masks Grace told them, 'I know they're horrible smelly things,' as she tied the straps tightly over their faces to secure the masks to their heads, 'but you got to have them.'

'I can't breathe,' Rene complained.

'You'll be fine. It's these things what are gonna keep you alive,' Grace told her.

Ann looked in one of the biggest boxes that their gas masks had arrived in, and saw a huge hood thing. 'What's that for, Mum?' she asked. Grace glanced at the box Ann was pointing to. 'That'll have to go back so's someone who can use it gets it. It's for the pram, but we don't need it, do we?' Like the big old Victorian pram that stood empty in the yard, it was a reminder of the absence of their baby sister.

Grace's tiredness and mood swings, coupled with having to raise her voice to be heard and repeat the same words several times over before Jack understood, was creating a lot of tension between her mum and dad, Ann realized. Grace didn't care about screaming at Jack in front of the children, who knew better than to ever take his side in an argument with her. As the year wore on in a kind of addictive suspense – everywhere she went it seemed to Ann that people were asking, 'When's Jerry gonna bomb, then?' – Grace seemed to become more and more nervous.

It was teatime when warning sirens began testing in late 1939, and Ann saw her mother almost faint. She dropped a frying pan into the sink, fell to the floor and crawled under the dining table. The younger children all thought it was funny, but when she began pulling at their legs in a rough way that hurt them, they soon got down with her. After a few minutes Jack came in and laughed at them, shouting, 'It's only a blooming test!'

From the beginning of 1940, though, planes and sirens began to be heard in the town at any time, day and night. It disrupted every waking and sleeping moment. The sound of aeroplane engines – which were felt as a rumble in Ann's chest before she heard them – was relentless. Both German and British planes droned on and on during the night. Grace's nerves were constantly on edge and, as was her way, she snapped and snarled at her husband and children over the smallest thing.

At the end of May 1940 the whole of Folkestone turned out on the seashore to see all sorts of boats off to France. Some of them didn't look to Ann as if they should be at sea, they were too small, surely. Alongside the trawlers the tiny little river boats looked like toys.

'Why are they all going, Mum?' asked Ann.

''Cos our boys need to be brought back 'ome sharpish, and the Germans are giving them a hiding over there, that's why,' Grace told her.

Ann spent the day going to and from the seashore hoping to see the boats return, and just before teatime she saw the first boats arrive back, overflowing with uniformed men. After they drew up on the beach, some of the soldiers jumped out and ran up to the nearest civilian, to push pieces of paper into their hand. One looked at Ann, trying to decide whether to give her his.

'What's that?' Ann asked.

'It's a letter for my wife, to tell her I'm safe. We can't go back home, we all have to regroup and get back to the fighting as soon as we can. Could you . . . ?'

Ann shook her head. She didn't want her mum to get angry with her, as she'd told her plenty of times not to ever talk to soldiers. He ran over to a middle-aged woman in a pair of jodhpurs and riding jacket, who did take his letter.

For the rest of the day and night, boats kept arriving and soldiers disembarked, some falling to their knees and putting their faces in the sand – the ferrying of troops into Folkestone from France seemed to go on all week. It was followed, just as Grace had feared ('You watch, them soldiers will get here and the Germans won't be far behind!'), by the first spate of heavy bombing that the town had seen. All of the bombs landed in a 300-yard-wide stretch of the town, and no one was sure whether that was intentional or if the Germans would bomb more widely at any time.

Grace became increasingly nervous and scared. One afternoon, she watched as two parachutists landed in the sea, and when a siren went off, Ann saw her begin to shake. 'We're leaving Kent. We can't stay here any longer,' Grace cried determinedly to the children.

That night, before going out on duty, Jack told the children that it was best for all of them to go to Cambridge. He didn't want them to end up working like slaves on a farm in Wales, which is what he'd heard happened to evacuees, and he didn't want them sent halfway round the world to Australia like some other kids had – especially since some hadn't made it at all, their ship had been sunk by German submarines. (Plus, Jack had told Ann more than once in the past, Grace had never liked living in Folkestone.)

He would have to stay though, Jack said, and held his hand up as the children began crying and shouting 'No!', trying to grab his big, calloused hands. He had to carry on in his duties as air raid warden.

'Don't you fuss,' Jack told them with half a smile, 'there won't be anywhere near as much bombing or dogfights in the sky over Cambridge like there are here, you'll be safe. Now get to bed . . .'

*

Three days later, Ann saw the tears in his eyes as Jack waved them off from Folkestone Central. 'When will we see Daddy again?' Rene cried, as the train pulled away from the station.

'I don't know,' snapped her mother. 'When Hitler says so, I reckon.'

'I can just see him coming in from the shelter in the middle of the night and playing some tunes that he can't really hear on the piano all by himself. He's going to be really lonely,' said Bet.

'We have to keep our promise and write to him. Every week. That way he'll have something to look forward to,' Ann told her sisters and brother.

When they reached London, Uncle Bill was at the station to meet his sister-in-law and children, to help them across town to King's Cross and then back to Cambridge. He recognized Ann straight away, she was almost thirteen years old now, he knew, but was probably just as shy as she had been two years earlier. He had never met his younger nieces and nephew, though. He had been told that Bet was almost eleven. 'She's got an artistic temperament and has a bit of a temper sometimes, like her mum,' Edie his wife had told him. Derek had just turned nine, and was 'gentle like his father' while Rene at just seven years old was 'bright and chirpy'. No one in the family had met the new baby, and Edie had told him not to mention her. 'Grace won't want to talk about it. So don't ask,' Edie reminded him several times before he left the house. Grace didn't want Ann going on about Joy all the time, either, she'd warned her oldest daughter as they packed to travel to Cambridge. It was as if Joy had never been born, Ann sometimes thought.

The family had arranged for the children to stay with various aunts and uncles in Cambridge while Grace and her sisters would be sharing the care of their mum Agnes, Ann's Nana

Wolfe. The old woman had suffered a stroke not long after her husband Samuel passed away six months earlier, and her health had deteriorated to the point where she was now bedridden and frail. Queenie and Elsie, the younger of the six Wolfe sisters in Cambridge, had been taking it in turns to care for their mum.

Grace assured Ann and her other children that they would only be separated for a few months. 'It's to give Elsie a break, really. You know she lives with your nana all the time, and it's not really fair on the others to be away from their children. Queenie's little boy Brian is only two. It's a good job Elsie never married really, and lucky for Mum she's around.'

Ann was sad that she'd never again climb into her nana's bed with her grandparents. One of the last times she'd seen her granddad was a Sunday morning in 1938 when she'd clambered up to ask him all about the university and the people who went there.

'What's it like? What do they do? Have they got posh voices? I bet they have lovely manners. What do they say to you when you're there?'

'I don't know, Nance. I don't take much notice,' he told her. 'I just go in and do what I need to do. I don't hang around.'

Samuel Wolfe travelled to each of the colleges to mark their billiard tables, but he really couldn't recall a time that he had actually spoken to any of the students. Come to think of it, he told Ann, he couldn't for the life of him remember how he had started to work there in the first place. It must have been his brother Jacob who recommended him. 'He probably told the head porter,' guessed Samuel, '"My brother has a steady hand, what comes from him being a professional plumber, an' he knows his way around a table, on account of being the best billiard player in town!" Not that I were, but he told them that, and that's why I got to be the billiards marker for them.'

Ann's Great Uncle Jacob was a porter at 'one of the bigger ones', and not long after arriving in the town in 1940, Ann pestered Grace to let her stay with Queenie, who lived near their uncle, so she could hear more tales of university life. She would help out her aunt with housework, Ann told Grace, and look after Brian, 'so I'll be useful.'

Jacob was as much a talker as his departed brother had been, and was flattered that young Ann wanted to know about him and his life. He'd pop round when it was alright with Queenie who'd make Ovaltine for Jacob as he told his stories about the colleges.

'They live a good life,' he told Ann. 'Ooh, the food is grand, and the silverware is worth a lot of money. When I go waiting there on a Friday night, if any fish is left over I tuck it into the tails of me jacket and bring it home.' Ann imagined a shoal of fish swimming in the tails of his jacket and laughed.

'Oh, and the May Balls they're great fun,' he continued, with a wink. 'I see all sorts at them. Come in from London some of the ladies, just for the night you know.'

He winked at Ann, but she didn't know why.

'They sure can put away a lot of booze those students, and they don't mind if we help ourselves to a few drinks neither!' He laughed. 'But it's R.A.G. week is what I like the best. Everyone can get involved in that, the students and us locals. It's ever such fun.'

Ann sat up and said, 'What, you can go to the college? You can do stuff with the students? What does "R.A.G." mean?'

Uncle Jacob laughed, 'It means Raise and Give, but really it's about pestering and badgering people for money. It's all for a good cause, though, you know, charity. The students come up with some batty ideas for raising money, and they often pick on pretty young girls from town to help them.'

'Like what?' The thought of being spoken to by a college student thrilled Ann, in a scary way.

'Like running around the town with a pretty girl from a shop like Woolies in a bed, that seems most popular, collecting money in a bucket. You're far too young for any of that, Nance, and God forbid they pick on you when you're older.'

What on earth did he mean, she thought. They were gentlemen, they were educated, why would they pick on her? 'What do you mean, Uncle Jake, they don't know me, why'd they pick on me when I don't know them and would never do nothing wrong?'

'That's enough now, Jake. She don't need to hear all that,' Queenie told him. 'Don't want her thinking it's all debauchery at them colleges. Little mite's afraid of her own shadow at the best of times, an' I can't imagine what she will be like if she came face to face with a gown!'

Ann thought Uncle Jacob was making the stories up. They seemed a bit far-fetched to her after what Nana and Edie had told her.

'I've seen them students. They look like gentlemen to me in their robes and gowns,' she said, which made both Queenie and Jacob laugh.

ROSE HOBBS

Rose Hobbs was born in Cambridge in 1923 ('or 1922, I'm not really sure,' she'd laugh if asked) to Emily, who was listed as being a seventeen-year-old servant on Rose's birth record. Her father was 'unknown'. Emily cared for Rose for the first few months of her life and then handed the baby over to an 'aunt' who lived in Clay Street, Soham, about twenty miles from Cambridge. Twenty-nine-year-old Gladys Dunn wasn't a real aunt to Rose, but she wanted a child and Emily couldn't look after one at that time, so they agreed that the older woman would bring up the illegitimate Rose.

Gladys was married to a sailor named Randolph who was hardly ever at home and sent money to her only intermittently. She took in washing for a living and spent most of her days, whatever the weather, in a lean-to in the garden of her tiny cottage where she washed the sheets and curtains, cassocks and surplices from the church, which was her main source of work.

As soon as Rose was old enough to understand, Gladys let her know that her mother had run off to America ('or somewhere like it') and was supposed to come back for her, but that might take a long time. After five years, Emily still hadn't come back for Rose, and Randolph had written to say that he was coming back 'for good' having had his left arm severed in an accident. Gladys, complaining of not having enough food for herself let alone a child and a husband, told Rose that she was going to have to go somewhere else to live. Rose was to go with another 'aunt' named Mary, Gladys told her, adding that she lived 'in the country, off a farm track outside of Burwell' with her husband Adam Sturgeon.

Rose didn't know what to think about that. She didn't care too much for Gladys, and had learned little from her. She couldn't read or write (in fact she didn't know what either were), knew a couple of hymns from repeated singing in church, but she'd spent most of her short life up to this point feeling hungry, cold and tired. Rose thought that 'Mary and Adam' sounded as real as Emily did to her. Which was not at all.

To Rose's surprise, they did turn up. The couple were significantly older than Gladys, just as poor, and had no children despite Mary desperately wanting them. They arrived to collect her in an old, dilapidated gypsy wagon, pulled by a horse that had been borrowed from the farm where Adam worked. He and another man unloaded a large, new-looking iron tub from the back of the wagon and carried it through to Gladys's lean-to. Rose was dressed in the only coat and bonnet she owned, with her two dresses, vests and an ancient, naked doll, all wrapped up in half a sheet tied into a bundle with a big bow, by her feet. As the men passed them on their way through the house, Gladys put the bundle in Rose's arms and pushed her out the door towards the tall, gaunt woman who stood nervously waiting. Rose was transfixed by the large, scuffed and unlaced men's boots the woman was wearing.

'Here she is then, missus,' Gladys said. 'Thank-ee for the washtub and I'll say the girl here won't be no trouble and she don't eat much.' Rose looked up at Gladys who glanced at her, said, 'Bye Rose, be nice to your aunt,' and turned back into her cottage as the men emerged.

The slow, meandering journey to Burwell was the only one that Rose ever took in the caravan. As soon as they reached Mary and Adam's one-up, two-down cottage, the horse was unhitched after backing it onto a bare patch of scrubby grass that served as a garden. Adam removed the wheels, which he'd borrowed for the trip to Soham, and the fading, slightly warped vehicle sat on bricks, merging into the scenery for the next few years. Rose was shown the corner under the stairs where her bed lay, fed some stew that sat in a big black pan on a rack in the enormous fireplace, and settled down to sleep. That trip from Soham was the last time that she'd be so far from the Sturgeon house for the next few years.

Rose's happiest times with the Sturgeons were when she played in the caravan and made up stories about the windmill she could see across the field. But after a few months, one early evening, Adam followed her to the caravan and introduced her to a new 'game' that she was uncertain about to begin with. But he insisted, so she gave in. That game, which he made her play different variations of over the next few years, became more and more repulsive to Rose, and she grew to hate the slowly rotting caravan with its smell of soft, mulchy decay, and yellow light filtered through the ragged curtains that had to be drawn when Adam was there with her.

Sometime around the age of seven Rose discovered that she could fly. It first happened one muggy early evening when Adam was touching her in his rough, smelly way. From feeling as if she was suffocating, Rose suddenly found herself floating up to the top of the caravan, where she flew around, examining the top of the window and curtain rails. If she turned her head slightly she could see horrible Adam playing with a doll – or rather, the body that Rose was now floating free from – out of the corner of her eye. But that wasn't a nice sight, so she flew around and looked out of the window.

Learning to fly was the best thing that had happened to Rose, and after discovering that she could, she'd lie in her 'bed' under the stairs and screw her eyes up tight, willing herself to float away, around the house, watching Mary and Adam, seeing her empty shell of a body curled up on the floor. She didn't tell Mary or Adam about her flying, because she knew they wouldn't understand. So, she got better at it, and before long – but only when Adam was in the caravan with her – Rose began to fly out of the caravan window, even though it was closed, and explore the fields and woods. She really liked that.

Rose was not sent to school because they needed her, they said, to help them out at home where she learned how to clean house, do the washing and cook basic dishes. She'd be locked in every morning just after dawn when Mary and Adam left to go to work – him on a beet farm just outside the village, her at the houses she cleaned from dawn to midday in the town, after which she'd return and, when able to, spend the afternoons cooking, cleaning up and occasionally teaching Rose the basics of writing and reading from a small, ancient book of common prayer. Many afternoons, though, Mary's headaches were so bad that she had to lie in the dark and Rose wasn't allowed to make any noise or disturb her. Rose had no friends of her own age. Or of any age, in fact. There were few visitors to the house, and on the rare occasion that anyone called, Rose was made to lay on the floor of the caravan and pretend to be 'dead', as Adam ordered her, 'Otherwise I bloody will kill you, missy.'

When Rose was eleven years old she felt the terrible disappointment of not being able to fly any more. Try as she might, she couldn't leave her body – and that meant that she felt hurt, sickened and shameful whenever Adam came to the caravan with her. One evening, when she felt really angry about not being able to float free, Rose stabbed Adam in the leg with a potato scraper as he tried to get her to play with him in the caravan. He clutched his leg, screamed, and Rose jumped out and ran across the field towards the windmill. That night she slept in a ditch, in sight of the house, but neither Mary nor Adam tried to find her. The next day, hungry, tired and cold, and when it was long enough after dawn to know that they'd be gone, Rose made her way back with a vague plan to get some food, her old doll and a coat and run away. She had no idea where to run away to, just that she had to leave.

She slid inside the back door but Mary grabbed her by the arm as soon as she got in, then dropped to her knees and hugged her tightly. Rose was astonished to see that Mary was crying, silently, and continued to for five minutes, while Rose stood straight-backed, unflinching. Finally, she got up without letting go of Rose's arm, took down both their coats from the back of the door, pulled her outside, and they walked quickly away from the house. Rose had no idea what Mary was going to do, she'd never left the house with her alone, and Mary never spoke to Rose as if she was a person, she only ordered her about, usually.

They made their way to the train station without a word. Mary bought a third class and a child's ticket to Cambridge and they sat at the very end of the platform, as far away from the entrance as they could, to wait for the train. 'I'm sorry, Rose, it's not fair, you need to learn proper, so I'm giving you to my sister and her husband, they've got two boys but Sal always wanted a girl, and she'll look after you real good. Maybe I'll see you sometime in the future.'

'Not him though?'

'No, not him, he don't know what I'm doing. You cut him good and proper Rose, he's right hurt and angry but I don't want him to hurt you. Not no more, anyway.'

*

An hour later, Rose was being shown her room in a new, strange house, albeit one that was smarter, lighter and cleaner than she was used to. Rose was surprised that so many houses could be gathered together in one place. She'd seen a few terraces of half a dozen houses together, but in this place all of the houses seemed to be attached to each other, and there were a lot of them. 'It's the smallest room, but it'll do, won't it, love?' asked Aunty Sal, as she asked Rose to call her. The room was properly decorated with wallpaper, unlike the bare plaster and brickwork of the Sturgeons' house. It had a small fireplace and a window that looked out over the back garden, which was thin and long and slightly overgrown. The bed had a thick-looking candlewick cover on it, not a rough horse blanket that she was used to. Rose thought it was a right luxury.

'It's lovely, missus,' she said with a hint of amazement in her voice.

Sal had an idea that something bad had happened at Rose's former home, and not just because Mary had been a surprise visitor that day. The women were not sisters, although they'd often been mistaken as that when young girls. They'd become firm childhood friends back then, and spent all their time together. The pair had lost touch a bit after Mary married and moved to Burwell, but Sal would make an effort every year to see her friend at least once a year and she always sent birthday and Christmas cards. She felt sorry for Mary and had felt a deep distrust of Adam from the moment she met him. Her own husband, Paul, wasn't keen on him, either. 'Gives me the creeps, he does,' he'd admitted to Sal after their first double date, in 1918.

Rose's arrival meant that Sal's sons Bobby, sixteen, and Jacky, fourteen, had to share a bedroom although, as Paul said, 'It won't be for long. Bobby'll be off to the army soon enough, won't you, Bob?' The prospect clearly didn't fill the boy with joy, and he muttered something inaudible under his breath.

'Bloody hope he does!' shouted Jacky, who was a good six inches taller than his 'big' brother. Bobby flicked out a hand and clipped Jacky on his ear. 'Ouch! You . . .' The boys fell into a loosely brawling mess on the sitting room floor, until their father stepped between them, grabbing each by an ear. 'Get out of it you two: no fighting 'less you want to fight me.'

Paul was as tall as Jacky but twice the width, his hands looked as if they were made of leather, his fingers the size of the sausages that Sal had served for tea. Rose hoped that she wouldn't have to 'play' with Paul; she wasn't sure if stabbing him in the leg would hurt enough to make him stop.

After a few sleepless nights in her new home, during which she smuggled a knife into her room and tried to stay awake in case anyone came in, Rose decided that Paul didn't want to play games with her. After a week she began to get a clear idea of how safe it was in their house, and how she could behave. School was another matter, though. Within days of moving in, and persuaded that she wasn't going to be too much trouble to look after, Sal organized for Rose to attend a church school sited just a few streets away. She told the headmaster that Rose was a 'charity case' that they'd taken in after her parents had died, and she was allocated a desk among other eleven- and twelve-year-olds.

Having never attended school and quite unused to being around so many children of her own age, Rose became a virtual mute on her first day. When her teacher realized that she was severely behind in her learning, Rose was taken out of class and put in with six 'slow' children, as they were known by the rest of the pupils. It didn't help that, although only just twelve years old, Rose had physically developed and looked at least three years older. Seated among her peers Rose looked like a teacher who'd taken the wrong desk. It didn't take long for the humiliation to become too much for her, and she simply stopped going to school.

She'd set off for school at the usual time, but instead of turning right at the end of her street to go to school, Rose would turn left and make her way to the bus station if it was raining, where she'd sit in a shelter and talk to anyone who talked to her. If it was a warm, sunny day, she'd sit on Parker's Piece or Christ's Piece, big green areas in the centre of town with flower beds, benches and lots of trees. If a grown-up asked why she wasn't at school, Rose would usually tell them that she was off to the doctor's and waiting for her mum, or some such story. Most people believed her – which was when she discovered the power of lies. Everyone, she realized, expected a nice-looking girl like her to tell the truth, and didn't want to hear a truth if it was not to their liking. More than once when Sal asked Rose what she'd done at school, Rose replied truthfully, saying things like, 'Oh I went to the park instead and cadged some cigarettes off a boy who's got a motorbike,' and Sal just laughed, or said, 'You'd better not, my girl!' and go on to something else.

When a truant officer called at the house one day, though, Sal had to confront Rose, who stood in front of her shaking her head, not speaking. I told you, thought Rose, but you didn't believe me! Sal had an uncomfortable look on her face, she thought, as if she doesn't want to do this. But when Sal said she'd take Rose to school, she shrugged and said, 'Fine.' All the next week Sal took Rose to school and made sure that she entered the building.

Rose never caught up with her peers academically, but she persisted with her attendance for the most part in order not to alarm or agitate Sal and Paul, who she only had to see dish out punishment to Jacky for playing truant to know that she didn't want any of that.

Rose grew in confidence as the months passed, though, and she discovered that she could easily persuade older boys at the school, including Jacky, to protect her from the jibes, digs and physical threats of girls jealous of her looks and her growing popularity. She stole cigarettes from Sal's purse in ones and twos, and held smoking parties behind the boiler room with the fourth and fifth form boys. Despite consistently getting bad reports from the teachers, Rose did enough housework at home to help Sal that she wasn't blamed for not performing well at school. 'Them teachers don't give you enough time, do they, girl?' Sal said sympathetically after getting Rose's first end of year report card. 'Or maybe you just can't learn. I had a brother who were like that, he can't hardly read nor write, but he makes his way over at Lowestoft on the trawlers. It'll be alright in the end, eh?'

During her first summer in Cambridge, Rose worked at keeping the house clean in the mornings, and roamed the city during the afternoons and early evenings. She was growing out of her clothes almost as fast as Sal could adjust them for length and width, and began attracting the wrong kind of attention from men on Parker's Piece where she'd sit under trees with Jacky and his friends, smoking and laughing.

Jacky became obsessively protective of Rose, and was made uneasy by the way that strangers looked at her. One night in late August, he and Rose were escorted home by the police who explained to Paul that Jacky had started a fight with a drunk who wouldn't leave Rose alone, and kept offering her a drink from his bottle. Paul brought in an 8 p.m. curfew for them both for the rest of that summer.

The following school year, Rose showed a small improvement academically, but clearly wasn't going to be staying on past the age of fourteen if she could help it. Sal had agreed with her that there'd be little point in enduring another year of schooling, and even though the leaving age was to be raised to fifteen in 1936, because Rose was born before 1925 she could leave earlier.

Paul told Sal that he'd be happy to see Rose in work and earning money so that she could think about moving out; he was aware of his youngest son's feelings for the girl and didn't like it. Jacky had refused to even consider following Bobby into the army and had remained at home, working with his father at the wood yard in order to do so. Paul was sure that he only wanted to be close to Rose and Sal also suspected her son had more than brotherly feelings for her.

Neither parent was really surprised to discover the pair asleep in Jacky's bed early one morning in the summer of 1936. That didn't mean that they were going to accept it, of course. Paul wanted to frogmarch Jacky straight down to the army recruiting offices and put Rose on a train to Burwell, but Sal calmed him down, and he had to accept that Jacky didn't want to join the army and Rose couldn't go to Burwell, because Mary and Adam had moved and she didn't know where to, so what was the point?

'The point,' said Paul, 'is that I don't want that little hussy in my house no more!'

By the evening, Sal had arranged for Rose to move in with the grandmother of a friend who lived across the city in Chesterton, and needed someone around the house to cook, clean and help out. Rose's all-too-brief and chaotic childhood ended that day.

*

For two years Rose acted as nurse, cook and carer for the old woman, who was mostly quiet and complacent, accepting of how she had become reliant on a stranger, a girl who didn't talk much, but wasn't cruel, at least.

Rose spent her days doing housework and making sure the old woman was comfortable. She'd put her to bed by 8 p.m. and then she'd either stay home and save enough money from the old lady's pension, which she had to make to last all week, or sometimes go and buy herself a drink in one of the many pubs that littered the area.

Rose never had to buy herself more than one drink, though. She was a good-looking girl, as many a man told her, and she was friendly enough, too. A few boyfriends came and went during the time Rose lived with the old woman – none of them were taken back there, Rose knew better than that; she'd be kicked out instantly.

Rose was evicted after the old woman died and, in desperate need of a roof over her head, she searched out one of the men she'd met in The Grapes on the Histon Road. He had asked her recently if she wanted to work for him. Rose knew he was a pimp and that his last girlfriend was serving time for soliciting, which was why he had what he called a 'vacancy'. Charlie dressed well, wore a big signet ring on his little finger and promised to give Rose a life of fun and money that she could only dream about. He was good-looking, and sometimes when they kissed Rose could almost feel something for him.

Rose didn't think her new life was difficult and the work didn't bother her – she simply switched off while on the job. A few times she thought that she could almost fly again, and felt detached from what she was doing, but often the 'job' was brief and easily forgotten about. She worked Parker's Piece, the market place and, on busy Saturday nights in June, Rose walked among people wearing fur stoles and top hats, looking for a light of her cigarette which, naturally, led to an offer to escort her home. In the winter months, Charlie brought clients to their three-room flat on the Histon Road where they kept the other bedroom for 'entertaining'.

It didn't take long for a kind of normality to settle over Rose's life, and she enjoyed the drinks and trinkets that Charlie bought for her (London Gin was a particular favourite). They had fun when not working, and took trips to London and stayed a couple of nights in West End hotels while he sorted business deals with men who looked like him, all thin moustaches, big shoulders and dropped aitches. They made Rose laugh, and she liked that.

The early years of the Second World War were difficult for Rose and Charlie, and they had to move from the north of Cambridge to the east, into two rooms on the first floor of a terraced house in Barnwell. Rose worked outside or at a few select clients' homes when she could through 1940 and '41. After the Americans arrived in numbers, her services were more in demand, and while she still plied her trade on Parker's Piece and Christ's Piece, she also began to attend parties at hotels in rooms booked by GIs out on a furlough. Soon she and Charlie had enough money that they could buy an old car which they used to travel outside Cambridge, to barracks and makeshift airfields within an hour or so drive of the city.

One of her regular GI customers, an officer, became so involved with Rose that he would book her for up to a week at a time when he was on leave. He told her that he wanted to take her away from England, back to Iowa with him when the war ended. Rose never believed him, but she played along with his fantasy, all the while feeling sure as she'd ever been about anyone who professed to 'care' for her that he'd disappear just like they had. Which, of course, he did, in June 1944 and she never heard from him again. Still, there were plenty of other men who'd pay to spend time with her.

Rose's life might have continued on that path indefinitely, but she became pregnant just before Christmas 1945, and didn't tell Charlie until March 1946, when it was too late to do anything about it. She didn't want a back-street abortion, at least two girls she knew had suffered terribly after having one. The pregnancy was, if she was honest with herself, a deliberate attempt by Rose to try something different. She knew that Charlie wouldn't want to marry her and that he knew no other way to make a living anyway, and she was curious ('Yes,' she thought, 'curious, that's right') to see if she might actually get to care for or even 'love' a baby if she had one.

Rose had stayed in touch with Sal over the past few years, and although Sal kind of knew what Rose was doing, she had preferred not to know for certain. She felt guilty that she and Paul hadn't been able to help Rose more when she was in their charge. When they bumped into each other one Saturday morning in the market place, Sal was shocked to see that Rose was pregnant. 'You . . . you're . . .' Sal couldn't find the words and Rose laughed.

'Yes, Sal, I'm with child! I feel a bit fat to be honest but I 'aven't bin too sick. How are you?'

'I, I . . . never mind me, what does Charlie think, is he alright with it?'

''Course not! I 'ave to get somewhere else to live sharpish. He's got another girl on the go and needs the room. You don't know anywhere do you, Sal?

'Too right I do! You can have Jacky's old room. Come back and live with us again, Rose. Please?'

Sal loved babies and Paul was easily persuaded, even though he had to grumble that it was 'against my better judgement'. Rose moved back in and gave birth to her first son in the house. She wanted to call the baby boy Parker in memory of all the good times she'd had on the Piece, but Sal told her that was cruel to the child, so he was called Clark, instead, in memory of the American lieutenant from Iowa.

The baby was only three months old when Paul brought a new workmate named Joseph home for tea. Quiet, dark and kind of shy, Joe spent that night gazing in awe at Rose as she nursed little Clark. He had moved to Cambridge from Grimsby, and came from a family of fishermen. He'd hated the sea, though, and had taken an apprenticeship as a carpenter at the age of fourteen. Ten years later he'd followed another pal down south in search of employment, eventually ending up at the wood yard where Paul worked. Paul took a liking to Joe, and Joe fell in love with Rose and Clark.

Rose and Joe's courtship was brief and uneventful. Neither of them could afford to go out much, and any money Joe had after paying his rent went on the baby. Rose didn't exactly tell Joe about her past life, but she guessed that he knew. Kind of. Occasionally if they were out at a pub (Sal would always babysit), men recognized Rose and would offer to buy her a drink. She'd always refuse politely and say, 'Meet my fiancé, Mr . . . er?' and they'd always fade back into the crowd at the bar. Joe didn't ask directly who any of the men were, so Rose didn't tell him. 'Ignorance is bliss, ain't it?' she replied when Sal enquired what Joe knew.

Within nine months of their meeting Rose and Joe married at the registry office, and the party was at Sal's house. After which, Joe moved in with Rose at Sal and Paul's until they could afford a place of their own. Within a year Rose had a second son, named Maurice after Joe's father, and suddenly the small house seemed too small and people started getting on each other's nerves.

Joe would never shout and barely argued with her, or anyone else, which meant that Rose, and increasingly, Sal, had been getting at him because they knew that he wouldn't respond. They could have a go at him out of spite, frustration, boredom or sheer malice, and he'd never shout back. Arguments with Joe were always over insignificant things, like his leaving dirty boots by the hearth, or forgetting to close a window on leaving the house empty. Rose hadn't bothered to confront him with the sad fact (as she saw it) that he'd given up on almost everything, because she knew it would make no difference and only upset her. He hadn't been looking for a house for them because he hadn't managed to get a better paid job, and they'd never save enough money to move out, as he saw it. He'd accepted whatever fate had in store for his family, it seemed to Rose. But she wasn't made that way.

When Rose heard Sal and Paul arguing loudly and almost violently one night, she thought that it was the first time she'd known it be that bad between them. Listening to them, Rose realized that they were fighting about her. She only knew of one way to earn a lot of money in a relatively short space of time, and she'd been going out every other night for two weeks, having told everyone that she was working as a bar maid at a pub in the Kite area, safe in the knowledge that Joe would be home with the babies and that Paul always drank at the Hearts of Oak. In fact, she'd been turning tricks, and earlier that night, she now realized from listening to the argument, Paul had seen her walking to the back of the Grapes with a bloke.

Rose went downstairs to the kitchen and shouted 'Stop!' at Sal and Paul. 'I know you don't like me doing it,' she said, in as even a voice as she could manage to Paul, 'but it's the only way I know how to get out of your hair. I can see it's making everyone here bloody miserable, but I've gone and made a bit of money. It's enough for me to pay some down on a slum place over by the railway, and that's what I'm going to do. I'm not taking him though,' she jerked her thumb at the ceiling, meaning Joe. 'He's bloody useless and I don't want him hanging round my neck an' all. I've got enough to do with the kids, so please let him stay here. Paul, make him stay, and I'll take the boys with me tomorrow.'

True to her word, Rose and her two boys set up home on their own, while Joe drifted back to his old home in the north and lost touch with Rose and the boys. Rose thought that he was too proud to tell anyone in his family up there that he'd failed in love, and had his kid taken away from him. It was the easiest way for him to go on, she figured. It was natural, wasn't it – after all, it was probably what she'd do if she had to.

JOYCE

'What's that noise, Mum?'

Joyce Jones, four years old and sharp as a pin, as her gran always said, looked out from under the table. Joyce knew what the air raid warning sounded like, and she'd run downstairs from her bed and ducked under the table when it had started ten minutes earlier. Her mum, who grabbed the babies and ran downstairs after Joyce, was feeding them to stop them crying. Since she couldn't do that properly under the table, she'd settled into the armchair by the fire. She couldn't easily move with them both on her, but anyway, the Germans didn't want to bomb them, did they? That was what her parents-in-law, who were under the stairs together, kept saying.

'Shush, Joyce,' Celia Jones comforted her daughter, 'it's only those 'orrible German aeroplanes again, on their way to London.'

Joyce knew what aeroplanes sounded like, alright. She'd seen with her own eyes a dirty great big German bomber – it had caught Dawn next door's runner beans in its propeller as it hopped over her hedge, just a few weeks back. But the sound that caught her attention now was different. It kind of sounded like whistling and whooshing at the same time, and it was getting closer. 'Mum!' Joyce screamed. Celia lifted both babies from her lap and flung herself forwards, head first under the table, twisting round as she dropped. She landed on her back with the twins atop, as Joyce scooted sideways to get out of the way. The whooshing sound stopped, the air hung still for a second, and then it exploded with a thud. With Celia panting, the boys crying and the windows rattling fair to break, Joyce's hands covered her ears and she screwed her eyes shut.

The silence that followed was like being underwater, Joyce thought, as she lay with her back against her mum's legs. A light kick made Joyce jump, and as she sat up, the sound of her baby brothers' crying reached her as if through a seashell she'd picked up on Brighton beach that sunny day last month, when Gran and Mum had taken them on the train. It really was as if she could hear the sea. Looking around her, Joyce was amazed to see that everything was just the same as it had been before the big bang. The big mirror that hung from a chain on the wall over the little fireplace was slightly crooked, but nothing was smashed or broken. 'Mum?' she asked, as Celia began crawling out from under the table.

'Yes, love?'

'I want an ice cream.'

'Ha!' Celia laughed and with a smile on her face looked at her daughter. 'You and your ice cream!'

Joyce's earliest memory would always be of her dad trying to get her to wave to Mum as she went off to the hospital with her big belly, in order to collect the twins. But all Joyce could see, looking in the other direction, was the ice cream man. 'I wan' ice cream,' she'd kept saying, refusing to wave at her mum. Celia now helped her up from under the table, saying, 'Out from under there, go get your gran and granddad. Then, when it gets lighter we'll pop next door to Mr Perkins, and ask if we might have an egg or two for breakfast.'

Joyce didn't get any eggs for breakfast that morning, though, because all that could be found of Mr Perkins' fifty hens were a lot of feathers and a head or two that sat in the churned mud of his garden, their beaks pointing at the sky, looking as if they were watching their bodies fly away. Mr Perkins suspected 'that rotten lot' who went out risking their lives during air raids in order to thieve bombed houses, had taken the opportunity of the raid to grab his birds. Mum said that, whether it was them or the bombing, it was really all the fault of the bloody Germans.

Mum, Joyce and the twins, Douglas and Trevor, were staying with Gran and Granddad in Caterham in Surrey because the Luftwaffe had been dropping bombs on Redhill, where they usually lived, early in August 1940. But now the barracks of the Guards nearby them in Caterham was probably the Germans' target, and bombs and a whole plane had landed among the fields and houses nearby. Celia was beginning to think they'd be better off living somewhere else altogether, leaving Caterham and Redhill behind, as she kept saying when the air raid sirens sounded. Especially after what some were saying was the landing of German spies in the woods near their back garden. It was mid-August when word got round that parachutes had been spotted in the night, landing in the trees over Coulsdon Road way, and that next morning a couple of men came marching down the Coulsdon Road from that direction, dressed in army gear, and got to the front gates of the barracks. The dogs there wouldn't stop barking at them, so they were taken in at gun point. No one knows what happened to them after that, but Celia had heard it from the landlady of the Arms that they were spies. Celia was beginning to seriously worry about being so close to the barracks, even though they were with her in-laws.

The Germans were bombing Redhill, near their own house, with some force, though. To begin with it seemed that they were aiming at the railway tracks – they hit the railway bridge at the top of Cronks Hill – and didn't seem to know about the aerodrome where Polish airmen had been training until earlier that summer. But not long after that a bomb landed in the grounds of the Hawthorns school at Gatton Point, blowing out windows and part of the roof. At least that was sort of closer to the aerodrome, said Celia to her father-in-law – the Germans were still not after them. But then there was the time, one morning, when a Stuka bomber had flown really low over the treetops at Petridge Wood Common and fired his machine guns at a poor milkman and his horse in Prince Albert Square; the milkman had run off to a house, but then turned back to cut his horse free of the wagon, all while the German plane was firing into the street. Luckily there was no one else around, and neither milkman nor his horse were hit. The following week, though, some houses in Clarence Walk and Hardwick Road close to the golf course had to be evacuated after bombs landed nearby, and the houses had to be demolished.

So no one knew what the bombs were meant to destroy in Joyce's old home town. It was a hot topic in the queues for the butcher and grocers. As soon as women were finished cooing at the babies in the pram, Joyce noticed, they'd all start damning 'Jerry' and wondering 'what they thought they were doing'.

When Celia had asked the same question at lunch one Sunday in September, Joyce's granddad had said, 'Hitler thinks we're done for.' Then he'd switched off the radio and said, 'At Dunkirk his planes shot at our boys who were in the water and on the beaches, and now he's sending bombers to hurt the women and kids over here. Bloody Hun!'

'Shush,' Gran had said sharply. 'We won't let 'im get us, will we, Joyce?' Her granddaughter looked over the bowl recently licked clean of blancmange pudding, and nodded emphatically. Whatever Gran said, Joyce always agreed, especially when food was involved.

'Hadn't you better get over to see that boiler's still stoked proper?' Gran almost barked at her husband. He harrumphed, got up from the table, put on his work jacket and took his bicycle out from the backyard. He'd recently added the work of caretaker to his usual job of orderly at the Earlswood Asylum, at least for as long as the war was on. His son Charles – Joyce's dad – had joined the army almost as soon as the news about Dunkirk had begun coming in over the radio. Initially, he'd wanted to go to the coast and try to help, but they didn't know anyone with a boat and he wasn't a great sailor, so he thought better of it and enlisted in the end.

As a trained medical orderly, Charles would be an army medic and possibly a stretcher bearer. 'At least you won't be firing guns,' Joyce's mum had said, 'so you're less likely to be shot at.' Her husband smiled at that and said nothing, before heading off for basic training somewhere up north. He'd only been gone a few weeks when the bombs started landing in Redhill.

In early October 1940, in broad daylight on a Sunday as the churches were holding harvest festival services, air raid sirens went off and, as a neighbour later told them, a bomb was dropped in Ridgeway Road, not far from Joyce's old house in Redhill. It was a time bomb and luckily it had been spotted landing, so the street was evacuated and the army managed to defuse it. The following week air raids began coming thick and fast after dark, and the Germans dropped incendiary bombs that were designed to spread fires everywhere. Joyce's grandmother had heard that even if it seemed to them that the Germans were dropping bombs wherever they wanted and for no good reason except to scare, maim and kill ordinary folk, they were better off than her old chums who lived near the docks in London. They were being bombed and set afire every night, all night.

'Why,' she'd proclaimed one Sunday morning, as she read

her *Sunday Express*, 'they're only trying to get the King at Buck House blown up!' Bombing normal folk was one thing to Joyce's gran, but trying to get the royal family was a bomb too far. 'Is nothing sacred?' she asked, and got a soft raspberry from her husband, which made Joyce laugh.

'It's been every night since September seventh,' Gran said, reading, 'and now people are not only hiding in the Tube stations at night to escape the bombs, but they're living there too! Imagine,' she looked over the top of the big grey paper at Joyce, 'sleeping on the dirty, mucky tube platforms with a lot of smelly people, and no loos to use.'

Joyce wrinkled her nose and shook her head.

'Well, we're not doing that,' Gran continued, 'but we shouldn't be hiding under the stairs nor tables neither, it says here, not if we've got an Anderson shelter.' Gran turned to stare over the top of her spectacles at her husband. The sun reflected off them into Joyce's eyes. 'Hear that, Les? Are you ever going to finish the damned thing?'

Granddad worked hard over the following week to complete their shelter. He'd already tied the corrugated iron sheets together and bowed them over the patch of the garden that he'd cleared of grass. Old doors for flooring were delivered on a horse and cart by the rag and bone man on Sunday morning, and Les set to work sawing them to size. After settling them on the earthen floor he called Joyce inside the shelter to walk and jump all over them, getting them to lie flat. Then she helped him drag carpets and rugs from the house to put over the doors. Grandpa's old army cot was set up along one side, and a double mattress along the other (also from the rag and bone man, who promised that he'd just got it from a woman whose house had the front wall blown off and it was 'like new'). Using old beer crates as tables and shelves, Les set up a small store along the back wall, and put candles, a kerosene lamp and tin cups on it. The little ones each had a special toy inside, a doll for Joyce and teddy bears for the twins, all of which lay on the mattress, on top of the ex-army blankets, old cushions with stuffing coming out and one of Gran's old, threadbare shawls. Once Les had put a layer of earth on the corrugated tin roof it was finished and ready for use. It wasn't exactly cosy, but it wasn't too dark and scary, thought Ann.

Not long after they'd finished the shelter, Joyce was asleep with her mum one night, the boys in their bassinets at the end of the bed, and the air raid siren went off. They all jumped out of bed, left the house by the back door and ran into the garden in their pyjamas and nighties, even Gran, which Joyce thought was very funny. But after an hour or so the shelter had turned cold and wet, and she didn't like the damp, dark place that smelled of paraffin from the lamp, which didn't do much to keep the place light. Granddad's cigarettes were smellier than they usually were, and one of the carpets on the floor was old and musty, which they hadn't noticed before. Joyce understood that it was better than having the house fall on top of her, even if she was under the table, but it was still not nice. After that first night, whenever the family was in the shelter after dark she'd cuddle up close to Mum, who always had the twins on her, and try to keep warm and not cry as the world outside rumbled and banged and whizzed and whooshed. During daytime raids she could at least play cards with Gran or do some colouring in.

On the night of 27 October, Joyce was asleep on the floor in the parlour next to the fire when the siren went off and they all traipsed to the Anderson shelter. After about twenty minutes they began to hear a low drone from the sky. They were used to it; usually the flyover lasted a few minutes at most, the drone of the German bombers punctuated by the ack-ack of the big anti-aircraft gun that was on a train nearby and moved along the rails as best it could when under attack. The attacks had been growing longer over the past month, and were more frequent too, sometimes three or four nights in a row. London was being given a right pasting, Gran had said more than once recently, and even though our boys in the RAF were giving as good as they got (according to the radio), there were simply too many of the bombers to stop them all. The Germans had started bombing other cities, too, with the radio reporting that Birmingham, Coventry, Liverpool, Manchester, Hull and Glasgow had been hit with as many bombs as London in the previous week. By the length of time that the planes were flying over it sounded as if London was in for a bad night.

When the all-clear sounded, it was nearly 11 p.m., but knowing that there might well be another attack, Granddad said they'd best stay in the shelter for the rest of the night. It was about 2 a.m. when the biggest bang Joyce had ever heard woke her up, and she thought that the roof was going to fall in. Douglas and Trevor started screaming and Mum said 'Christ!' at the same time as Gran. Granddad shot bolt upright from his camp bed. Again, Joyce could hear the sea, and the voices of everyone seemed to come from a long way away. 'Oh Les,' Gran sounded shaky, 'is the house . . . ?'

Her husband pulled the heavy piece of blackout material away from the door, opened it a crack, and peered out. 'It all looks alright, love,' Granddad seemed to be whispering, 'let's wait till sun up, eh? Try to rest until then.' He closed the door, pulled the curtain back across, and shifted back onto his bed, reaching for his tobacco pouch. Gran slowly sank back onto her mattress next to Mum. 'It's enough to make me take up smoking an' all.'

Joyce didn't really sleep after that, or at least didn't feel as if she did. Neither did anyone else except the twins, after being fed by her mum, who hadn't said anything since the big bang and looked very white. Even after the sun had come up they couldn't make it to the house for breakfast, because another siren sounded just before 8 a.m. But she was too tired to feel hungry. Despite there being no bombs, and it sounding like only a few planes, the all-clear didn't come until two hours later. 'It's sounded nearly twenty minutes after the London all-clear had gone off, as usual,' said Granddad, who kept poking his head out of the door to reassure everyone that their house, and Mr Perkins' and Dawn's were all OK. The all-clear had sounded pretty much straight after the one in London in the early days of the bombing, but after a couple of returning German bombers who hadn't emptied their bays over the capital city's docks and railway lines dropped bombs over Redhill and Caterham, that changed. Now the wardens in the surrounding area waited for all German planes to get to the coast before sounding their all-clears.

Now, Granddad climbed out of the shelter and said he was going to go and see where the big bomb had gone off, and if he could be of any help. Inside their home, Joyce went straight to her and her mum's room, and found everything as they had left it, except for the mirror which was hanging askew.

Granddad didn't come home until after they'd had their dinner. 'The big bomb two roads over didn't do too much damage, but I got a lift from a mate in his delivery van and went down to your old place, Celia,' he looked at Joyce's mum. 'There was a big bomb landed in Emlyn Road,' he said as he put his cap on the table, 'they got poor old Eliza Gates and her daughters, and one of her grandsons, too, as like. Her house and three others, smashed to pieces.'

'Oh no,' Gran cried, 'from the grocers?'

Joyce felt a shiver run down her neck. She knew the greengrocer lady, and liked how her hair – which stood on top of her head like an ice cream whirl – always looked perfect, even in high winds. All she could think of was how her hair must look after being bombed. Perhaps it fell off in one large cone, just like ice creams sometimes did if you weren't careful.

'Yes,' Les replied, 'them and a couple of people they reckon in the other houses. Silly buggers hadn't gone to the shelters – like mad Dawn next door, who I keep telling to get in our shelter if she wants, and not to stay under her table. Lots of people in the street were hurt by stuff falling on them.' As he sat and ate his egg salad, Granddad went on to say how the houses were all smashed up, their walls torn down, but showing off bedrooms and bathrooms with pictures and mirrors on the walls, coats and the ironing hanging off wardrobes and furniture all undisturbed-looking. It was as if they were giant doll's houses with the front left open.

Gran kept saying, 'Poor old Eliza.' She said Eliza had run the greengrocers in Emlyn Road near Earlswood station for years, and she only had her daughters Alice and Mabel and her teenage grandsons with her because the men were off in the army. Mabel had only moved from the East End in order to be safe from the bombing a few weeks back, and now look – they'd all been killed in a bloody air raid anyway!

All the time Granddad and Gran were talking, Joyce noticed that her mum was silent, and sat in the armchair by the fire, the twins asleep in her arms. She looked funny, thought Joyce. And then, 'Right,' her mum snapped, looking at her own mother. 'That's it. I'm not stopping here with these kids any longer. I owe it to them to get them away from all this bombing, and I ain't gonna to let them be taken away from me, neither. I don't want 'em evacuated, I'm going to sort us out a place to go and live together, where there ain't no bloody German bombs!'

Feeling excited by her mother's mood, Joyce jumped off her chair and threw her arms in the air. 'Whooo-ee,' she shouted, 'we're goin' where the Jerry's ain't gonna be!' The adults all stared at her for a second in silence, and then her mum burst out laughing. Soon everyone in the room was laughing, so Joyce danced around whooping some more, until – tired – she stopped and grabbed her still laughing mum's arm.

'Mum?' she asked, watching tears roll down her cheek.

'Ohhh, yes my lovely?'

'Can I have an ice cream?'

ANN

Cambridge 1941

'I s'pose Nance could work up at one a' the colleges as an assistant to one of them old bedders if there were any men left to bed for. Uncle Jake said there're only a few old ones left at his college. The RAF have taken it over.'

Ann's ears pricked up at her mother's mention of her nickname, Uncle Jake and the colleges. How on earth could I work at one of the colleges, Ann thought, I'm not yet fourteen and far too young. The eldest of the Pilcher children was seated at the table in her Nana Wolfe's house in Cambridge in the spring of 1941, glad to be there with her mum who she hadn't seen for two weeks. Ann, her two sisters and brother had been separated and lodged with different aunts around the town a few months earlier, while their mum lived with her own, elderly and poorly mother. This Saturday, Ann had been delivered at Nana Wolfe's house for breakfast by her Aunt Edie, who gave the girl some lumpy porridge and turned her attention to what Grace was saying.

Grace had been talking to the pot on the stove as much as to anyone in the room, but she turned to her sister and continued in an offhand manner. 'Anyway, when those students were here they din't really do anything useful. It's not like they was making any money, is it, Edie?'

'No,' Edie agreed cautiously. 'They just sit 'round talking

without really saying much. Maybe they can make a living out of that, but I'll be blowed if we can.' They both laughed.

Ann wondered where this conversation was leading. It was past nine in the morning and her sisters and brother hadn't arrived yet. When Aunt Edie had picked her up from her Aunt Violet's house, she'd told her that she thought Grace had a surprise for her, and Ann was hoping for a rare family reunion.

'What's all this talk about bedders for, Grace?' asked Edie.

Grace looked at Ann, seated at the plain wooden table with its leaves folded down. The girl rested her feet on what looked like flowers carved into the bottom of a leg at her corner. 'We would still have to lie about your age and I'm not so sure we'd get away with it at them colleges, what with all their "education". They're sticklers for details, them bursars.' Her mum seemed to think about that, before adding, 'I really wouldn't have wanted you there, anyway. It's like begging for scraps, being a bedder.'

'No, Grace, don't,' Edie said in defence of the job. 'It's not bad pay and there are perks, you know. Back in our day the tram used to smell lovely of the bread that the bedders had sneaked out of the colleges on their way home. They got a lot of free things at the job. At the end of term they'd get given old cups and clothes that the students or fellows had left behind.'

'No, no,' Grace continued, paying no attention to her sister's reminiscence. 'No child of mine is ever going to work there, they think they're so superior and do you know what? It's beneath us, that job.'

Ann furrowed her brow and asked, 'Why are you talking about me being a bedder?'

'You're not!' Grace said firmly. 'You're going into service for some horse owners in Royston, like I used to do. I was fourteen but there weren't a war on then, and I got a room in the attic to share with an older, ginger girl named Mary. I learned how to make silver shine and fires burn proper. The sooner you can get a job like that and learn them things, the better. You can live with them like I did, before I got married to your dad.'

Ann was shocked. So her mum was planning on getting rid of her, just like she had Joy. Perhaps Bet, Rene and Derek would never get to live with her again, neither. Although Grace wouldn't say that she was planning on getting all of her children off her hands, she was about to attempt to get Ann a full-time, live-in job.

Quite simply, she needed Ann to start earning for the sake of the family (and her mother's peace of mind). Grace told all of her children when they had reached school age, 'None of you are going to go to posh schools. You can take that there eleven-plus exam, but don't bother passing it, 'cos there's no point. We can't afford the uniform, and you're going to be working as soon as you're able.'

An hour later Ann was being half-dragged by her mum to a big house near Royston Heath. She was going to try for a job as a house servant, said Grace, who had put on her smartest dress and hat. They'd dressed smartly in order to 'make an impression', she said. Ann wondered about the 'impression' she was going to make with her short, unruly, curly dark hair that made her look like a boy, as did her skinny frame on which Grace had made her wear a plain grey smock. She looked much younger than she was.

'I don't look smart like you, Mum,' she told Grace.

'It's where you come from that's important, not what you look like,' her mum replied.

Ann didn't think that where she'd come from – Folkestone – was going to do her much good. The houses that they were passing were all big, and stood apart from one another. There were only a couple of streets with houses like that in Kent that she could remember, and she'd never been near them. All

Ann knew were long rows of small terraced houses with two bedrooms, a larder and an outhouse for the washing, with the toilet at the end of the yard. Anyway, Ann had decided that she would much rather work in a college than anywhere else. Even as a bedder.

Grace yanked Ann's sleeve and turned into a driveway, they passed under an arch that had the letters 'Hat n Ho se' carved into it. Instead of going up the stone steps to the front door, Grace led the way round the side of the house, to a back door. She pulled the metal bell handle and tried to stick Ann's hair down with a lick of her fingers as they waited.

A young boy who looked about Ann's age, wearing a blue shirt under a brown waistcoat, opened the door and, before Grace could say anything, turned his head back into the house and shouted, 'Mrs Hedges, it's for you.' He turned back to Grace and Ann, said, 'Wait here, please,' and disappeared through a frosted-glass inner door into the darkness behind.

Ann looked into the porch, which had black and white tiles on the floor, and coats and hats hung on the wall to the left.

'Who is it?' boomed a rich voice, before the glass-panelled door swung open and a large, florid woman in a black dress with white collar and cuffs emerged. She looked mother and daughter up and down. 'Yes?'

'Hello, Mrs Hedges,' Grace put on her 'posh' voice, Ann noticed. 'It's me, Grace Wolfe, that was, I used to work here, do you remember me?'

The housekeeper screwed her eyes up and pulled her head back into her shoulders, as if she were trying to focus properly on something that was too close to see all of it. 'Grace? From 1922 or thereabouts? You've changed a bit. What do you want, dear, it's washing day.'

'Yes, I remember; how's that old mangle holding up, Mrs Hedges? Used to fair make my wrists hurt that did.'

'It's gone, Grace, we had a new one a few years back. You've not come to ask to do our laundry, have you? Because we . . .'

'No, no, missus,' Grace said hurriedly. 'This is my Ann,' she pushed her daughter forwards, and Ann reluctantly stepped in front of her mother.

'How do, dear,' Mrs Hedges lowered her eyes to Ann and then looked over her head at Grace with a puzzled look. 'And?'

'Well, I was hoping that you'd take her in like you did me, and teach her how to be a scullery maid. She's a good girl.'

Mrs Hedges took a half step backwards and put both hands on the door edge, as if about to slam it in their faces. 'Lord no, dear,' she said, and pointed at Ann. 'Look at her, skinny little thing. She wouldn't last longer than a week.'

Ann felt a sense of relief rise in her chest, and then apprehension at what Grace would do.

Mrs Hedges continued, 'And anyway, if you haven't noticed we've got a war on and we can't afford to take in any more girls. I'm sorry, but it's been nice seeing you again, Grace.' With that she closed the door.

Grace looked as if she was about to kick it, but instead took hold of Ann's hand and turned to stalk back along the gravelled path, her head held so high that Ann wondered if she could see where she was going.

The trip was never talked about again.

The next Monday, Grace, along with three of Ann's aunts, went to Histon and got part-time work at Chivers Farm.

At school, Ann was dying to tell her sister Bet what had happened on Saturday. 'Mum took me to some house. Wanted me to start working in the kitchens or as a chambermaid . . . it was embarrassing, Bet, they took one look at me and said no. I wanted the ground to swallow me up, I did.'

Bet looked outraged. 'You can't work yet! You're too young.'

'That's what the housekeeper said.'

'Blimey, she don't waste any time, do she?'

Bet was staying at their Aunt Win's house, and had been for two weeks. The sisters who'd been so close when they lived in Folkestone were only able to spend any time together in Cambridge at school. They sat at separate desks but next to each other, with just enough of a gap for the teacher to walk between. She hadn't arrived yet – the sisters wouldn't dare talk when she was in the room. They learned from their first day that Mrs Smales didn't take kindly to talkers after she'd marched along their row and dealt Bet a hard slap on the back of her hand, just because she had leaned across to her sister and asked to use her inkwell.

'I don't mind getting a job if it's going to help us get a place where we can all live together,' Ann told Bet. 'Really I don't. It's not like I'm any good at school, is it? I'm not like you, Bet, you're good at everything. I wish I could make things like you can, sew and draw like . . .'

'Ann!' Bet interrupted her at the mention of drawing. 'You know that Uncle George paints? Well, he's given me his oils so I'm painting a lot at his house! I love it there, it's bloody luxury, Nance. I've got my own bedroom and my own bed! They're so kind. You know Aunty Win gave Rene a bone bracelet when she stayed there?'

Ann nodded, used to her sister's jumping from one subject to the next mid-sentence. Bet continued without a pause. 'I don't want to leave. Every time me or you stay at Aunty Queenie's we have to look after her baby Brian, and 'cos Rene's too young really, Queenie likes one of us to do it. I don't know why we have to keep swapping all the time. I can look after myself when Aunty Win's at Nana's.'

'Mum said none of us should be left alone ever,' Ann reminded her. 'Think about it; if Uncle George is out on volunteer duty with the fire brigade and Aunty Win's at Nana's and you're in the house and a bomb hits it – what then? You'd have no one, and the council don't know we're here yet, so how would people know if you're dead or alive?'

Bet smiled sweetly at her. 'There won't be any bombs here, Nance. It's Cambridge, not Folkestone.'

'You don't know what Hitler's planning, Bet.'

Bet didn't want to argue with her sister, so she nodded and smiled. After all, it was their mum Bet was angry with – not that she'd let Grace know it, of course.

'And,' Ann remembered, adding cheerily, 'Uncle Bill said he thinks he might have found somewhere for us all to live. So we should all be together with Mum soon.'

'Wonderful,' Bet muttered under her breath, as Mrs Smales marched through the door barking, 'Sit down, be quiet and face the front!'

The day began with a session of needlework in which Ann was forced to start again on a piece of embroidery that was almost finished when she dropped a stitch and so was told to unpick the lot. Towards the end of the afternoon, Bet was shouted at by Mrs Smales for asking Ann if she could borrow a pencil, and the teacher strode over to Bet's desk. She stood with her back turned to Ann and smacked at Bet's hand just as Ann lifted the lid of her desk, looking for the pencil. She hadn't noticed how close Mrs Smales was to her, and the lid caught the teacher's elbow. The shock made Ann laugh and the rest of the class joined in.

Enraged, Mrs Smales smacked Ann across the face. Bet jumped up, pulled the teacher's arm and yelled, 'You leave my sister alone!' which was countered with a smack from Mrs Smales.

Ann opened her desk lid again, this time knowing that it would hit Mrs Smales's elbow. Her face glowing red, the teacher turned, quick-stepped back to her blackboard and shouted, 'Get out, get out!' at the sisters.

Bet and Ann started the walk to Nana Wolfe's house in silence. The girls were thinking about what Grace was going to do to them when they got there and had to tell her that they'd been sent home by the school. Ann felt desperately glum. She really wanted to explore Cambridge on her own and maybe visit some colleges. Her mum had said no once, because it was supposedly 'too dangerous', her reason being that, 'If anywhere is going to be bombed in Cambridge it'll be one of those colleges, you mark my words.' Now Ann knew her mum would punish her by making Violet keep her in the house all the time, just to spite her. She also worried what Grace would do to Bet when they got to Nana's house; Bet was bound to give her lip.

As they turned into their nana's street, both girls had their eyes fixed firmly on the ground, their apprehension growing as they neared the house. Bet was about to tell Ann not to worry, that she'd say it was all her fault, when their brother Derek could be heard shouting, 'It's Dad, we're with Dad!'

They looked up to see their father Jack in his Sunday suit, his boots all shined up and his trilby tilted back on his head, half-skipping along the road holding Derek and Rene's hands. Bet ran towards him shouting, 'Nance, it's Dad, it's Dad!'

Ann stood rooted to the spot, not believing what she was seeing. Jack smiled and hugged Bet as Derek yelled, 'He can't hear anything!' and Rene added, 'He's completely deaf.'

'I don't care! We've got our dad back,' Bet cried.

'Come here, Nance,' Jack called out, and Ann ran over to become part of a family hug that seemed to last for hours.

The greeting from his children after their three-month separation was in stark contrast to the one that Jack had received from his wife a little earlier. 'What are you doing 'ere?' Grace asked with a scowl when he pushed open the kitchen door. He stood and smiled and she asked again. 'Why you 'ere, eh? You got leave?'

Jack, still smiling, said, 'Hello, love, I've come to live with you and the kids for good.'

Grace clenched her fists. 'Oh yeah, and where are you going to work?' she shouted at her bewildered husband.

He shrugged his shoulders and held his arms wide. It wasn't that he didn't know the answer to her question, he simply hadn't heard it. In the last few months, under fire from German bombs in Folkestone, the deafness that had started in the trenches of the Great War had become profound. Jack brought his hands together at chest level and mimed writing on his palm.

Grace stamped her foot in frustration, turned on her heel and pushed past him, out of the kitchen. Jack looked around to see where she had gone just as she reached the toilet. She strode back into the house carrying scraps of paper and found a pencil on the mantelpiece. In her large, child-like scrawl she wrote: 'WHAT ABOUT WORK? MONEY?'

Jack shrugged and tried to smile winningly.

Grace strangled a scream and wrote again, 'Nearly all our coupons gone.' Then she turned her back and returned to the bread she had been making.

She hadn't smiled at him once, but determined not to show how hurt he was, Jack asked, 'Are the kids at school? St Luke's?' Grace nodded without looking at him, so he left and went to fetch Derek and Rene, knowing the school would let them out early if he asked nicely.

When they all returned, Jack explained to the children, as much for the benefit of his wife as for them, that he had been asked to leave his job as an air raid warden because, 'I couldn't hear a thing, so I was no good to man nor beast. They had to write everything down, and last week the head warden wrote, 'Go on Jack, join your family.' So here I am, I'm going to stay with your mum for now, but we'll all have somewhere to live together soon. Your Uncle Bill's sorting it.'

Jack hoped that his brother-in-law could find them somewhere decent to live and get him a job, too. But it was not going to be easy, as Grace pointed out to him more than once – his lack of hearing made him a liability on the kind of labouring jobs he was used to doing.

With the surprise of Jack arriving and the fuss that the family made of him – Bill and Edie joined them for tea – nothing was said about why Bet and Ann were heading to Nana Wolfe's house when they should have been in school.

When, a few weeks later, Ann explained about hitting Mrs Smales's elbow with the desk, Grace replied sternly, 'If she hits Bet again, you tell her to keep her hands to herself or else I'll come up there and show her how to give a smack.'

A few days after this, just as Mrs Smales was about to deliver her first smack of the day to Bet, Ann stood up and said with a slight wobble in her voice, 'You don't ought to do that, miss, or my mum says she'll come up to school and show you a proper smack.'

The teacher turned in the aisle between their desks and raised her hand to smack Ann, who, although trembling, kept her gaze levelled at her. Mrs Smales paused before lowering her hand to straighten her blouse, trying to make it appear as if that's what she was going to do all along. 'Right, well, we'll see . . .' she muttered, returning to her place at the front of the classroom.

Bet was not smacked that day, nor in the months that followed, before bombing hit Cambridge so hard that classes were suspended.

Uncle Bill said he'd have to find Jack some paid work before he found them a house – which didn't take too long, as it happened. Jack had been in Cambridge only a few days when Bill announced that he'd found him a job on a pig farm. 'You won't have to do it for long,' he said, although both men knew that it was unlikely anything else would come up that Jack could do while there was a war on.

Jack's pig farm work began when the sun came up, lasted for as long as there was daylight and involved a lot of dirty work. He was caked in mud from pushing barrows of beets and roots around and making sure that the pens were secure. It was hard, physical work, but he did everything asked of him, didn't complain, and his boss liked him.

Jack hadn't been in the job long, cycling the three miles out of the city every morning and back at night, when the family discovered that there were 'perks' to it, too. One night he returned home carrying a dead piglet in his front basket. It had been killed by its mother rolling on it, and since Jack was the only man working with the herd, he was given the corpse to take home to do with what he wanted. Which was a lot, as it turned out.

Jack made black pudding, smoked sides of bacon in the back garden, left trotters and tail in a bucket of brine in the shed and hung the rest on a hook above the buckets. Jack, Grace, Nana Wolfe and Elsie ate pork for five days, which was as unexpected as hearing Grace say that her husband was good in the kitchen. 'I'll give him that,' she told Elsie. 'He's a good cook.'

Over the following week it wasn't only piglets that Jack sometimes turned up carrying at the end of the day. Sometimes he brought a rabbit home, often there'd be root vegetables, too. While she was glad he was working and bringing home the bacon (as Bill liked to joke), Grace wasn't overly happy with Jack's new job because, apart from the smell that he brought back with him every night, as she was always complaining in front of the children, the pay was low.

Still, it did mean that if Bill found them a house they'd be able to afford the rent.

JOYCE

Christmas 1940 had been a jolly one in the Jones house, which was strange, for wartime. Joyce's dad wasn't home, but he'd been there for three days a couple of weeks before, and he brought a few things wrapped in brown paper for Joyce and her baby twin brothers, Douglas and Trevor – Joyce was delighted with her little nurse's outfit. Although rationing was on, it wasn't too bad, said Gran, totting up what she had in a normal week: four ounces of bacon or ham, six ounces of butter or margarine, two ounces of tea (which was doubled for Christmas week), eight ounces of sugar (made up to twelve for Christmas), two ounces of cooking fats and meat to the value of one shilling and ten pence. Sadly, Mr Perkins didn't have a chicken for them, but they'd managed to get a bit of brisket instead and Gran had made trifle. Gran bought Granddad a new tin helmet, and he bought her a snazzy-looking gas mask, and they both chipped in for a gas mask thing that could fit over the twins' pram, although it made it look like a tank or something, said Granddad. Celia got a half-dozen bottling jars from Gran, and promised to make jam for her. The Germans didn't stop dropping bombs just because it was Christmas, though, and Boxing Day was spent running in and out of the Anderson shelter.

When Joyce's dad had been at the house, she heard him tell her mum about a place called Cambridge, where one of his new mates in the army came from. 'It's a quiet place he reckons,' Charles had said, 'there ain't been anywhere near as much bombing as round here, and there's countryside all round it. There's only the university, a Chivers jam factory and farms there, so no reason for Jerry to bomb the place.' Which sounded good to Celia. Charles promised to send names and addresses of some people who his mate knew and that might put them up for a while. With the kids being so young, and their house in Caterham having being made uninhabitable by a bomb that landed in their street, and because Celia would make arrangements herself rather than going through the Ministry of Health, she would get free train travel and payment of billeting expenses.

After a couple of letters to a woman named Aggie, who was the wife of the soldier in their dad's regiment who lived in Cambridge, it was all arranged. Aggie was used to having people stay, she explained in a letter to Celia, because she used to rent rooms to university students. Since she'd lost them due to the war, she said how handy it would be for her to get the government's billeting allowance for the family. So in early January 1941, Joyce's family said goodbye to her grandparents and joined the still growing number of evacuees from London and the south-east.

Joyce had never been on a train for so long before, let alone been to London. Their funny little electric train rattled along through muddy fields and Joyce didn't see a single cow or sheep on the way. In places there were patches of snow covering the landscape as it flew past, which gave off more light than the low, grey clouds in the sky above. As they neared London, Joyce began to notice the backs of houses facing the railway line, most of which reminded her of Caterham, but increasingly as they approached the centre of the city, lines of terraced houses would have sudden gaps, and it reminded her of looking at her own crooked smile in the mirror when her teeth fell out.

'Bombs,' her mum nodded when Joyce turned from the window to ask why some houses were missing. As they drew into London Bridge station it was getting dark, but Joyce could clearly see the destruction and devastation of the area around the station. The sight made her heart beat faster, and she wore an ever-deepening frown as they walked from the station. There were wide-open spaces with huge mounds of rubble between the soot-blackened skeleton buildings, their windows gaping like Halloween lanterns. In some places bricks fanned out from the open fronts of buildings as if they were a carpet, welcoming people inside. In others, walls stood lonely and detached from anything, their arched, glassless windows now spaces that reminded you of what was no longer behind them. Spots of grey snow added an oddly softening touch to what were obviously sharp, cold and hard iron rails, metal pipes and blackened, charred beams. Dark human shapes moved quickly, giving the appearance of knowing where they were headed and why, but Joyce couldn't imagine wanting to move about and live among that mess. She wanted to get away from the chaos and destruction as quickly as she could.

On 30 December 1940, more than 100,000 incendiaries and 24,000 high explosive bombs had landed around St Paul's cathedral. The *Daily Mail* had called it 'the second great fire of London', and showed a photo of the cathedral standing defiant against a sky lit by flames, with smoke all around that made it appear as if the clouds had come down to the level of the great dome. Now, as Celia pushed the pram along crowded platforms towards the Tube, Joyce could see that dome from the newspaper picture across the river, shadowed against the darkling sky. They didn't know it, but a couple of days later, a massive bomb would score a direct hit on the Bank underground station just across the river from where they were walking, killing 111 people who thought that they'd be safe sheltering inside.

The train that took the family north and east of King's Cross – which was amazingly still functioning, despite its tracks having been hit at least four times so far – was drawn by a slow, steam-spouting, big old engine, and the small, stuffy compartments were full of men: most of them in uniform. Joyce had to stand by the window, her arm on her mum's shoulder, the twins as usual taking up Celia's arms and lap. The men smoked and talked in low voices, occasionally laughing. A couple of them kept looking over at Celia, who had her head turned permanently towards the blackout blind that covered the window, or down at the sleeping faces of her boys. Whenever the train stopped, which was often, sometimes in the middle of a field (or so it seemed), Celia would get nervous and shift in her seat, making as if to get up. A man opposite, wearing a uniform with stripes on his arm, noticed after a couple of stops, and started talking to her. 'Don't worry, love, we're not there, yet, it'll be a stop to check the wheels or something. Where you going?'

'Cambridge!' Joyce blurted. 'Where you going?'

The man with the stripes laughed. 'Can't tell yer that, little 'un, don't choo know loose talk cost lives, and that walls have ears?' The men next to him all laughed.

'No they don't, look!' Joyce pointed above his head, at the carriage wall below the wire luggage rack. 'There's no ears there.'

'Ah, yer right, not that you can see, anyways. It's alright, we're going past Cambridge and I'll let yer know when we get there, OK?' He reached out a hand to Joyce, as if asking for a shake. She shrank back against her mum's arm.

'Thank you, if you would, that would be most kind,' Celia said in a posh voice that Joyce didn't recognize. The man saluted, nodded and leant back in his seat, continuing to stare at Celia, who'd once more directed her gaze at Douglas and

Trevor. 'He's a lucky man, your old man,' the soldier said in a low voice. Celia ignored him. Eventually Joyce saw him close his eyes, his arms crossed over his chest.

True to his word, whenever the train pulled into a station he'd pull aside the blackout blinds, slip the window down and lean out, searching for someone to ask where they were. The signs had been taken down in every train station in the country, Granddad had warned them before they left, so they had to ask. The soldier would try to joke and get a smile out of Celia – 'Blimey, that guard looked just like Rob Wilton!' he exclaimed, and, 'Oy, that's Will Hay!' – but Celia wouldn't react. After what felt like a hundred stops and forever in time to Joyce, the train stopped and all along the platform they could hear doors opening and people getting out and in. 'This is it, love, time for our sweet parting . . .' the soldier pulled up the blind and lowered the window. Celia leant forwards, her head out of the window. She searched along the platform, and shouted to the guard, 'Hello? Can you help me with my babies, please? There's a pram in the guard's van.' With a half-smile at the soldier who'd been so helpful, she turned the door handle and stepped down onto the platform. The soldier lifted Joyce under her arms, which surprised her, and swung her down onto the pavement in one easy movement. Then he pulled the door shut, saluted them and pulled down the blind. 'He was nice, Mum. Wasn't he?'

Celia sniffed. 'Come along, Joyce, let's get the pram and our bags and find Aggie, shall we?'

She wasn't hard to find, since she was holding a piece of paper with 'Celia' written on it. Aggie looked to be about the same age as Celia, and could have been her sister, almost. The two women got on immediately, and although the walk from the station to Aggie's house wasn't short, it flew past in a whirl of conversation for the grown-ups. Joyce half-listened to them as she looked around her. All of the buildings seemed to be low, and the sky looked bigger than she'd ever seen it in Redhill or Caterham. There were no hills, she noticed. Some tall houses stood impressively grand but dark, their front doors all in dark colours too, their windows covered with net curtains and some still had their blackouts closed (in the middle of the day!). Looking up, she saw a couple of thin chimneys poking up above the rows of small houses, and lots of church steeples – or she thought they were. It was quiet, Joyce realized, and somewhere she could hear bells ringing, even though it wasn't a Sunday. Joyce couldn't interrupt the adults to ask about the bells, though, because they were chattering on.

Aggie didn't have kids. 'Yet!' she laughed, and her husband was also in the army, like Charles, training to be a medical orderly. When Joyce tried to butt in, Aggie thought she wanted to be carried, so she picked her up, grunting as she did so, and carried her for a while as they made their way along closely lined streets of small terraced houses. Aggie smelled of carbolic soap, powder and some kind of food that Joyce couldn't make out.

'Are you hungry?' she asked, and Joyce nodded. 'Good, 'cos I've got some soup on the go, some bread I baked and a special treat' – which turned out to be some Cadbury's Teatime chocolate biscuits.

Aggie's house was in a terrace just like the ones that they'd passed from the station. Joyce wondered if she'd ever be able to find her way back if she got lost, they all looked the same to her. Aggie lived there alone until now, she said, because her husband was away and the young men that they used to put up for the college weren't coming any more. One of the bedrooms on the second floor, and the front parlour downstairs, used to be for university students before the war, Aggie explained. She'd decided to take in evacuees in order to 'help out – and not be so lonely, like'.

'Well, we're very glad you did,' said Celia, slurping her soup slightly and smiling at Aggie as she rocked the pram to keep the boys sleeping. Feeling full and happy, Joyce put her head on her arms at the smoothly polished dining table, and promptly fell asleep.

The following day, Aggie told them tales of Cambridge, and of how there had been some bombs dropped by the Germans – bringing down some houses in Vicarage Terrace just up the road, she said, waving vaguely in the direction of where the street was – but there hadn't been much of anything to speak of since October. According to Aggie, the Germans did more damage to a farmer's beet fields the previous spring than they had done to the town since then. It wasn't that there were no air raids in Cambridge, she explained, just that there were not many actual bombings. No one knew why the Germans had gone for Vicarage Terrace, since it wasn't exactly near the railway lines and as far as anyone knew had no secret buildings around it. 'But then,' Aggie said, 'them bloody Germans don't need a reason to kill us, do they? Maybe the pilot had been at one of the colleges, and didn't have a happy time,' she laughed.

Joyce and her mother set about exploring Cambridge for the first few days of their stay, and Celia told her it was like most other places she'd been to in England, only it had more pubs, more even than Brighton, and that was saying something. Joyce couldn't think of much except how freezing cold it was, and not just because of the snow that hadn't let up since the New Year. Aggie told them that there was a constant bone chilling wind that blew through Cambridge in winter and it came all the way from Russia. Due to everyone being wrapped up in layers of clothing and hiding half their faces with scarves, Joyce didn't notice the black capes some of the men around the market square had on weren't made to keep the wearer warm. She was too busy trying to not get snow and hail in her eyes.

One morning, a week after being in the town, Joyce spotted a couple of young men in their pyjamas and dressing gowns, carrying towels and walking across Parker's Piece. Admittedly it was early, not yet 8 a.m., but it was very odd, she thought. 'What are those funny men doing?' she asked her mum. Celia shushed her and said they'd ask Aggie when they got back home with the fresh milk they'd gone out for (the milky hadn't arrived).

Celia explained what they'd seen, and Aggie laughed. 'They're just going for their morning baths, that's all.'

'Eh?' Celia replied. 'I thought you told me the public baths were up off Mill Road, in that funny-sounding street, what was it, G-why-deer?'

'They are, in Gwydir Street. Those blokes you saw were going off to their colleges for a bath. The places they stay, like mine here, don't have any bathing, just a tin tub in front of the fire. None of the gentlemen I had staying ever wanted the tin tub, though, they'd always go and have a bath at college. Then they'll go back to their digs and have a cooked breakfast. You see 'em in their 'jamas all weather, some of 'em. Funny bunch. None of my gents ever went out of the house in their night-clothes, though, I can tell you.'

'Cooked breakfast!' exclaimed Joyce. 'Every day? How come? Can I have one every day please!'

'Shush,' Celia told her, and turned to Aggie. 'Must cost the earth to feed grown men of that age?'

'Yeah, but they paid a fair price to live here, and they paid in advance every term, so we always knew what we had to spend on them. There's lots of us university landladies who've had eminent young gentlemen living with us, and it's a good way of making a living. Better than the jam factory, anyway. Some of my young gents send Christmas cards and sometimes pop in and visit when they're here for May Week. Or, at least they used to. Bit different with the war on, naturally.'

On the night of 16 January, the sirens went off in Cambridge just before Joyce's bedtime. Rather than battle their way through the snow and icy wind, Aggie suggested that they stay put, and if they hear any planes near them, they get under the stairs and the table. Joyce was asleep by the time that the drone of aeroplanes was close enough for Aggie to lift her and put her on a pillow under the table. For the following half hour or so there was a constant thud and bang of what turned out to be mostly incendiary bombs landing about a mile away from them. Long after the planes had gone, there was a bright light in the sky over towards Regent Street, reckoned Aggie. She hoped the Regal hadn't gone up in flames, ''cos that would be an end to dancing on Saturday night'. The following morning Aggie went out 'to 'ave a look-see at what happened last night'. When she returned she told them that 'Hyde Park copped it proper last night!' Celia looked confused. 'What, in London? How d'you know?'

'No, silly,' Aggie unwrapped her head and neck from the thick scarf she'd only finished knitting two days earlier, 'Hyde Park Corner over near the Catholic church. One of the air raid wardens reckon that 200 fire bombs got dropped round there. A warehouse went up, and bits of the posh school, The Perse. He said the firemen couldn't get their pumps going 'cos they couldn't find the water taps, and them they did find were frozen solid. It didn't take long for some of them to thaw with all that burning, though, I bet.'

'Was anyone hurt?' asked Celia.

'Don't think so. Sorry, loveys, we didn't have any of that

kind of thing before. 'Ere, you don't reckon Jerry's after you, do you?' Aggie laughed, but Joyce noticed that her mum looked worried.

Aggie repeated the question a couple of weeks later, on 30 January, when the women were caught in an air raid on Mill Road at four in the afternoon. With no shelter close enough to run to as the siren went, which was closely followed by the thrum of engines overhead, Celia and Aggie crept under a big lorry that was just high enough that they didn't have to lie down to get under. 'At least we won't get wet in the snow,' Celia said to Aggie, clutching her hand tightly as they squatted on their haunches. From their spot a few hundred yards from the bridge over the railway line, they watched – horrified – as first one, and then the matching cottage on the other side of the bridge, were hit by bombs.

'They just sort of crumpled at first,' Celia told Joyce when they got home, 'and lots of smoke came out and then bricks started flying everywhere, like in slow motion it was. I was glad we were under that lorry . . .'

'Yeah, until we got out from there, eh, Celia?' Aggie was grinning so much that her cheekbones looked as if they'd pop out, thought Joyce. Both women had had a giddy air about them when they'd burst through the door, their hair wild, their voices shrieking.

'Oh.' Celia stopped completely still, her coat half off and half on. 'Oh.' She sat down at the kitchen table. 'Oh.'

'Mum? What?'

Aggie was beginning to giggle so much that she could hardly speak. 'Ah . . .' She took a breath, leaning with both hands on the back of Celia's chair. Aggie breathed out slowly, giggles breaking into the breath like hiccups, while Celia sat, white-faced and staring. 'When we shuffled out from under the lorry,' Aggie said in a trembling voice, 'this warden came running towards us waving his arms, shouting and pointing behind us. "What's he want, silly old sod," I said to Ceel, didn't I, Ceel?' A nod. 'And he came up to us as we started walking back towards home, and grabbed my arm and says, "Din't you see where you was?" Well, I stopped and said, "Yeah, 'course. What, is it against the law now to hide from bombs?" And he said, "No, but it's bloody stupid to hide from bombs under a petrol lorry!" Then we both turned round and looked at where we'd been, and sure enough, it was a bloody big petrol tanker! And I said to Ceel, "You sure Adolf ain't after you personally?" Then we both burst out laughing, din't we, Ceel?' Another nod.

Aggie paused, her smile gone. 'But now, it don't seem so funny. I think I'll go an' have a lie down.'

ANN

'Good old Uncle Bill!' Ann shouted, hugging her sister Bet. They were at Nana Wolfe's house and he'd just told them that he'd found them a home.

It was far from being as 'decent' as he had promised, he said, but it was definitely big enough to fit them all in. As he explained to Grace, 'It used to be three houses but it's more of a warehouse now. The Baldry's drinks factory bought it and knocked them into one, and then rented it to the Premier brush-making company who kept their brushes there until recently. You lot will be OK. We can soon do it up.'

The family went to see the place the following day. 'It's a dump,' Grace said, none too quietly, as she stood halfway through the door as the children ran in. They were desperate to explore, and immediately saw the potential for den building and games of hide and seek.

Bill stood with his arms crossed over his chest and told Grace, 'I know that it's in the yard of the Hearts of Oak, but it's not a rough pub. It only ever really gets busy when the brush factory workers come in for a drink on pay day. And they're not a bad bunch, mostly girls, so it's never rowdy or too noisy.'

Grace didn't want to complain because she knew they wouldn't be able to find anything this size anywhere else in Cambridge, and certainly not as cheap as this. Bill had arranged with the brush factory for them to live there until the council could find them something permanent, and all they had to pay was for the gas and electricity.

'Presumably there is electric, is there, Bill?' Grace asked only half-sarcastically.

Doubtless because the houses that had been knocked through on the ground floor had been used as a warehouse, all three front windows were shuttered, so the only light came through the door. On closer inspection, Bill could see it was a smaller doorway cut into a larger pair of gates, so he began to unbolt it in order to let more light in. 'Yes, it's on, only I don't think there are any bulbs. Let's get the big doors open and then you can see.'

As he and Jack struggled with the rusted bolts on the top of the gate frame, the children began venturing further away from the light. 'Careful you lot,' Grace warned them harshly, 'you don't know what you might be stepping in, there'll have been cats and all sorts in here.'

Suddenly Ann screamed. 'Mum! Rene's legs have gone right through the floorboards!' Derek started to laugh.

Grace searched in the direction of Rene's shouts, just as Jack got to her and Bill swung half of the double gates open, allowing more weak sunshine in.

Derek continued to laugh as their dad pulled Rene out from the hole she'd made in the rotten floorboards. Laughter spread through the family, becoming hysterical when Ann pointed out what looked like a family of rats scurrying away from the light.

'They're going off to pack their bags,' said Bill, 'they won't stay now you're here, don't worry about them.'

Grace forced a smile, but her disappointment was hard to conceal. Jack caught her looking at him and could almost see the words 'disappointed with my lot' forming on her lips.

Although the ground floor had been knocked through so

that there was a huge space and three front windows looking onto the small street, only one of the former houses had retained a back room, in which there was a stone sink and cold tap. The upstairs hadn't been knocked through, so there were three staircases from the ground floor that each led to two bedrooms, a larger one at the front and small at the rear, making six bedrooms in total. There was an outside lavatory for each former house, but no bathrooms. The first floor rooms had beds in varying degrees of decrepitude, along with wardrobes and cupboards, so all they needed was some furniture for the ground floor. And some flooring, of course.

Over the next few days Jack, Bill and some of his mates carried in floorboards taken from bombed houses and fitted them where needed, while the aunts arranged for some of their furniture to be loaned to the Pilchers at the House of Brushes.

The younger children had great fun in the 'brush house', as they called it, and for the first week had no arguments at all, they so enjoyed being together again. They built dens and hideouts under each of the staircases, and in the three back-yards that had also been knocked through, but not fully, so some bits of wall remained. One provided support to the coal shed, another for the lean-to in which an old mangle stood, rusting away.

Derek and Rene were happier attending the Brunswick, a non-religious school not far from the house, and they soon made lots of friends in the area.

For a while, as the brush house began to look like a home rather than a warehouse, the Pilchers were beginning to seem like a family again, and Grace felt that they were more pro-tected from the war. There had been raids on the outskirts of Cambridge, and one of the boys at Brunswick claimed that he and a pal had been dive-bombed and shot at by a German plane one morning when they were playing in Ditton Fields, but there hadn't been a major raid on the city to compare with what the family had escaped in Folkestone. 'At least there won't be any bombs dropped on us, they're all falling in the sugar beet fields miles from here!' Grace said one day at teatime.

'Drops on the crops,' Jack had told her when he read about the bombs falling in the fields on the outskirts of the town.

As summer 1942 bloomed, the family settled into their new home. On warm Friday evenings, the turbaned and dungaree-wearing women from the brush factory took to sitting in the Hearts of Oak yard with their pints and port, smoking and joking with Grace as she took in her washing, or emptied rubbish into the bins out back. Ann and Bet always smiled at the brush girls and Bet even sneaked a sip of beer from a couple who took a shine to her.

Air raid warnings had gone off occasionally, and the family knew where to go if a raid happened – although Grace, knowing that they were rushing to the cellar under what used to be a petrol station on Occupation Road, was worried that there might still be a tank filled with flammable material nearby. It was the designated shelter for a large number of people from Newmarket Road, and the Pilchers often found themselves sharing a 'bed' of an old mattress with strangers for several hours. It was dank, uncomfortable and, Ann thought, embarrassing. Women who did manage to sleep, even when wrapped in old raincoats for warmth in that cold dark cellar, couldn't help showing their stocking tops, or that they'd drawn a line up their legs because they didn't have any stockings. Ann noticed men looking at them, with strange expressions on their faces, and confusingly she felt embarrassed for the men as much as the women.

When bombs dropped close to the shelter, Ann could feel a sense of fear sweep through the place. When it did, some people cried uncontrollably, one man would recite the Lord's prayer over and over, and an old woman kept saying 'This is it! This is it! This is it!' as the ack-ack guns sounded, long after the major bangs and thuds had faded. On such nights Grace lay with her hands over her ears, on her side with Derek clinging to her front while Rene clung to her back. Ann and Bet sat either side of Jack, against the cobwebby wall in a corner, holding hands, their eyes closed.

Even in the bright glare of the morning sun the dark sounds, smells and sense of fear followed the family as they entered their house. Finally, one morning as Ann thought she couldn't stand it for much longer, her sister spoke up. 'I hate it in there, Mum,' Bet murmured, as Grace found the loaf and some margarine for their breakfast.

'Me too!' said Rene and Derek in unison. Jack looked puzzled, so Ann wrote on the scrap paper pad that was always kept on the table, 'We hate being in the shelter.' Her father nodded. 'Me too.'

There were no air raids for the next couple of nights, and so they got to stay in their own beds all night. On Friday after tea Grace chatted with some of the brush girls in the yard. On re-entering the kitchen she looked triumphant.

'Right,' she began, 'the girls from the brush factory have said that we can go to their new shelter if there's enough room.'

Jack looked up from his newspaper and Bet wrote it down for him. He smiled and said, 'I'll make sure to take us some mattresses.'

Admittedly the brush factory shelter was close and usually the Pilchers were the only people in it if the sirens went late at night, but it was another cellar and the workers didn't knock off until eight or nine sometimes, and if a raid occurred before the end of the working day, things could get very tight in the airless, arch-roofed rooms. Most of the women who worked at

Premier smoked like chimneys and at times Ann couldn't see the end wall of the shelter because of the blue fug in the cellar.

But when it was just them and the night watchman in the brush factory shelter, the raids kind of became an adventure for the children – and while they played games and ran around Grace would sit silently in a corner, her back to her husband. Ann thought Grace looked scared and miserable, and that she only didn't tell them off because of the watchman being in the shelter. Her dad looked as if he was trying to sleep, but that wasn't easy and more often impossible.

Just before Christmas, Jack told Grace that he'd decided to buy a Morrison shelter with the little money they had plus a loan from Bill, who helped to assemble it in their kitchen. It was like one they had back in Folkestone, made up of a metal table with steel mesh sides.

Now, they'd all cram into it when the air raids were on and ask their dad to tell them stories about his time in India and the 'Batsman' and especially the one called Christmas. After the third or fourth telling, a clearly fed-up Grace shouted, 'Oh no! Not again,' and so they had a sing-song instead. Ann noticed that her mum never sang along, though, and kept her thin lips firmly pursed together. She seemed as stiff as a board to Ann, every moment that she spent in the shelter with them made her tense. For the next year whenever raids happened the Pilcher house of brushes would resound to the sound of 'Underneath the Arches', 'Roll Out the Barrel', 'Down at the Old Bull and Bush' and 'When You Wish Upon a Star' from *Pinocchio*, the cartoon film that the kids had loved when they saw it at the Regal in February, but Grace's voice was never raised in unison with her family.

By the summer of 1942, the age of conscription had increased to include men aged between eighteen and fifty-one and all women aged twenty to thirty. Thousands more people had been called up for duty, which meant that there were more jobs going in Cambridge, and Jack finally found employment at the gasworks, despite his disability. It was dangerous because it was a likely target for German bombers, but it was a lot closer to home than the pig farm and meant that Jack was working inside, at least. Now aged fourteen and thirteen respectively, Ann and Bet took jobs at Premier, but money continued to be short. Even if there was little to buy, with rations restricting much of what shops could stock, the cost of coal and keeping four growing children in clothes was stretching the family budget beyond breaking some weeks.

One Saturday afternoon in May of 1943, Ann called Bet, Rene and Derek together in the kitchen and gave each a duster or a brush, and told them that they were going to have visitors. 'Mum's bringing home some of them evacuees to stay. So we have to tidy up.'

'What do you mean?' Rene asked. 'There's thousands of them here in Cambridge. We've got some at our school and they've been there ages. How come we're having them now?'

'Hardly safe here are they?' Derek laughed. 'I nearly fell through the floor this morning up in the back bedroom.'

'Oh, it's because Mum'll get some extra shillings for each one, isn't it,' Bet realized. 'She's always moaning that Dad doesn't earn enough up at the gasworks, and she says I can't go to art college. She got us into that 'orrible brush factory before me and Nance could get our school bags off our shoulders.' She slumped into a chair and looked at her older sister. 'It'll never be enough though, will it? Who's going to look after them when she's at work?'

Ann sat down opposite her sister and explained. 'They're coming from Aunt Lily's, where they'd been billeted. She's had them on her farm but she can't cope any more. The evacuees are too young to be of any help and she's got Herbert to see to, and he's only a year old. We've got enough space here. Look at it – it's huge. We'll all help, too, won't we?' She reached over and rested her hand on Bet's arm. 'They're probably really homesick and petrified – have some sympathy, Bet. And anyway, Derek,' Ann turned to her brother, 'there hasn't been any bombs for ages and there's talk of there not being any more neither! There's a girl and two boys, so you'll have them to play soldiers with.'

All three looked reluctantly at their cleaning implements. 'Please come and help me,' Ann asked, 'we haven't got long and I've got a rabbit stew on.'

Bet and Rene knew that they couldn't leave Ann to do everything because she'd forget about the stew, and never get the cleaning done well enough so she'd be scolded by their mum. 'I never get it right, sorry, Mum,' Ann had told Grace after one of her regular housework inspections only a couple of weeks earlier. 'I don't know why, but housework just doesn't like me. I'd rather be cooking.' Grace liked Ann to do the cooking when Jack wasn't home, although she could never muster a meat pudding quite as good as her dad's.

'OK, Nance,' Bet rose from her chair, 'you stick with the stew and we'll clean upstairs, get their rooms ready for them.'

An hour later three tiny figures stood in the door cut from the double gates, staring inside. Iris, Tony and Derek Lashmar from Poplar had no suitcases or bags. The oversized clothes that they wore were the ones they had arrived in weeks previously. Grace ushered them in. 'It's alright, they won't bite,' she snapped.

'Come on,' Ann beckoned to them. 'We've got some gooseberries we picked yesterday, and I'm going to make us a crumble later, but you can have some now.'

She held out a large bowl of gooseberries and the children walked towards her smiling. They took as many as they could fit into their tiny hands and munched happily. Hearing their mother's voice, Bet, Rene and Derek came down the staircase furthest from the kitchen and trundled across to the new arrivals, who shrank back against the table and put all the gooseberries they had left into their mouths.

'Coo blimey, you wouldn't find me stuffing that much in me mouth,' Derek pointed at the Lashmars, 'or any at all, I only like gooseberries in crumbles!'

It took less than five minutes for Derek to have Tony and Del ('You can be Derek,' the evacuee told the older boy, 'I'm Del') running around the staircases shooting at each other. Iris sat at the kitchen table watching Ann making the crumble. This will work, she thought to herself.

The following morning, though, Grace came blowing into Ann and Bet's room and shouted at her eldest daughter, 'Just bloody marvellous! Those gooseberries you fed the little ones have given them the runs.'

Although there was plenty of room at the house of brushes, it was never cosy or even really comfortable, and so when one day Jack shouted to the family scattered around the ground floor, 'We're going to move house!' there was a general feeling of happy expectation. In recent weeks the kids had heard their parents and Uncle Bill talking about how he and Edie were about to move from their Histon Road house to Albert Street, and that the Pilchers were taking over their old place. 'It's a lot smaller than Brush House, but we'll manage,' Jack had told Grace, forcing an air of optimism. He was too aware that the seven children would be crammed into a three-bedroom house. Plus, in a few months' time, another Pilcher would be joining them.

Ann didn't know what to feel when she overheard Grace telling Aunty Edie that she was pregnant. Ann was sitting quietly reading a book under the kitchen table when her mum and sister came in through the back door. 'I thought that you had gone through the change,' said Edie.

'So did I,' her mum had replied, 'I'm forty-three and too old for another one. I jump out of my skin every time I hear a bang or even thunder. I'm a nervous wreck and can't bear the idea of a baby screaming all night.'

Edie's voice was sympathetic. 'Oh Grace, you'll manage, you always do,' she told her. 'Me and Bill will help as much as we can. He's sorted it with the council for you to have our place, so that's a new start. There's been no bombs dropping over our way.'

Ann almost stopped breathing, not daring to make a sound in case her mum noticed her and told her off. Grace changed the subject anyway, and she and Edie soon moved into another part of the house, allowing Ann to breathe out and think about there being another baby in the family. She hoped that it would be alright, and promised herself to take extra special care of it. No matter what her mum said, she wouldn't let her give this new little sister or brother away.

On the Saturday after the council had agreed for them to take over the tenancy, Jack, with Rene and Derek and the evacuee children, began decorating the Histon Road house. But as they tore down the old wallpaper, bugs ran all over the walls, floors and ceilings. 'Disgusting!' Rene shouted. Jack shooed the children out and the whole house had to be fumigated before they could decorate, let alone move in. However, a few weeks later they were back and stripping paper in rooms that smelled like a hospital due to the distemper. It didn't take long to clean up, paper and paint the three bedrooms, front room, living room and kitchen, and soon enough the younger children were settling in.

Ann tried not to think about the impending arrival of a new Pilcher, but Grace's stomach grew, her moods worsened and she constantly referred to the 'terrible burden' she was carrying, which made it impossible to ignore. Grace's morning sickness became all-day and often night sickness, and she grumbled, moaned and snapped at everyone in the family over the first six months of living on Histon Road.

The baby was due in less than a month when Grace, standing at the sink, gave a loud cry, grabbed the stone sink and doubled over. Gasping, she shouted as loudly as she could, 'Get someone, Nance! The baby's coming.'

Rene, who was still at the table, jumped from her seat as Derek sat, frozen and staring at his mum reaching backwards for something to steady herself against. After pushing a chair towards Grace, Rene ran up the stairs shouting, 'Nance, Nance, Nance, the baby!'

Ann ran to the corner of the next street and the telephone box, covered in posters asking if she really had to make this call and to remember that loose talk costs lives. 'Blimey,' she thought, trying to get her penny into the slot, 'you'd think making a public phone call was an offence.'

Less than an hour later the ambulance arrived, but as they were about to carry Grace into it on the stretcher, the driver said, 'Sounds like she's too far gone. She's going to have to stay here I'm afraid. We won't get her there in time.'

'What's happening?' Derek asked Ann.

'It's OK, Mum's going to have the baby here,' interrupted Mrs Sumpton, a neighbour who had taken charge of the front room, where Grace lay in labour. 'We'll let you come and see her later, but for now go back upstairs,' she told the younger Pilchers and the evacuees, and ordered Nance and Bet to get some hot towels.

'Where's the black bag, Nance?' Rene asked from halfway up the stairs, as the older Pilchers carried the baby bathtub laden with hot towels through to the front room.

Ann said, 'It's in there with Mum, now off you go and look after Derek.'

Standing by with the towels, Ann turned to Bet and said, 'Something's not right.'

Bet looked worried. 'You mean about us using the best room? Mum said it was only for best and this ain't "best", is it?'

Ann shook her head. 'No, I mean with the baby.' Grace was moaning louder and for longer each time when she was told to 'breathe' and 'push' by the ambulance man and Mrs Sumpton. Ann and Bet could barely watch, fascinated by what was happening but repelled at the same time.

When the baby's head crowned, Bet had to sit down and hold a fresh towel in front of her face, peeking at the bloody scene in front of her when she dared. As the baby emerged, Bet buried her face in the towel. Ann continued to watch, and was horror-struck by the sight. Something was certainly wrong, the baby's head looked the wrong shape and it wasn't making much noise.

Outside the room, Derek and Rene sat on the stairs, listening through the bannisters as their mum screamed. After a couple of minutes of silence, Mrs Sumpton left the front room briefly to fetch some clean rags, and they saw their mum laying on the floor with the good rug underneath her, crying. At her feet was a tiny little baby, looking as if its brain was oozing out of its head. Ann stared, transfixed, until one of the ambulance man said, 'We'll get them to the hospital now. They'll be fine.' But it was clear, even to the children, from his tone of voice that all was not fine, and from what she had seen, it certainly didn't look fine.

Jack had been working late at the gasworks that night when Uncle Bill came to take him to Mill Road hospital, where he stayed until well past midnight. When he got home he found a large piece of paper with the words, 'Mum at hospital with baby' on the table. Ann had scribbled it down before she went to bed, unaware that he had already been told. Jack sat at the kitchen table with his head in his hands, and wept silently.

The next morning, the children found Jack cleaning the front room. 'I need all of you to meet me in the kitchen with pencils and paper.' They quietly obeyed their father, and within a couple of minutes were all sitting at the kitchen table, looking at him. Jack held his shoulders back and announced proudly, 'We've called him Johnny. He's a strong fella and handsome like me and you, Derek.' He paused for what seemed hours before continuing. 'But he's got something wrong with his brain . . . some of it's missing, there's like a hole in the front of his skull. I've got it writ down what they called it.' He took a crumpled piece of paper out of his pocket and handed it to Ann. The word 'Encephalocele' was typed on it.

Answering the querying looks, he told them, 'They're going to take him down to London to Great Ormond Street for more tests and treatments. They're going to have to operate. Your mum will have to go with him.'

The strain of telling them became too much for Jack, who rested his head slowly on his arms folded in front of him on the table, and began to cry in huge, racking sobs.

The children didn't know what to do, they had never seen him cry before, he was always happy and laughing. No matter what the situation, they knew they could always rely on their dad to be positive. 'We have to pull together,' Ann said to her sisters and brother, who all nodded, stood, and gathered round their dad to hug him.

Johnny was taken to London before the rest of the family could properly meet him. Grace had asked Jack to bring her a bag of clothes for the trip to Great Ormond Street, but said not to let the children visit. The operation involved doctors attempting to ease his brain tissue inside his skull, draining fluid and hoping that as little damage had been done to his neural functions as possible. Grace and the newest member of the Pilcher family were gone for two weeks, and when they returned it was not a joyous occasion.

Grace and Johnny got to their house in the middle of the afternoon when everyone was out, at work or school. She greeted Bet and Ann as they returned from work, holding Johnny in her arms, seated at the kitchen table. 'He's probably going to be severely brain damaged,' Grace said matter-of-factly. 'And he's deaf and completely blind, not the same as Joy.' As if to soften the shock, she added the only positive that the doctors had been able to find. 'But look, his skull has been closed up. They've had to fit a plate so they could repair the area.' Grace turned the tiny infant so that they could see the stitches in his battered-looking and grotesquely swollen head.

Ann was filled with pity for the child, but she was seriously concerned about her mum, who looked more worn-out and weaker than she'd ever seen her. Ann reached out and took the baby from their mum's arms and handed him to Bet. Then she turned back to Grace and put her arms around her, gently putting her mother's head onto her shoulder. 'It's going to be alright, Mum,' she comforted her, even though she knew that it wouldn't be, ever, for Johnny.

While the children loved having a little baby in the house, after Joy they were prepared for the inevitable. It wasn't long before Grace announced that Johnny would be joining Joy at the Sunshine Home, 'in a few months'. Before then it fell to Bet and Ann to take it in turns to look after him during the night, and their ten-year-old sister Rene to look after him during the day when she returned from school. It was a job that Rene relished.

'You can't help but love him, can you?' she would say to the others whenever she was sure that she was out of earshot of her mum. Rocking Johnny gently, she'd add, 'He's beautiful.'

Ann found it heartbreaking to watch the bond form between Rene and Johnny, and tried to tell her not to get too fond of her little brother. But Ann didn't know how to put into words the sense of loss and emptiness that she'd felt when Joy had been taken away, and which had been doubled when leaving her behind on the single, solitary visit she'd made with her mum and dad. Grace must have noticed how Rene was becoming so fond of Johnny, because when the day came for him to be taken to East Sussex, she ensured that Rene was out. No one knew the actual date of Johnny's departure, which turned out to be the day that Rene had to take Derek to Mrs Sumpton's house.

When she got home, Rene was hot, tired and hungry – and immediately disturbed to discover the house cold and empty. Grace had told her that Aunty Edie was coming to help her with Johnny that day, so why was no one about?

When Ann and Bet returned home a couple of hours later, Ann immediately realized what had happened, and had to break the awful news to Rene, who ran to her room, slammed the door and stayed there, even when Jack and Grace got back and tried to talk to her about how happy Johnny was to meet Joy.

Rene cried all night.

*

Sisters Ann, Bet and Rene, together with the evacuee Iris, shared a bedroom in Histon Road, with the older girls sleeping in the same bed. They were as close as they'd ever been, but working at the brush factory had shown Bet how much she needed to look after her older sister – Ann's bad hearing on her right side meant that Bet had to keep both an eye and ear out for her in case any of the lorries came along on that side while her back was turned. Ann had also given money to a few of the women who'd begged off her, giving some sob story or other about needing it for their children. Bet knew what a soft touch her sister was, so she had to be harder-hearted for her.

Not that they worked there for too long after the move, because Grace found them better paid jobs at the Star Brewery on Newmarket Road. The girls didn't like that much, either, but had little choice other than to take it. There was a terrible stench from the fermentation section, and they were asked to shovel spent grains out of the brewery all day. It was hard, physical work that a woman wouldn't do if there hadn't been a war on.

'Can we take a few bottles home to our dad?' Bet asked Walter Locker, the foreman, on their first day.

'No you bloody can't,' he half-joked. 'Cheeky blighter. It's alright for you to taste a few brews, mind, but you're not to take any out!' The girls found shovelling thirsty work, and when they learned that they had to do the same thing every day, Bet soon got to like the taste.

A couple of weeks into the new job, Ann noticed some crates of beers stacked up high that had the coat of arms of one the colleges stamped on them. She figured that they must be waiting for collection or delivery, and went into a daydream about her future husband being served the beer with the other fellows and dons at what Uncle Jake had called high table.

They would be talking about politics and important issues, she daydreamed.

But before the first course was finished, she was brought back to the real world by Bet shouting at her, 'Here, old Locker said we can try some of the new brew! Come and have a tipple and a smoke with me, Nance!'

Sitting in the yard with her sister, Ann used her firmest voice, and sounded as if she was talking to a child as she told Bet, 'I don't really like beer, Bet, and I am never going to try smoking again no matter how much you try and persuade me. It's disgusting.'

'Give over, Nance, it's lovely,' Bet said, lighting up another one. 'Look at me, see how sophisticated I am,' she said, swigging the beer and taking a long drag on her Rothmans cigarette. She started to cough.

'Mum won't like you spending money on them.'

'I'll buy Woodbines then, they're a lot cheaper,' Bet stuck her tongue out at her sister. 'She's got to let me have some luxury for Pete's sake. I can't wait to get out of there, Nance. Hey, let's go dancing this weekend. We can go to the Beaconsfield! Please say you'll come.'

Ann hesitated. She didn't like going to the dances, it cost a shilling to get in and a tuppence for the cloakroom, and she was trying to save for her future. Ann had opened a National Savings account as soon as she started working at the brush factory and put away all the money she had left over after she had given her mum her keep.

She also found it too difficult to hear anyone who talked to her in the ballroom, what with the band playing and the chatter going on all around her. Ann was embarrassed about her dancing, too, because ever since her operations her balance and co-ordination had been affected. She offered a different excuse, though. 'I don't want to spend hours ironing my hair,' she told Bet, 'and I haven't got nothing to wear any more. Those damn moths have eaten all my clothes.'

Bet countered with, 'Nance, listen, don't worry, if you keep your new jacket on you'll look lovely.'

Ann had been given a stylish bolero jacket by her Aunt Win for her birthday, and felt like royalty when she put it on. She had to agree that it was the perfect opportunity to wear it.

Bet knew she wouldn't be able to go without Ann as her chaperone. 'You can only go if our Nance goes with you,' Jack told her every time she asked. 'You're not old enough really, Bet.' Neither girl wanted to upset Jack, and so when they had gone out the first half-dozen times, they made sure that they were home before his bedtime. But still he would walk towards the dance halls a full five minutes before they were due home, in order to meet them. Every time they burst out of the dance hall they'd see him standing there, hands in his pockets with the same phrase ready, 'Better not have danced with any Yanks, you two!'

Although there were a fair number of Americans in Cambridge by the end of 1943, neither Bet nor Ann had spoken to any, let alone danced with them: their mum and dad were forever warning them about the 'Yanks' and their wicked ways with women. 'Nice girls don't date Yanks!' Grace was forever yelling as they left the house for an evening out. And anyway, Bet, who loved dancing, had taken a liking to a cheeky local boy nicknamed Barrel who was no slouch on the dance floor. They first met when he was on leave from the navy and planned to meet this weekend when, Ann knew, they'd spend the whole of their evening together jiving and doing the foxtrot.

The chance to show off her jacket was too tempting, and Ann liked seeing everyone dressed up and dancing, even if she didn't like joining in herself, so she said yes, even though she was unconvinced about what else to wear that night.

Bet was dressed and made up before Ann had changed, and in an effort to hurry her along took the fine wool pink sweater Aunt Win had bought Ann the year before from the wardrobe and handed it to her. 'But it's been eaten by moths,' she told Bet, disheartened. Bet tutted and reassured her, 'Don't worry, you can still wear it, it looks fine from the front. Look.'

She forced it over Ann's head and ordered her to put the jacket on. Ann did so, and Bet pushed her to the mirror. 'See! It's fine. You'll be fine, who'll see it if you keep your jacket on? You look lovely.'

Ann had to admit that it looked OK, and the jacket was lovely.

'Now come on!' Bet urged her. 'Barrel will think I've stood him up if we don't hurry.'

Ann smiled – it was good to see her sister so happy – took Bet's hand and ran down the stairs and through the front door, calling as they left, 'See you, Mum, Dad, we'll be at the Beaconsfield, won't be late.'

At the hall a local accordion band from New Street were playing, and Barrel was standing by the door tapping his feet. 'There he is, Nance! My Barrel!' Bet almost sprinted away from Ann. 'I'll see you in there, Nance,' she said, making a beeline for him.

Looking delighted, he planted a great big kiss on her cheek, looked Ann up and down and said, 'You scrub up well, girl, don't you, Nance?'

Ann smiled, she liked Harry Reynolds because he reminded her of Lou Costello. 'Don't you think it's a little cruel that he's nicknamed Barrel?' she'd asked Bet after their first meeting.

'No, he doesn't mind, it's not just because he's short and a bit round that he's called that,' she laughed, 'it's because he likes a bit of a tipple from the brandy barrel!'

As she watched them skip onto the dance floor giggling, Ann found herself thinking that if they would hurry up and get married, she wouldn't have to go out with Bet any more.

Ann looked for somewhere to sit that would enable her to have her back to the wall. She knew nobody could see through her bolero jacket, but it was enough for her to know that her sweater was full of holes to make her feel uneasy. Heading for a chair at an empty table, she was stopped in her tracks by the looming figure of a tall, besuited young man. 'Good evening. It's Ann, isn't it?' he asked. 'Winifred and George's niece?'

Ann blushed a bright scarlet as she recognized the man. He was a lodger at Aunt Win's house, where they'd met a couple of months earlier at Nana Wolfe's funeral party. His existence had come as a surprise to Ann. 'I didn't know Aunt Win had a lodger. What do you know about him?' she had whispered to Bet after narrowly avoiding being introduced to him by Win. Bet had already taken a glass (or two) of sherry and was looking flushed.

'Aunt Win's started a lodging house for the colleges, and he's a fellow.' Noticing how Ann stared at him, Bet continued. 'Bit old for you ain't he, Nance? Must be at least thirty! Although he is educated, and he's from Kent, I've been told.' She looked him over. 'He is rather handsome though, ain't he? I reckon that's what Errol Flynn will look like in a few years.' Knowing the actor was Ann's heart-throb, she nudged her and drew a smile out of her desperately shy sister. Ann had run away on some pretence when Win tried to introduce them. But now, here in the semi-darkness of the dance hall, during a lull between numbers, Peter Constable was trying to get her to talk to him.

'I love this band. I've seen them a couple of times here,' he said, and Ann, in complete contrast to when they had previously met, began talking and didn't know when or how to stop.

'Erm, yes, my dad used to play the accordion before he became deaf. He played it out in India, to the batmen mainly. They loved his playing, he said. He can play the banjo as well, although he likes to play like the minstrels used to, how his dad had taught him. He doesn't play any more though really. Well, he bangs some tunes out on the piano but he doesn't know if they're in tune because of his deafness. Better than me though, I can't play any music, I had trouble with my ears when I was a little girl so I can't play a tune, neither.'

When she did stop talking, Peter had a slightly lopsided smile on his face, and didn't say anything immediately. Oh no, she thought, he doesn't want to hear all of this. He's just being polite, he only said 'hello', he didn't ask for my life history. She should have just said yes, and that would have been it.

'Would you like to dance?' he asked.

Now tongue-tied and blushing, Ann looked down at the dance floor. 'Oh no, you're alright. I don't dance,' she replied.

'OK, well at least let me get you a drink?'

'No, I don't drink. Thanks, though.'

He laughed. 'Actually, neither do I, we can have a soft drink.'

What was she going to do? He wasn't going to give up, she thought.

Peter stepped to Ann's side, gently took her elbow and started walking her towards the same table that she'd been heading for. 'There's a table, please come and sit down,' he said softly. 'It would be a pleasure for me to spend an evening with someone with a true appreciation of this style of music.' He pulled a chair out for her, and as she moved past him, Peter put a hand on the collar of her jacket. Ann froze.

'Let me take your jacket. I'll put it in the cloakroom for you on my way to the bar.'

'No, please don't, I . . .' Peter gently pulled the jacket backwards and down her arms. As the pink sweater was revealed he stopped and stared just long enough for Ann to shrug the jacket back on. Then she ran.

'Sorry . . . Ann, I, I didn't realize . . . Don't go!' Peter called after her as she escaped him.

Watching from the dance floor, Barrel nudged Bet. ''Ere, ain't that your Nance running to the lavs?' he asked.

Bet turned in time to see her sister fleeing towards the toilets, and ran after her. By the time she got through the door Ann had already locked herself into a cubicle. 'What's happened, Nance, are you in there?' Bet asked, knocking on the door.

'It's Aunty Win's lodger, he's here,' sobbed Ann from behind the door. 'He saw the holes in my jumper, oh Bet, I want to die!'

Bet put her forehead against the door, closed her eyes and tried to bully her sister out of the locked cubicle. 'Don't be so blooming stupid, come out.'

'I am not coming out! Go and get me a drink, lemonade or something. I'm going to stay in here until Dad comes to meet us!'

'Oh great. Just great. You can't stay in there all night!'

Getting no reply, Bet turned on her heel and marched back to Barrel and threw herself into a jive, as if kicking her legs could free her of the guilt and shame that she felt for her sister. True to her word, Ann stayed in the toilets for two-and-a-half hours. Bet twice returned to check on her, and saw Ann watching from the entrance as she approached and dodge back into the cubicle as she got closer the first time.

'Where's my drink?' she demanded through the door, as Bet

pushed into the room. 'I'm not coming out until I at least get a lemonade!'

Bet sighed in exasperation and left without a word. Half an hour later she returned, and as Ann watched, she saw Bet had a drink in her hand, and so stayed in the entrance, half in and half out of the loo.

'Oh, Nance. Don't worry, no one saw it,' Bet tried to cheer her sister as she handed the lemonade to her.

'He bloomin' saw it, alright. Is he still here? 'Cos I'm not coming out until he's gone home and that's for sure.'

'He's gone, about ten minutes ago,' Bet said. 'He looked ever so sad, stood there all alone, for an hour, he was. Then he just left.'

'Oh. Right.' Ann felt miserable. 'Can we go now, then?'

Bet sighed. 'Give me a couple more dances, Ann. Then we'll go. OK?'

Ann nodded and stepped out of the toilet completely. She sidled along the wall sipping her drink as Bet returned to Barrel. Their dad would be outside in a short while and then Ann could go home and throw away the horrible sweater.

JOYCE

Cambridge 1941–46

From that day in January when Joyce's mum came back giddy after sheltering under a fuel lorry, the bombing of Cambridge intensified. The air raid sirens went off almost daily, although the actual raids were fewer and further between than Joyce, her mum Celia and the twin babies had known in Surrey. The sky was often filled with the sound of aeroplanes, but they were more often 'our boys' as the grown-ups called them, either on training flights or in fighters passing over on their way to one of the many bases situated further north and east in Norfolk, or south in Suffolk.

Late one night at the end of February 1941, the highest number of people killed in a raid on the city occurred when three waves of bombers targeted Cambridge. Eleven people met their end in the attacks. Heading from east to west over the town, explosives hit Cherry Hinton Road on one side of the railway tracks, Hyde Park Corner again and Grantchester Meadows on the other. Incendiary bombs were dropped in some number, but following the January raid when firemen had trouble getting their hoses attached to pipes, the council installed static water tanks by the side of major roads for easy access. They proved useful three months later when more than fifty houses between Hills Road and Trumpington (again on either side of the railway) were hit. All of the fires were put out within minutes, the local paper reported.

It was odd, as Aggie their landlady kept saying, that none

of the university buildings had been hit. King's College still stood proud and untouched, even if its windows were covered in a black tar paper and you could no longer see the pretty designs on them. That new, tall tower library should surely be a plain target, Aggie said she heard lots of blokes in the pub say, only it hadn't been. There were always lines of army trucks parked up on the backs, by the river, behind all the old colleges, too, but they were never hit.

Aggie took the family for a stroll along the river and the backs when the sun came out in May. She explained that it was called the backs because all you could see was the backs of the college buildings from there. She pointed out King's and St John's, which was having a lot of building work done near the round church and on Bridge Street, too. There were rumours, Aggie said, that they were putting in a bomb shelter under a house on Bridge Street that only the college people could use. 'Typical,' she said, 'always us and them, gown versus town.'

Their wandering took them over a pretty little bridge and along a lane that brought them out in Trinity Street, in the town centre. There were lots of men in uniforms walking about, both army and RAF. 'There's a lot of cadets stationed at St John's,' Aggie explained to Celia who commented on the number of fly boys about. 'They're using up the space where the students used to be, in their rooms I think, though they have some tents too. According to a lady I know who works in the kitchens, there's a right to-do between the RAF blokes and the bursar about food and supplies going missing from the college kitchens.'

That warm Sunday proved to be the first of many in the summer of 1941. There were no air raids in the summer months and Joyce and Celia got to know the place well by walking Douglas and Trevor around in the pram, crossing the many green commons and 'pieces' as the locals called them. Joyce

soon learned which college was where. Many of Aggie's friends
and neighbours seemed to either work there, or used to, before
war broke out.

The summer months always used to be less busy in the
town and at the colleges, Aggie explained to Celia, due to there
being no students around until October. Although there were
still the fellows who needed to be cooked for and cleaned up
after, their shoes blacked and laundry done.

Joyce, whose ears always pricked up when mention of the
colleges was made, interrupted the adults. 'What do you mean,
"fellows"? Ain't they all fellows?' she asked.

'I mean their teachers, them what live at the colleges,'
Aggie smiled at the young girl, always happy to tell her what
she knew about the colleges. 'Most of them don't have a wife
and don't 'ave a home to go to, neither. A lot of them are
ancient an' all, these days especially,' she continued. 'They might
have never lived nowhere else since being students themselves,
I reckon. There's one old boy, I heard, who couldn't dress himself no more, and the housekeeper has to do it, she's more of a
nurse to 'im if you ask me. Mind you, some of them fellows
are young men, too. Or was, until they all got called up, of
course, or joined up. The ones that are married don't live in the
colleges, of course, they get houses what the college own and
rent to 'em. I sometimes had what they call a graduate student
lodging with me, he was a bit older than them that are undergraduates, and he was going on to become a doctor, though not
in hospital.'

'So they have a hospital in them colleges too, do they?'

'No Joyce, love, not really. There's a lot of hospitals round
here, though. There's the one round the corner on Mill Road
near Gwydir Street what used to be a workhouse and where all
the babies are born – if you can make it there in time, of course,
and afford it. Up the road a bit further there's Brookfields,

which is a disease hospital, but the big one's called Adden-brooke's and it's on Trumpington Street where there's a lovely kiddies bit, only about ten years old, that is. There's another old workhouse over the river at Chesterton that's a hospital. Of course, some of the villages have one too, like the TB clinic at Papworth where my Uncle Ted spent his last days in the twenties. The students what study medicine get to go an' prac-tice on the poor buggers in them hospitals. I wouldn't have any of them looking at me, though. I mean, it's not decent, is it? They're not proper doctors and one time I was in the hospital having my appendix out when a bunch of them came round the ward, and they stopped at my bed and asked if they could see my scar. "Not bloody likely!" I told 'em.'

Joyce giggled with delight at the idea, and Aggie continued. 'There was only one of the students in among them who'd lived in my house the previous year, wasn't there? Dougal, it was. A lovely, quiet boy, he was Scottish, used to have lots of birds' skulls in his room. I thought he was training to be a vet.'

Celia and Joyce laughed together. 'How do you know the kiddies' hospital is nice?' Celia asked Aggie, who had a basket of washing that she was taking into the yard to put through the mangle. Resting the washing basket on the doorstep, Aggie wiped her brow and looked at Joyce, folded her arms and leant towards Celia. 'I'm not sure it's a good idea if your Joyce hears why I know. She takes it all in, I'm sure she does.' Joyce was told to stay inside, and the women stepped into the yard, closing the door behind them. Joyce sighed with frustration. She found the conversations of grown-ups much more inter-esting than anything she heard in school, even if a lot of it didn't make sense to her.

After the relative quiet of the summer months, the Germans attacked Cambridge at the end of August, when two houses around the corner from Aggie's were hit, and again in September when the main road near Castle Hill was bombed. After that, though, there were no more raids for ten months, not even when the Luftwaffe began their 'Baedeker Raids' of April 1942 when they chose historical sites in cities like Norwich, Exeter and York out of *Baedeker's Guide to Great Britain* to bomb, said the radio news. The last big raid on Cambridge happened in late July of that year, during the school holidays. Earlier that day Joyce had been out with her mum and the twins looking at the shops on Sidney Street which were then hit by fire bombs during the night. They hadn't aimed at the town centre before. Joyce was scared.

Two days later as she walked down the same street, Joyce felt a funny fluttering in her stomach and a nervousness that she hadn't had since leaving Redhill. The town had changed. Slowly and surely, the streets of the town had seen railings and metal gates disappear 'to help make bombs and guns', said her mum. The remaining iron was painted white, so that they could be seen during the blackout. The spaces opened up by the loss of gates and fences, along with the newly created holes and missing buildings, made the town seem different after every bombing. For the seven-year-old Joyce, Cambridge was an ever-changing series of streets, alleys, over-grown gardens, open spaces and cobbled lanes that she could easily get lost in.

Even after bombing raids dropped off, Joyce still wouldn't want to go into the centre or even too far from her street without an adult to hold her hand. She took it on herself to 'look after' the twins as much as she could, and would play with them in the street along with other kids around her age. Douglas and Trevor were too young to play with the bigger boys, so Joyce rolled up newspaper into a ball and let them kick that between them, as she sat on the doorstep half-watching them and half-watching other kids run about, the girls skipping or playing hopscotch in a grid chalked on the road, the boys playing war, football or marbles that would occasionally turn into brief fights.

At school Joyce and all the children were given a spoonful of cod liver oil and another of malt every day. Occasionally they'd be given foodstuffs to take home, it having been donated by countries in the Empire unaffected by the war. The best one, Joyce would always remember, was a tin of powdered chocolate from nice Canadian People (the teacher wrote it on the board for them). Her fingers and her mouth were all brown by the time she got it home. Joyce would go home for dinner at noon, when she would make jam sandwiches for herself and the twins, before going back to school for the afternoon. If there was any, she'd have a glass of milk at school before heading home again at the end of the day.

When Joyce felt brave enough, she began to explore further afield than Newmarket Road and East Road, where she had lived ever since being in Cambridge. In Gwydir Street she discovered a baker's shop that made fresh pies every day, a chip shop that still fried fish, at least at the end of the week, and gardens in which people kept all kinds of livestock, everything from chickens to pigs and goats. None of the houses had electricity (neither did hers), but all seemed to have very smart front rooms half-hidden behind net curtains that covered only the bottom half of the window. Being nosey, Joyce would stand on front walls where railings had been removed and peer in, wondering who lived in such a nice, tidy house. She supposed that those rooms were only used on Christmas and Boxing Day like in her old home, and the rest of the house was as crowded and plain as her own.

After the Americans entered the war ('about bloody time', Aggie had said, who was listening to the radio with them when it was announced in December 1941), everyone had said that it would soon be over, and that the Yanks would help get Jerry on the run. In 1943 lots of American soldiers and flyers started to turn up in the town. Aggie was excited at first because she thought she might be able to get one or two in as lodgers, if Celia and the kids could find somewhere else. But because she was a 'single' woman, what with her husband away in the services, she wasn't allowed to even apply. She was annoyed when she found out that landladies who did get an American also got bigger rations, including tinned fruit and even fresh bananas.

There were plenty of US soldiers billeted around their area, and Joyce became as brazen as every other kid in the street when they saw an American soldier; she'd shout to them, 'Got any gum, chum?' and was more often than not rewarded with a stick or two for her cheek. Joyce thought that they all sounded funny, and it made her laugh when they told her what a funny accent she had. Although not quite five years old, Douglas and Trevor were more brazen with the American soldiers, and would ask for anything that they might want to part with, from marbles to uniform patches. A couple of times they were given American comic books which were all about the war, with American soldiers beating the Germans and Japanese in battles on land, sea and in the air, and they were passed between each other until they fell apart.

Following the invasion of Italy in September 1943, the family heard that Charles had been a part of the invading force and was somewhere near Pompeii. Not long after Christmas that year, foreigners wearing loose uniforms with badges on them started appearing in Cambridge. 'They're prisoners of war,' Celia told Aggie as they watched from the upstairs window as a line of them walked down their street. 'They're going to be working on the farms and that, till the war's over. Italians, Madge at the grocers reckons.'

'Don't look Italian, do they?' said Aggie.

'How's that, then?' Celia asked.

'I dunno,' Aggie thought for a second, 'maybe smarter or something, like that Frankie Sinatra.'

'He's not Italian, Ag,' Celia laughed.

'Close enough though, ain't he? Italian-American. And gorgeous, eh?'

'Who's gorgeous, Mum?' Joyce asked, walking into her mother's bedroom where the two women stood.

'Your dad, love', Celia said sweetly. 'And I hope we'll see him soon, eh?'

They didn't see him for another nine months, but Charles returned for a two-week leave in one piece and sun-tanned in June 1944, just after the Normandy landings had taken place. The boys were delighted to have their own war hero at home, even if he wouldn't talk to them about what had happened during the invasion. His nightmares, night sweats and dark moods told Celia that something terrible had happened, but he wouldn't say a word. Instead he'd take her and Aggie to the pub as often as they'd agree to go, leaving Joyce to 'look after' the twins.

Aggie's husband hadn't been heard from for some months, but she hadn't received any telegrams from the war office about him, so she supposed he was 'having a whale of a time with those Italian girls', although she said it with more hope than humour.

When it came time for Charles to report back for duty he told Celia that he didn't think he was going back to Italy, and that it was more likely to be France, but not to worry. He was still giving dying men medical care and carrying stretchers away from the battlefield. Celia couldn't read much in his eyes as Charles said goodbye, there was a determined hardness to the set of his features, as if a front had been pulled down on a shop window, she thought. Joyce felt it, too. She knew her dad was inside that uniform and under the little hat, only she didn't think that she could see him, just the shape of the dad she'd known and loved. As he walked away from the house, Joyce noticed his usual light step turn into a stiff, jerky march as he got further away from the house, and by the time he turned the corner out of sight he'd become just another soldier like the ones she saw marching across Parker's Piece, or along Newmarket Road.

When Charles returned from the war for good he was physically in one piece, but it seemed like he'd left a bit of something in France and Germany. The Jones family all survived the conflict, bombings, separations and privations of the war. Joyce's grandparents picked up their life as if the previous six years hadn't happened (although they'd pass away within months of each other, from natural causes, before the 1950s began). However, the ensuing peacetime was not as successfully navigated by one of the twins.

Two weeks before their seventh birthday in April 1946, Joyce took the boys to Newmarket Road intending to go to see the circus tent being put up on Midsummer Common. As they reached the public toilets in the centre of the busiest part of the road, Douglas said he had to go to the lav, could they wait for him? Joyce sat on the steps and listened for the sound of Douglas singing 'It's a long way to Tipperary', as he always did when he went to the toilet. Trevor made his way around the traffic island because he couldn't sit still. As he climbed around the railings a bunch of bigger boys crossed the road to where he was and started calling him ginger, pushing him and poking him. In a panic, Trevor jumped off the railings and ran across the road, trying to hide between the pillar box and telephone box, but the boys followed him across and chased him. As he got to the roadside again he stepped backwards, into the road – the driver of a passing lorry had no chance of missing him. Trevor was dragged under his wheels and left in a small, crumpled heap.

Traffic stopped and people ran to the boy, forming a ring around him. Someone went to the doctor's office opposite where the accident had happened, and as Joyce fought her way through the crowd to her little brother, Dr Cameron, a middle-aged GP wearing tweed and small, rimless spectacles, reached the boy at the same time. He bent over Trevor, who was still conscious, felt his chest, held his limp wrist for a few seconds and straightened up.

'Sorry, nothing I can do for him, and he's not my patient anyway. I'll call an ambulance for him, though.' He turned and walked stiffly back to his office.

Joyce sat crying beside Trevor as adults tried to comfort her. One man put his jacket over the boy. Trevor's eyelids flickered and he looked up at his sister. 'J-J-Joyce,' he stammered, and lifted his hand towards her, 'give this to Mum . . .'

She took the brand new ha'penny from him and Trevor sank into nothingness. She knew when the ambulance men arrived and set about lifting her brother that it was too late, they wouldn't be able to do anything for him. He was dead.

MAUD COOPER

Cambridge 1945–50

Maud Cooper was twenty-one and desperate to get away from the house she shared with her grandmother when she met Hugh Ingram in 1945. She vowed to herself that she would never go back to see her after she married and moved out. She had not really known either of her parents, and her last memory of them being together was from when she was about three years old, standing at the garden gate. Her dad was wearing a sailor's uniform, waving goodbye and promising to write. But he never returned, and according to her nan, Maud's mother had collapsed when she received a telegram telling her that he had gone missing after the ship he was serving on as a bo'sun had disappeared somewhere in the China seas. She never recovered, according to Nan, who soon had her only daughter committed to the local psychiatric hospital at Fulbourn, and moved her granddaughter into her decrepit house on Mitcham's Corner.

They lived a very private and frugal existence. Her nan never mentioned her mum, and Maud was discouraged from asking questions about her. Nan kept Maud busy when not at school by giving her housework to do, and as a result she had few friends and didn't know how to behave when around boys. By the time she reached her teens, Nan was forever telling her that she wasn't good enough for marriage. 'No man wants a miserable sour-looking girl like you,' she told her. 'You'll be a spinster, you will. Good for nothing, too.'

Her nan's obstructiveness didn't extend to Maud's imagina-
tion, and as a teenager she spent plenty of time practising
'smooching' in the bedroom she shared with the old woman,
when sent to bed before her. Maud attempted to master what
she imagined would be the perfect kiss, until one evening she
was caught in the act by Nan. 'Bloody mental you are, Maud.
Just like your mum,' Nan said with mild disgust, after finding
her with eyes closed, kissing her hand and dancing a waltz;
the noise her heels made on the wooden floor had brought the
old woman to the bedroom door. 'I don't mind you play acting
some romantic nonsense,' she scolded Maud, 'but keep your
lovemaking down. Why are you such a stupid girl? I don't
want old shorty pants from downstairs banging on his ceiling
again! I'm fed up fighting with him.' Maud didn't fancy their
downstairs lodger Mr Golding's chances in a fight with Nan,
so she was careful from then on to take her shoes off when she
waltzed to music that only she could hear.

Throughout her late teens, during the Second World War,
Maud admired scores of men from a distance, never daring
to talk to any of them. It was inevitable that when a relatively
good-looking young man did speak to her, she would fall
finally and fatally in love with him. So it was when Hugh
Ingram started to tease her one fine day by the River Cam in
1945. They had both come to watch the annual college boat
races known as the Bumps. This year Maud decided to support
the St John's Lady Margaret crew, simply because it was their
'turn' – she chose a different one every year. She and neighbour
Gladys Burnett were visiting the river in Chesterton, enjoying
watching the crowds of people, soaking up the atmosphere and
excited to be close to college people, who were rarely seen in
such numbers away from the university.

The girls sat watching the races, and when the Lady Margaret crew came into sight they jumped up and ran alongside

the river shouting encouragement. It was when they were running along the river bank that she first saw her future husband. He was there with another young man, helping old Dewsbury the lock keeper at Baits Bite to turn the boats round using punting poles. The Lady Margaret crew had just lost to a Jesus College boat, which was declared the winner and it was being set alight as Maud and Gladys reached the Bite.

'That's a damned waste!' the nice-looking young man shouted.

Slightly annoyed that he should question a college tradition, Maud forgot her shyness and addressed the young man directly. 'Does seem like it, don't it?' she said as snootily as she could manage. 'But it's their tradition.'

Looking wryly amused, he asked, 'And who are you, Miss . . . ?'

Blushing she stammered a response. 'Maud, Maud Cooper.'

'Well, I'm Hugh Ingram,' he lifted his straw boater to reveal a fine head of auburn hair, swept back over his crown. 'Pleased to be of acquaintance, Miss Cooper. What are you doing here?'

Deciding to be what her nan would call 'brazen', Maud proceeded to carry on a conversation with an older male stranger (he's a good four or five years older than me, she thought). 'Me and Gladys started coming down here a couple of years ago. It's become our tradition, like.' Maud could hear Gladys giggling next to her, and she hushed her with a backwards wave.

Hugh looked directly into Maud's eyes. 'Well, we've been helping Dewsbury since we were boys, so for years,' he pointed to the other young man, who had moved away, along the top of the lock gate. Hugh continued, 'I'm on leave at the moment, and thought I'd help him out for old time's sake. I suppose it's a tradition for me, too.'

Maud thought she had never met anyone so well spoken and polite. She didn't want him to go, and desperately tried to think of something to say. 'Is rowing your thing then, is that what you did at school?' she blurted. What am I thinking? she asked herself silently, I sound proper daft.

Hugh laughed. 'Goodness no. Didn't do rowing at school, just cadets. But I love boats. I'm in the navy, although not a sailor. I'm based up in the Orkneys. I get terrible sea sickness,' he laughed, 'so I'm a dry land sailor.'

'Oh dear,' Maud laughed.

Hugh pointed at Maud's dress and asked, 'And you? Did you like needlework at school?'

'Oh very funny,' she replied, with as much sarcasm as she'd allow herself. Her dress was home-made from an old patch-work blanket she had found in the bin outside her house. 'But yes, I did, and I still do. I make dresses out of sheets and all sorts, but you can't always make a silk purse out of a sow's ear, can you? At least, that's what my nan says.' She looked around at Gladys for some support, but she had wandered off.

'I didn't mean to offend you, I'm awfully sorry.' Hugh seemed genuinely contrite. 'Can I make it up to you?' he asked. 'Do you want to meet me at the Beaconsfield tomorrow night? There's always a good band on.'

Maud smiled, and feeling brave replied, 'OK, yes.'

It would be Maud's first date – and she already had butter-flies in her tummy thinking about the prospect of being held in his arms when he said, 'I'll see you there. Seven o'clock.'

Those butterflies almost died of boredom by the time Hugh arrived the following night. He was slightly dishevelled, clearly flustered and full of apologies. 'It was very embarrassing wait-ing under this lamp post,' Maud said pointedly. 'Not sure what I looked like.'

'You look very nice and I'm so sorry,' Hugh replied, regaining some composure. 'I got caught up with something and there was no way of letting you know.'

Maud looked closely at him and saw a trace of blood on his shirt. His nose looked red. 'Have you had a nose bleed?' she said with concern.

He touched his nose to check for blood and looked down at the area of his shirt to which Maud was pointing. 'Oh yes,' he said quickly, 'yes, I had a nose bleed. That's why I'm late. I've had them since I was a young boy. I'm so pleased you waited. I didn't expect that you would.'

But Maud did wait, and she would continue to do so, for months. She waited for Hugh to call round when on leave from the navy, and then, on his return, for him to visit after his shifts at the Post Office. Because she had been brought up to wait for everything, and never do anything without permission, she waited for him to kiss her. She waited for a proposal, and had to defend him against her nan's sneering questions about their future when he didn't. 'We've been courting for a year,' she told her when asked what Hugh's intentions were, or if he even had any, 'and he's never done nothing he shouldn't with me.'

'Huh. Well, if you ask me he don't seem very keen,' came the snorted response.

Maud angrily snapped back, 'Oh but he is. He told me he likes me. He's just not very good with words. Bit like me. That's why we're suited.'

'Well, just tell him you can't afford to hang around for him,' Nan replied dismissively. 'You're not getting any younger and you're sure not getting any prettier.'

As usual Nan's barb hurt, and almost in tears Maud replied, 'OK, OK, I just don't want to pressure him. You know, be too keen. I'm surprised he even looks at me, he's so very handsome and so dapper.'

Nan folded her arms and sniffed. 'They're the ones you should stay away from. Don't trust them. They'll always be sniffing around for something else. Think a lot of themselves, that sort.'

While waiting for Hugh to get out of the navy, Maud continued to work at the Pye radio factory, which she hated. 'Don't know why I couldn't 'ave been a land girl so I could be out all day. But no, I'm stuck working here,' she'd moan to Gladys regularly. 'All day I count and pack valves, springs and all sorts.' Finally though, Hugh did propose to Maud, on his last visit home before being demobbed, although it wasn't anything like the way she'd seen it done in the movies. They were sitting on the wall outside the Beaconsfield and he mumbled under his breath something about a wedding and Maud said, 'Are you asking me to marry you, Hugh? If you are, it's yes.' Looking back, she would often ask herself if it had been intended as a proposal.

The wedding was a modest do at the local registry office. Maud's nan and Hugh's mum were the only guests. 'I'm an atheist,' Hugh had told her after she had accepted the 'proposal'. At the time Maud wasn't sure what he meant by that, but she explained that she had only ever been to the church for Sunday school and 'I'm not bothered where we get married.' Although, really she was more than bothered. She longed for a church wedding and lots of fuss made about her. But instead she accepted what was to be a quiet and cheap affair. 'As long as I'm married to you, Hugh,' she told him, 'I'm the happiest bride you'll ever have.'

Hugh's smile seemed to be tinged with something, Maud thought. Was it regret?

*

After the marriage, Maud moved in with Hugh and his mother in their house in Ditton Fields, on the east side of Cambridge. Maud tried very hard to get and keep Hugh's attention. She bought a couple of new dresses and some fancy underwear from Joshua Taylor, but he didn't notice. She made him his favourite meal, beef and ale suet pudding, but he asked if his mother had made it. He was rarely home. His mum told her that he had always been like that. 'Never in, comes home all hours. I'm afraid you'll just have to be patient, dear. Takes men a little longer to adjust to married life.'

It wasn't long before Maud felt very hard done by. She had imagined married life to be very different and thought that her mum must have loved her dad very much. She often wondered if she would ever 'fall madly in love', and so far reckoned that she hadn't. Before the wedding Maud thought that Hugh was a gentleman because he'd barely kissed her and never tried to touch her anywhere he shouldn't. But she had expected him to seduce her on their wedding night, and while they had managed to do something, it was over quickly and there had been no intimacy.

Back home after the honeymoon, Hugh had refused to touch Maud again in the same way, and when she asked him why not he said that they needed to get to know each other better. 'Let's just try and be friends to start with, and then see what happens?' After further rejections, Maud gave up asking for any form of physical affection.

Then he announced they would have separate bedrooms, because, he said, 'I don't want you waking me up during the day when you get up, so it makes sense.' Maud wasn't convinced. Although he was doing shift work, he wouldn't always be on at night and she would be out most of the day so how could he be disturbed.

After a year of married but single life, Maud felt defeated

and had no one to confide in about how she felt. She was determined not to prove her nan right and ask to move back there, and she didn't want anyone to know that there were problems in her marriage. She went through a period of asking Hugh if the problem was her. 'Is it because I'm not as clever as you? Is it 'cos I'm not pretty? Is it my clothes?' She begged him for an explanation. 'Tell me what should I do?'

But Hugh replied, 'I am very fond of you, Maud. We will always be friends, isn't that enough?'

For the next few years Maud tried to be a dutiful wife, but it was difficult when her husband was absent, which proved to be more often than not. When he wasn't working nights Hugh went night fishing. When they took a holiday together – to the same caravan in Felixstowe every time – he spent all night down at the shore, fishing. 'It's totally different from river fishing, Maudie,' he told her, 'I can't pass up the chance of it.' The funny thing was, he rarely caught anything, and when he did he always brought a single fish home, already cleaned and wrapped in newspaper.

So Maud and Hugh Ingram were never 'happy' in ways that she expected from the films she'd seen at the cinema. But then, they were never exactly 'unhappy', either, in that they never fought, rarely argued, and on Sundays often slept side-by-side on the sofa after lunch (cooked by Mrs Ingram), as the radio played.

Finding work after her marriage had not been a necessity, since Hugh had his naval pension as well as his job. Maud had had to leave the radiogram assembly line at the Pye factory when she married, and she soon became bored and bewildered by days spent watching her mother-in-law do housework. It was not easy for Maud to find work. Many places wouldn't take young married women on because they expected them to leave and have children (fat chance of that, Maud had thought, when she first heard the excuse for not hiring her), and anyway, it was a woman's place to be at home and take care of the house for her husband, apparently. She couldn't tell anyone that her husband didn't need or want her at home keeping house for him; the shame would be too great.

Maud searched wanted ads in newsagents across the city and eventually found work as a cleaner at a large house on the Grantchester Road. For a few months the novelty of going into the grand dark house filled with enormous Victorian furniture – one of the wardrobes was as big as the kitchen at her nan's, she thought – kept her occupied, if not exactly happy. The work wasn't hard but it was lonely. Mrs Kemp, whose husband was a bigwig at a museum, seemed either to go out when Maud arrived for work or keep to her study during the three hours Maud was there. There were no chats over tea and biscuits, and Maud wondered if Mrs Kemp even remembered her name sometimes, since when she did address her it was as 'you there', or 'I say, Miss . . .' There was a cook who did everything in the kitchen to keep it clean and tidy, but she made it clear from the start that Maud wasn't needed or welcome in 'her' kitchen. The single solitary cup of tea Maud had on the two days a week she cleaned there would be left on the mantelpiece of the dining room at 11 a.m.

After a year of cleaning for Mrs Kemp, Maud decided that she would learn to make dresses, for something else to do. She'd been pretty good at needlework and knitting at school – it was the only subject that she was really any good at – and with her pay from the cleaning job she began to buy patterns. It soon became clear to her that she'd need more than a thimble and some needles to do things properly, and so she asked Hugh to lend her the money to buy a new Singer sewing machine.

'I'll pay you back weekly,' she told him. 'I would rather borrow from you than go on the never, never.'

'I don't want your money, Maud,' Hugh said, 'I'll buy you it.'

He did, but every Friday evening Maud put three shillings in an envelope and slid it under his bedroom door. Since they didn't live together as man and wife should, Maud didn't think she could accept being kept by Hugh. She longed to feel loved and looked after by her husband, but since she wasn't she felt that it was best if she didn't depend on him for much.

It wasn't long before Maud became well known in Ditton Fields for being able to make do and mend just about anything, and for not charging a great deal for it, either. 'Just give me what you can, I don't really need it,' she'd tell people who brought her a dress that needed lengthening, or trousers that needed letting out. 'Hugh looks after me alright,' she'd fib, and push their hands away if they tried to pay her what she thought was too much.

But some of her customers wondered how Hugh looked after her, because Maud had stopped taking care in her appearance. She wore her work pinafore all the time while awake, she had no use for make-up or high-heeled shoes and thought she certainly didn't need to look 'done up'. 'No point, is there?' she asked Hugh when he commented on her unbrushed hair one weekend.

'When was the last time you cleaned your teeth?' he asked her, looking genuinely puzzled.

'Would it make a difference?' she shot back, to which he bowed his head and left the room muttering apologies. Hugh hadn't kissed her since their honeymoon and Maud had never been taught by her nan that she had to brush her teeth regularly.

Maud stopped looking in mirrors when she passed them,

but when she caught her reflection in the window of Eaden Lilley one Monday after work, she felt something like shock, and was struck with a sadness that seemed bottomless. I look just like my nan, she realised with a sinking heart. Same dumpy figure, old-woman's shoes and shapeless coat, I could pass for forty-five, not twenty-five.

But what was the point anyway? she sighed to herself, as she headed from the department store to Woolworths. If Hugh didn't want her, no one else would so there's no need to bother trying to find anyone. What I need, she decided, as she pushed through the swing doors and onto Woolies lovely wooden floor, heading for the cottons and needle counter, is another job to take up more of my time. Then she bumped into Bertha Mizen, the mother of an old schoolfriend, coming round the underwear counter looking the other way.

Maud politely asked after Bertha's daughter, Marjorie, who had been in her class at school. Bertha, a little taken aback at Maud's wild hair, bare face and unplucked eyebrows, dismissed Marjorie with a wave of her hand.

'Oh hell, that girl,' she said without a smile, 'you know 'er, she's not changed; never happy 'less she's arguing with someone. The latest is her mate Doris, who Marj asked to be her bridesmaid for when she and Deryk get married in the summer. Doris agreed but she's always slagging off Deryk, an' says she wants to choose the dresses.'

She paused and stared at Maud, who opened her mouth but nothing came out. 'What's wrong, Maud?' she asked.

Bertha always had a soft spot for Maud. Her daughter had told her one day that most children kept away from the poor girl at school. 'She stinks,' Marjorie had said, to which Bertha responded sharply, telling her not to be so nasty, it wasn't Maud's fault that the house she lived in was so damp. Poor Maud always smelled of mildew back then, and while she

seemed healthy enough today, there was an air of despera-
tion about her, and she looked as if she was on her way to the
madhouse, just like her mother.

'Come on, love, what's up?'

Maud explained how she was married and cleaning houses,
but really wanted a job that would take up more of her time,
because she didn't need to be at home as her mother-in-law
did all the housework. ('It is her house, after all.')

'Right,' Bertha squeezed Maud's upper arm reassuringly
and told her, 'I'm still working as a bedder, so just you let me
talk to the housekeeper at my college and I'll have you join
me as my assistant in no time.'

True to her word Bertha talked to Mrs George, her boss,
about Maud the next day, telling her that, 'She's a grafter, just
got married to a postman, and you know how it is, they're
just starting out, they'll be saving for a house of their own, no
doubt, and I can vouch for her. Honest.'

Maud started working alongside Bertha a fortnight after they'd
bumped into each other in Woolies. The work wasn't hard, it
was more of the same as she'd been doing at Grantchester
Road (which she now did in the afternoons). Sweeping, dusting, making beds, emptying bins, setting fires. Cleaning up
the gyp room was new, but it was tiny, almost as small as her
kitchen at home, although with far less stuffed into it.

The students were a bit intimidating, though, and she
hardly knew how to talk to them, preferring to mumble and
leave the room if she entered alone and there was already
someone there. Bertha treated the 'boys' as if they were her
own children, thought Maud. Some she scolded for making
too much mess (although without swearing at them, Maud
noticed), others she giggled with and let them off tidying
completely.

With certain students Bertha acted very properly, Maud noticed, and almost curtsied to two in particular. 'His dad's in the gov'nerment,' Bertha said under her breath after they'd left the room of a tall, thin boy with owlish glasses and a long, floppy fringe. 'That one's proper posh, got a "right 'onourable" on his cheque books,' she said about the other student, a rotund, oily-haired boy with piggy eyes and starched collars. 'I know how to do 'is collars proper 'cos my dad had to wear them when he was a butler, an' 'is lordship pays me sixpence extra for each.' Maud usually stayed away from those rooms and let Bertha handle them, which the older woman was happy to do.

The mention of extra ironing work made Maud wonder aloud whether any of the boys needed buttons sewing on or clothes adjusted, because she could do it if they did. Bertha told her to mention it to some of them, if she fancied it, but the May Balls were when Maud might make best use of her sewing skills.

'What's a May Ball?' Maud asked.

'It's the end of exams parties that every college has,' Bertha explained, 'usually in their gardens, but sometimes on the greens. All the students get properly dressed up in top hat and tails like they're bleedin' Fred Astaire, an' they invite their girlfriends, sisters and sometimes mum and dads, too. There's dancing, music, lots of food, candles everywhere an' naturally lots of drinking. 'Cos of the drinking and dancing the ladies and the gents are always ripping clothes, spilling things down themselves, losing buttons and their hems come down, straps break and all that. Every college gets a seamstress to sit in one of the tents and mend stuff as the party carries on.'

'So you get to go to the ball, like Cinderella?' Maud smiled.

'Yeah, but you 'ave to work like Cinders at home, and there ain't no glass slipper,' Bertha snorted.

'Well, May's not very far off, who do I ask about being a seamstress?' Maud could feel something like happy anticipation sending the blood to her face.

Bertha laughed, gave Maud a gentle push and told her, 'They're in June, and you ask Mrs George. Give it a few weeks then ask. You've got lots of time, it's only bleedin' March.'

The following weeks went by in a blur as Maud worked harder and made sure that Bertha noticed her extra effort. She did a few sewing jobs for students who expressed their thanks in words and pennies in envelopes ('thruppence a button, sixpence a hem', she'd tell any who asked), and gained a reputation at the college as the person who could sew, fix and adjust any item of clothing. Her sewing began to keep Maud from thinking too much about her failing marriage and earn her a good bit extra, too.

When silent week started – 'No talking to the students,' Bertha told her as they travelled to work one morning in early May, 'and only whisper to me if you have to when we're at work 'cos they're cramming for their exams' – Maud took a chance and asked the college housekeeper if she could work as a seamstress at the forthcoming May Ball.

The following day at tea break Maud found Bertha sitting, drinking tea with her back to the door in the gyp room. Tip-toeing up behind her, Maud whispered, 'Coooo-ee!' in her ear and Bertha jumped, spilling tea on the table. Maud stifled a laugh.

'What the . . .' Bertha dropped her voice, 'hell, Maud! Creeping up on me like that, gave me the frights. Blimey, my old man puts his cold feet on me in the middle of the night and I jump out my skin and you've just had the same effect on me!'

Maud covered her mouth to supress her laughter. Bertha's husband had been a driver of a horse drawn hackney carriage and now he was gas lighter on Histon Road, igniting the street lamps at night; Maud had seen him emerging from the occasional pea-souper fog wearing two jackets, a scarf, two hats and hobnailed boots. The thought of him and Bertha in bed made her want to laugh even more.

Bertha sat down again, her hand at her throat, and asked, 'What'd you do that for?'

'Oh, Bertha, I've asked if I can be the seamstress at the balls and Mrs George's said yes, isn't it great? Only, I'm worried that I may have to get up too close to them if I have to sew things on while they're still wearing the shirt or whatever. You know, they'll be able to smell my breath. Hugh's mum says it's really bad and I should have my teeth taken out. I don't know if I could bear that, and I can't do it now anyway, it's too soon to the ball, isn't it?'

'Oh dear,' Bertha patted the chair next to her. 'Sit yourself down you poor girl and listen to me. You'll be alright. You can ask 'em to take their shirts off, after all, they'll prob'ly be wearing a vest or something underneath if they're respectable. You 'aven't got to get up close and personal, like. An' you ain't got to have your teeth pulled out. Seems a bit extreme unless you wants to, 'course. I had all mine taken out years ago but that's 'cos they were falling out. Now, I always carry a tin of these around.'

Bertha put her hand into the pocket of her overall and pulled out a red and white tin. The label said 'Compound Glycerin of Thymol pastilles with AMC'. 'They're a godsend. You can 'ave my tin – it don't 'alf freshen your breath. There you go.'

Maud was grateful and thanked Bertha for the pastilles. 'Just make sure you 'ave a good time, Maud, while you're young enough to enjoy yourself,' she laughed.

Maud laughed too, nervously. She spent the next week

alternating between feeling as excited as she'd ever been, but scared, too. As a child she'd barely noticed the approach of Christmases, and couldn't understand the eager anticipation her classmates felt as December wore on. They'd talk about Father Christmas bringing them toys and fruit, and Maud would feel confused, bemused, even. Her nan had put her right about 'Father Christmas' almost as soon as Maud could walk, telling her, 'You'll be getting nothing from no one 'cos there's only me and we ain't got no money for presents.' At the age of nine or so, though, Maud got herself caught up in the excitement of Christmas approaching, encouraged by her school friends, and she convinced herself that on Christmas morning, somehow Father Christmas would have climbed down their dirty chimney and left a stocking full of toys on their smoke-smudged, teacup-stained mantelpiece.

Maud remembered her innocent sense of anticipation and excitement of that Christmas as she looked forward to the May Ball of 1950. She couldn't help feeling excited, but equally, she couldn't help feeling scared that she'd feel so let down on the day. Because, naturally, come Christmas morning when she was nine, she rushed downstairs in the freezing cold, pre-dawn gloom to see her much-longed-for bulging stocking from Father Christmas – and found only a chipped cup on the mantelpiece and the cold grey ashes of last night's fire in the grate.

ANN

Cambridge 1945-47

Ann wasn't surprised by the announcement, nor by the manner in which it had come about. 'I suppose we should get married,' Barrel said to Bet one evening early in March 1945.

It wasn't the most romantic proposal that Bet could think of, but still, it was a proposal and she accepted.

When Jack was told, he was happy for her. 'Mrs Harry Reynolds of Cambridge,' he said, 'got a nice ring to it, that has.'

Grace simply said, ''Bout time an' all.' Then smiled and added, 'Well done.'

Ann was almost as relieved as she was pleased about the announcement, because it meant that she didn't have to accompany Bet to any more dances.

Bet had changed their dancehall of choice to the British Legion, mainly because it was the only place that Ann could be persuaded to go and be confident that Peter Constable wouldn't be there. They'd been out dancing twice a week since Barrel had come out of the services with a slight limp, and as Ann complained to Bet, 'I'm always playing gooseberry to you and Barrel. I have to be up early you know. I hate late nights. I'm always tired.'

Bet laughed and said, 'Oh but you've got to admit he makes you laugh, Nance, doesn't he?' Which was true. Ann was also relieved that she wouldn't have to go out in a foursome with Bet, Barrel and his friend Albert, any more. She knew that they had paired him off with her because they felt guilty about her tagging along with them, and although the few times they'd all gone out were pleasant enough, Ann didn't dream of Albert at night, or think about him during the longest, dullest day at the brewery. For a few months, Ann was happy to stay home while Bet and her fiancé went out without a chaperone.

After the D-Day landings the previous year, it had become increasingly clear that the war was finally coming to a close. The Russians and Allies were advancing on Germany, the papers said, and nothing could save Hitler now. Just after the landings, though, a new type of Nazi flying bomb called the doodlebug had caused havoc in London. The 'rockets', as the papers called them, had been fired from somewhere in Belgium. But at the end of March the site they were being fired from in Antwerp was captured and now there were no more bombs landing in England at all. There was a general air of relief breathed in with fresh spring winds. Ann had begun to daydream about a life after war, one in which she could meet and mix with people like Peter Constable, perhaps, without feeling embarrassed or shy.

When the news broke that the war was over on 7 May, there was no hesitation from Ann about going out. She didn't mind dancing that night, she didn't care what people thought, she wanted to be out there with everyone else, celebrating, being free from falling bombs and the threat of death and injury from above. She and her sisters went to Parker's Piece where they found a huge area had been designated for dancing.

'I want to dance!' she shouted, almost running towards the bandstand, wearing her ordinary, everyday dress, pushing past women who were all done out in their best frocks, shoes and hats. She really didn't care who saw or heard her as she sang and danced with her sisters as the US army band played Glenn Miller tunes. Later in the evening they joined the other revellers in a torchlight procession to Midsummer Common, where an enormous bonfire had been built, as if it were 5 November. But it was not Guy Fawkes that sat at the top of the bonfire, it was an effigy of one of Hitler's henchmen, Josef Goebbels.

The Pilchers were giggling and singing along with everyone else when Ann realized how late it was. 'Dad's going to be worried,' she said to Bet and Rene, 'he'll be waiting on the doorstep you know, we're going to have to get going soon.'

Bet agreed, but Rene was clearly disappointed. 'We're never allowed to do anything!' She resisted her sisters' tugging at her sleeve. 'Surely tonight, I mean, there's no school, they've given us an extra two days off.'

'Don't matter,' Ann replied, 'we don't want to worry Dad.'

Rene took a last look at the bonfire and turned to grab the bottom of Bet's jumper so she wouldn't get lost in the crowd. It had grown very dark and, as they made their way towards Victoria Avenue, the mass of bodies on the unlit paths remained as solid and often unmoving as it had been for what seemed like hours now. A few beery-breathed men leaned into the sisters' faces and attempted to kiss them, usually mumbling, 'S'peace! Gisakiss . . .' Bet pushed most away with a laugh, Rene ducked down low, causing a couple of men to bang their heads and square up to one another as Rene urged her sisters onwards. Ann's cheek was feeling wet and sore, her being too shy to even say 'no' to the drunken kisses that headed her way. She could see the gate out onto the bridge was surrounded by people and would need some determination to get through, when her attention was caught by a familiar face.

'Are you girls alright? Do you need me to help you get through the crowds?' Fred Adams spoke from under a tree, where he stood with a torch in his hand, looking directly at Ann.

Rene looked over and squealed, 'But you've only got one eye!'

Fred laughed.

'Don't be so rude, Rene,' Ann scolded her, and turned a blushing face towards Fred. 'Sorry, she's overexcited. Yes, we would like that very much. Thank you.'

Ann and Fred had met at Drummer Street bus station a few weeks previously, as she was seeing Albert off on a bus. Bet and Barrel were otherwise occupied, and as Ann walked away from the kissing couple, Fred had approached her. He asked her if she wanted to go to a picture show the following week, and although she said she couldn't, she was apologetic enough about her refusal to give Fred the sense that she was interested. 'See you around, then,' he'd said as Bet approached them, and walked away.

'Who was that?' Bet had asked, watching Fred's back disappear around the corner.

'A boy,' Ann replied, blushing. 'He asked me out.'

'What? You said no, didn't you, Ann?'

Her sister blushed and said, 'Yes, but I didn't want to.'

'Eh? What about Albert?' Bet was amazed at Ann's blushing cheeks and candour.

'He's gone, hasn't he? And it's not like we're ever going to get married or anything,' Ann replied. 'He was kind of nice, actually.' She'd looked into the space where Fred had been with a feeling of slight frustration, wishing she'd said 'yes' to his invite.

Now here he was, smiling and being playful with her and her sisters.

'It lights up in the dark, this glass eye, so people tell me,' he said to Rene, 'so it's good for things like this.'

He laughed, turned, and the girls followed as he made his way towards the gate. Pushing through the people with 'Excuse me' and 'Warden coming through!', Fred waved his torch into people's eyes and they moved away to let the small line through with barely a comment. He did have an armband on, although no helmet, of course – 'We don't need them any more!' Ann realized with a smile.

As they made their way along the road, all four could walk closely enough together to talk, and being as inquisitive as ever, Bet asked him, 'So what do you do?'

'I've been working in the chef's core but I'm working on my dad's farm now, and I've been working at the air raid shelters.'

'What's your name?' she asked. Ann held onto Rene's hand, desperately wanting Bet to stop bothering him.

'It's Fred,' he replied, 'Fred Adams, but I get called Tiny Tim 'cos I'm the runt of the litter.'

'How many of you are there then?!' Bet asked.

'There's the girls Rose, Violet, Iris, Lil, Daisy, and then there's five of us boys.'

'Blimey, that's a lot, ain't it, Nance?' Bet laughed and turned to look at Ann, who wanted to tell her that this was the boy she had met at Drummer Street. She wanted to say, 'Oh, I didn't know that all your sisters are named after flowers.' She wasn't sure if he recognized her, though, and she was too shy to speak to him.

Fred asked the group, 'Have you got far to go?'

'No, we're on Histon Road, thanks. I'm Bet by the way. This is Rene, and she's Nance, but she may want you to call her Ann.'

'I know Ann, don't I, Annie?'

Relieved to hear him use her name, Ann tugged at Bet's sleeve, and stepped up to his side. Bet stepped back to take Rene's hand as they neared the corner of Histon Road and Victoria Road. Amazed at how brave her sister was being, she decided to slow her pace a little and let them have some time 'alone'.

Fred showed all the confidence of his four years over Ann,

who he had fallen in love with when he had seen her at Drummer Street. He had wanted to compliment her then, on her dark curls and brown eyes, but hadn't. He wasn't going to miss the chance now, though. 'You've got nice hair and eyes, Annie.'

Bet almost tripped over her feet at that.

Ann responded as calmly as she could. 'Thank you, and thanks for walking us through the gate.' She was relieved that he had acknowledged her.

'Can we go to the flicks soon?' he asked. 'They've got *Objective, Burma!* with Errol Flynn on at the moment. Meet me at Drummer Street at seven, tomorrow? What do you say, Annie?'

Without hesitating Ann said, 'Yes, OK.'

'Alright,' he said.

'Alright.'

All too soon the wandering party reached the Pilcher home, which showed lots of lights. Before Jack could open the door, Ann waved Fred off and turned to her sisters.

With a huge smile, Bet said to Rene, 'Must be the smoke from the bonfire, it's gone to her head.'

With butterflies in her tummy, Ann said, 'He's a real gent isn't he?' I'm going out with a real gentleman, she thought.

Ann and Fred's first trip to the cinema was one of countless others, and soon enough both their families were calling them a courting couple. They had to go to the cinema so often because they were not encouraged to sit in at Ann's house, which was too small to afford them any privacy. Grace would shoo them out after a cup of tea at the most. Fred lived with his family in Waterbeach and cycled the three miles to Ann's house on Saturdays, some Sundays and Friday nights, which was when they'd inevitably end up at the flicks. They both loved sitting close in the dark as the recently ended war was re-fought on screen by actors.

Their Saturday afternoons were spent with Ann on Fred's arm, window shopping and occasionally picking up a few things for their mothers. One Saturday in 1946, as they walked around Woolworths in Sidney Street in search of something for Jack's forthcoming birthday, they were passing the sheet music racks when someone called out, 'Hello there, Ann, isn't it?' Ann and Fred turned to see a short, dark-haired girl of Ann's age. 'It's me, Jane . . . Jane Granger, remember? How are you?'

Ann recognized her as a tough girl from St Luke's school. They'd never been friends, exactly, but they had known a lot of the same people and sometimes mixed in the same group of girls in the playground. 'I'm alright, Jane, how are you? This is Fred, by the way.' He nodded.

'What are you looking for, love?' Jane asked with a half-smile to Fred.

'It's my dad's birthday and I'm looking for something for him,' Ann smiled back. 'Seeing your sheet music's made me think it'd be a good idea to get him some. He's been given an old piano by our Uncle Bill what he sometimes bangs away on in the front room.'

The girls loved to hear Jack playing, although their mother was not as keen on it, and tried to stop the instrument from being delivered to their house. But as Bill had said as he pushed the piano into their hallway, 'It's not doing anything at mine. I'm sure you lot will get some use out of it. Deaf or not deaf, your dad will be able to play it better than I ever could.' Ann had suggested to Grace her idea of getting Jack some sheet music before leaving the house, but she'd been given short shrift, as usual. 'That's a waste of sixpence, that is,' her mother complained, 'it's not like he's going to be able to hear if he's playing it right or wrong, is it?' Discouraged, Ann had almost decided against it, but seeing a copy of 'Blue Skies' on the counter, and remembering how she'd loved Bing Crosby singing it in the film of that name, she thought it the best present she'd find.

Picking a copy up, she said, 'He can read music so he'll be able to play this, which I love, and so will he. It'll be great. Can I pay you, Jane?' Wrinkling her nose, Jane put her hand out with her palm towards Ann. 'No, I'll get someone to do that. I'm the supervisor, you see. Worked my way up.'

'That's great, Jane, really great.' Ann thought she'd better let her know what she was doing. 'Me and Bet are working at the brewery, which is a good laugh.' It was nothing compared to working at Woolworths, but she wasn't embarrassed and knew that it wasn't something Jane would look down on her for. 'How's the family, Jane?'

Jane's family had run a greengrocer's on Fitzroy Street before the war, but rationing and the Dig For Victory campaign had put an end to that, she said. When they had the shop, Jane's mum used to make ice cream in there, and her dad and uncle would go to the mart on King Street to buy rabbits and livestock while it was still warm, getting back to hang it outside their door in time for people on their way to shop for dinner. As well as running the shop, they went round the streets with a horse and cart, hawking fruit and veg. 'They're alright. I miss the cart. I loved going out with them to Histon Road when I was allowed,' she recalled.

'I know!' Ann remembered seeing her once, sitting up next to her dad as he gently reined their old horse along, calling out what sounded like noises rather than actual words.

'After the shop closed my dad went to work at the gasworks as a labourer. Your dad was there an' all, weren't he?'

'That's right, he was. How's your uncle, then?'

He used to mend bikes and sell them second hand to locals and students (who'd pay slightly higher prices). Ann remembered the house that Jane used to live in had a front shop window to it, which was where the uncle used to do up his bikes.

'He's alright, doing council work and at night a bit of pint pot clearing in the pub.'

'That's great, Jane, and well done on your job here,' Ann said sincerely. 'You'll do well for yourself, you will.'

Clearly proud, Jane smiled and pointed to a girl by a till. 'Lovely seeing you, Ann, go and see Mabel over there and she'll take your money. Lovely meeting you, Fred.' With that she turned and walked towards the back of the store.

A year later Ann and Fred bumped into Jane again, this time in a queue to get into the Regal cinema to see *The Bishop's Wife* with Cary Grant, David Niven and Loretta Young. 'Hello, Ann, what you up to? Still at the brewery?' Jane asked cheerily.

'Hello, Jane,' Ann smiled, 'no, me and Bet are at the laundry down Union Lane now. It's hard work, but better pay. You still at Woolies?'

'No way,' Jane put her hand palm out towards Ann, just as she had in Woolies a year earlier. 'I'm working for one of the colleges now, as a bedmaker's helper. My mum's a bedder, and she got me the job.'

Ann wondered, why would you want to leave Woolies? Every girl she knew wanted to work there. 'I don't get it, Jane, you had a good job at Woolies, you can't get paid much at the colleges, can you?' Ann was interested to know exactly how much the colleges paid, because she earned only fourteen shillings at the laundry and had to give ten of that to her mum. If there were bedmakers' assistant's jobs going and they paid more, or even as much, then she wanted one. Ann was still in awe of the colleges, their students and fellows.

'I had to leave 'cos all the old girls came back out of the forces,' Jane explained. 'Even though I worked myself up to supervisor, when all the girls came back, they was 'titled to their old jobs back. There was too many supervisors and they said to me, "You can go back behind the counter." Well, the manager, he's a proper old upstart and I just weren't having none of it. I wouldn't put up with him pushing me about. So I said, "No, that's it," and I put my notice in. Then my mum said, "Why don't you come and do bedmaking." An' I did.'

'What's the work like, then?'

'It's really tough, you have to clean all the rooms and they have coal fires and we have to make sure they've got coal for the rest of the day, so I have to carry that up all those bloody stairs.' She didn't look too unhappy about it, though. 'But it's only three hours, I'm usually home by 10.30. My mum is the real bedmaker, so she gets their breakfast ready and then comes back and has a sleep before going back in the afternoon to turn the beds down ready for them to get into.'

'Is that all you do then, Jane?'

'Well, I wash up, tidy up,' she acted out all the jobs, sighed, and continued. 'I need another job, though, if only there were any – there just isn't nothing. We make extra money if we take some of the boys' washing home, you know – wash it and iron it and bring it back for them.' She paused, and broke into a wide grin. 'Still,' she added, 'I'm eighteen now, and got married last year. I wanted a job, any job. You know how it is; you can't live without a job.'

Ann sensed Fred beginning to fidget beside her and he half-stepped back from them, turning to look along the road as if he needed to be somewhere else. They had been talking about marriage only that morning, and Ann was keen to carry on her chat with Jane, but the queue started to move and although she had still not learned how much Jane was getting paid, or who she had married, she and Fred soon reached the box office. 'Lovely to see you, Jane,' she said as they moved into the cinema.

'You too,' smiled Jane, adding, 'don't forget to tell your sisters I'm Mrs Kerr now.' She raised her left hand and wiggled her wedding ring with her thumb. 'See ya.'

Once seated and settled into their seats, as the organist played tunes in front of the curtain, Ann turned to Fred. 'Well, did you hear that? She's married and working at the colleges. She's only eighteen! I don't want to wait any longer. I'm nineteen and I want to get married before I'm twenty.' Ann didn't want to be like her mum and get married in her late twenties, she wanted to have children young, and was wary of giving birth to damaged children like her mum had. That had been caused, so she'd heard, by Grace being too old to have kiddies. 'Let's get it over and done with,' Ann and Bet agreed when they discussed marriage and children.

There was a long pause as they listened to the music. Fred seemed to be thinking hard. Then he leaned over to speak into Ann's good ear. 'She must of married Jimmy Kerr. He was in the Royal Artillery, based out in Woolwich. He was up in Scotland for a long time. I remember he was going to go out on D-Day but a few days before it him and his mates all went out drinking and he got his leg caught on barbed wire trying to get back into camp. He ripped himself up good and proper, so he didn't go to France in the end. And then he got stationed at Deep Cut. Blooming lucky he was.'

Fred became silent again. Clearly he wasn't going to talk about marriage.

'I might try and get a job at the colleges now the boys are back,' Ann said, as determined as she had ever been. 'Maybe I could do some bedding in the morning before work. I could start saving for my bottom drawer. I don't have anything left really, after I've paid my mum.'

'No, you're not!' Fred said firmly. 'I see a lot of them bedders walking or cycling to the colleges blooming early in the mornings. I used to see some of the old bedders about six o'clock, in the pitch black going up the colleges to wait on them old fellas. They're the type what have servants and that's all you are to them, a servant. Anyway,' he continued in a softer tone, 'you won't be able to work at a college, Annie.' He snuggled up to her, and lowered his voice as the organ disappeared into the floor in front of them. 'You wouldn't be able to get there every morning from my house in Waterbeach.'

With his softer voice Ann thought she'd misheard him, but hoped she hadn't. 'Are you asking me to marry you, Fred Adams?' she shouted.

'Yes, I am!' he barked back.

The whole cinema audience burst into applause. Embarrassed and excited, Ann buried her head in Fred's shoulder as he laughed with delight. So it was decided. Ann would be moving in with his family in Waterbeach when they got married, and that was the last time they talked about Ann working at the colleges.

As much to save money as it was a romantic idea, Ann and Fred had a double wedding with Bet and Barrel at St Luke's church, Cambridge, in the summer of 1947. 'It's a lovely do,' Rene was almost crying as she and her now married sisters stood in their backyard on Histon Road, having a quiet moment. 'I can't believe Mum said it was OK to use the front room for the reception! Dad did you proud, didn't he?'

'It's all been lovely, Rene.' Bet rubbed her sister's shoulder gently.

'You know he cooked all that food and made the cake? Didn't ask for any help,' Rene continued, as they looked through the window at Jack, who was taking a break from playing the piano and leading dances to share a beer with Fred, Barrel and Derek – who was clearly drunk. 'Are you going to be alright out in the sticks, Nance?' Bet looked squarely at her big sister, who shrugged her shoulders. ''Course we will, I'm more worried about you and Barrel being here with Mum and Dad. I don't want there to be loads of arguments with Mum telling you what to do all the time.'

'Don't worry about us. Poor old Barrel will be out most of the day and asleep the rest of the time, I reckon. That job he has as a stoker in the boiler house at Fulbourn is shift work, and he either has to do from six till two in the morning, or from two in the afternoon till ten at night. So either I'll work when he's sleeping, or I'll be sleeping when he gets in. Married life is great, in't it? I reckon I saw more of him when we were courting than I'm going to as his wife.' She smiled. 'Still, there's other things to be getting on with, aren't there? Like trying to find somewhere else to live. At least you're getting out of this place, Ann, and you, young Rene, you're so gorgeous it won't be long before a young man asks you to be his wife!'

Rene cringed, laughed, and said, 'Not blooming likely!'

Three months later the same sisters were seated in the kitchen on Histon Road, having tea and chatting. Grace and Jack had gone to visit Aunt Win and Uncle George. 'Are you alright, Nance? You look tired,' Bet asked.

Ann sighed. It was true that she had been feeling very tired lately, and she was sure it wasn't just down to the stress of living with so many people. Something else was wrong, she thought, but she wasn't going to trouble her sisters with health worries. Instead, she opened up to them about life in

Waterbeach. 'I don't like it much at Fred's place. You know, they're nothing like us. The sisters argue all the time. I miss you and everyone,' she sniffed and was grateful for the sympathetic looks from Bet and Rene. 'I was thinking about going back to work,' she continued. 'Fred only gives me ten bob a week, and do you know what his mum says about that? She said, if I went out to work she would put the rent up. So it's not worth it, I'm not going to bother.'

Thinking about finding work had naturally led to her thinking about the colleges again. Not that she'd said anything to anyone about that. Bet wanted Ann to realize that it wasn't plain sailing at home either, and told her, 'I miss you too, Nance. It's not easy here neither. I hardly see Barrel, you know.'

Rene got up to go to the outside toilet, and Bet confided in Ann. 'Joy is coming home for the Christmas holidays. Mum's moaning about the prospect already. It's not good. Me and Barrel are thinking about telling her that Joy can stay with us as soon as we find a place of our own, you know.'

Ann was always happy to see Joy, and like Bet always wary of their mother's reaction to having the youngest girl around the house, so she was genuinely delighted that Bet would offer Joy a room. 'That'd be lovely!' she exclaimed. Then her grin turned to a frown. 'What about Rene?' she asked. 'She doesn't look well either.'

'She's missing Johnny but she can't talk to Mum about him. You know Rene loves him like he's her own. But it was too much of a responsibility for a girl her age and Mum needs her to get a job.'

At the beginning of 1947 the Sunshine Home had told Grace and Jack that they were unable to teach their youngest son anything, because he wasn't like the other children, his disabilities were far too severe. Before her wedding, Ann (and Bet) helped Rene to care for Johnny while he lived on Histon

Road with them for a brief few months, but once Ann had left home, Grace decided that he wasn't being looked after 'properly' and so had to be put in another home. So she had Johnny committed to what used to be called the pauper lunatic asylum at Fulbourn, which was now known as Cambridge's 'mental' hospital. Ann and Bet felt terrible about it, and somehow responsible for him being sent there – because they weren't around to help out.

Bet's tone was becoming angrier. 'I know he had to go somewhere but . . . Now he's got nobody and he's in there with all them. There's over 900 patients in that hospital, Nance . . . it's not a hospital, is it though? It's an asylum, Nance, it's no place for a child. Barrel says there's some real violent patients in there. "The chronics, the incurables and the intractables", that's what they're called, the ones who have been abandoned. Barrel thinks that Johnny is left in a cot all day. He said he's going to ask Miss Fossey the matron if it's OK for him to see Johnny when he's on a break from stoking.'

'He's a good man your Barrel.' Ann was holding back her tears, trying to be strong. She knew Bet was holding back her anger. Neither of them wanted Rene to know the full extent of what Johnny would be experiencing in Fulbourn Hospital. She had been told that it was for the best, that they would be able to care for him better than Grace would manage.

'I would come back as often as I could, you know that, don't you?' Ann looked as if she was going to cry.

'I know, Nance. It wasn't our decision though, was it? It was Mum.' She reached over and patted Ann's hands that were folded round her mug of tea.

'What are you two whispering about?' Rene asked as she came through the back door.

'Oh, you know, married life . . .' Ann told her.

JOYCE

Joyce blamed herself for the death of her brother. She would never forget the cold, callous manner of the doctor who had done nothing for Trevor as he lay dying, and she felt anger at the boys who'd chased her brother into the path of the lorry. But she was supposed to look after the twins and keep them both safe, and she'd failed. Her mother was heartbroken, distraught and in her distress did once – but only once – ask pitifully, 'Where were you, Joyce? Why didn't you stop him running out like that?' Celia knew that it wasn't nine-year-old Joyce's fault, but she refused to let either of her remaining children go anywhere without her for a good two years after Trevor's death.

Despite the war having ended, Joyce's dad didn't return for the funeral, which was a small, miserable affair at the cemetery on Newmarket Road attended only by Celia, Joyce, Aggie and a handful of parents whose children were friends with the twins. Celia's grandparents came for the day only but the funeral made Joyce so sad that she couldn't even feel happy to see them again.

Charles Jones was demobilized in 1946 and arrived back in Cambridge with four medals that he put in the bottom of a drawer and didn't look at again until his grandsons asked about them, two decades later. With Celia having found work as a cleaner and Joyce so settled in the Fenland town, and with no real reason for them to return to Surrey, Charles took employment as a painter and decorator at a fast-growing company in Cambridge. The job allowed the Jones family to rent a flat of their own, next door to the Bird in the Hand public house on Newmarket Road, above a barbers' shop. Aggie was sorry to see them leave, especially after her husband failed to return, having been reported missing in action during what proved to be the final weeks of the conflict. She understood their need to be together as a family, though, and so reapplied to the university to register as a landlady and soon had two students lodging with her.

Her father didn't talk to Joyce about what he'd seen or done in Italy, but as she grew up he encouraged her to join the territorial army as soon as she could. Charles was proud of the service that he'd given his country and of the discipline and training that the army had given him. He must have considered that his daughter would benefit from the sense of camaraderie, well-being and sense of purpose that putting on a military uniform brought.

After living in the flat for a couple of years, Charles had found them a small three-bedroom house in Ditton Fields to rent. Two of the bedrooms were much larger than those above the barbers' shop, and Joyce had one of those to herself. On entering the house, a little door on the left hand side hid the toilet, which was still something of a luxury given that a lot of the other houses in the street had outside loos in their garden. Along a short hallway on the right there was a front room used for best, then a dining room in the middle, a kitchen and scullery with a copper sink used for the washing. It was a little further out from town and a lot further from the two houses that Celia cleaned for on the Barton Road, but it was their first family home.

Douglas, who'd withdrawn into himself following the death of his twin, seemed to enjoy being in a different place, away from so much that reminded him of Trevor. Joyce often sat quietly with him during evenings when they'd listen to the radio, not speaking, but not feeling the need to communicate. In the first few weeks after losing Trevor, Douglas had woken in the night and gone to his mother's bed. When Charles returned, sometimes Douglas would find his way into Joyce's bed, and she'd awake in the morning to find him there, having not been woken as he climbed under the blankets with her.

In their Ditton Fields house though, Douglas had never strayed from his own room at night. Slowly, it seemed to Joyce, he'd come to terms with being alone, and was no longer missing the physical presence of his twin. Still though, sometimes she'd walk past the closed door of Douglas' room and hear him talking out loud, even though she knew there was no-one in the room with him. He was talking to Trevor, she knew. And that was a good thing, she thought.

On leaving school at fifteen, in 1951, Joyce, along with her best friends Janet, Vicky and Rita, worked at the Lyons tearooms in Petty Cury. They waited on tables in shifts, which would usually see two of them 'on' at the same time. It was hard work, but they liked the uniforms and meeting customers, most of them being what the girls thought of as 'well-to-do', they'd leave tips of thruppence or even sixpence. Like all of her friends, Joyce gave half of her weekly wages to her mum for her keep, which now included her part of the rent on a house.

Working at Lyons made Joyce feel like an adult, and she asked Celia for more freedom to go out and about on her own, or with friends, particularly in the evenings. Reluctantly her mother agreed, albeit with a very early curfew time of 9 p.m. Joyce stuck to the time and made certain she was home from wherever she'd gone – often the cinema, sometimes dancing at a church hall youth club in Oakington (reached by bus) – to prove that she was sensible and obedient. Within a few weeks the curfew was loosened and before long Joyce could be home after the pubs closed at 11 p.m. – not that she was drinking, but the dances she went to kept pub opening hours.

By then, because Joyce had kept her tips stored away she could afford to buy a tight, bright green, flared-waisted coat that she'd seen and a black, tight pencil skirt to go with it. When she, Janet, Vicky and Rita went out dancing together they were always done up to the nines, and attracted a swarm of boys around them eager for a dance (and more, if they were allowed). The girls loved to dance but did not enjoy the 'taking a walk outside' with boys after a couple of turns on the floor. Joyce's solution to the problem was to invite Celia to go to dances in Oakington with her. On these occasions, whenever a boy asked if she wanted to go outside with him, she could point to Celia, apologize and say, 'My mum's here . . .' It worked every time; the boys would get embarrassed, mumble apologies and back away. Celia was happy to play chaperone, being all too aware of how attractive her teenage daughter had become. Whenever Joyce went out without her, Celia would warn her not to talk to, and certainly never dance with, any 'Yanks', disparaging the American servicemen who still populated Cambridge's pubs and clubs (it would take a few years for the U.S. services to decamp back to their homeland).

Joyce had only been at Lyons for a few months when she was accused of stealing cold meats from the kitchen. Being wholly innocent, she protested strongly against the accusation, and in an argument with the manageress about it, tore off the doily-like hairpiece and white apron that made up part of her uniform, threw them at the woman and marched out, slamming the door behind her. While Celia said she'd done the right thing in quitting, her father wanted to go to the tearooms and demand an apology from the manageress. Joyce told him that it wasn't worth it, and the following Monday went looking for a new job. By the end of the day she'd found one, working at Woolworths on the flower counter, starting the following Monday.

Weeks later, Joyce received a letter of apology from Lyons, in which it was explained that a kitchen porter had been discovered with a ham under his coat as he left work one night, and he then confessed to having taken the items that Joyce had been accused of stealing. She kept the letter and showed it to Janet, Vicky and Rita, who made sure that the manageress didn't forget what she'd done to their friend.

The job at Woolworths was better paid than that at Lyons, and even without tips to top up her earnings Joyce took more money home on a Friday. Now working full-time, Joyce began to go out at nights with her friends and without Celia. She went dancing at the Rex and even visited pubs beforehand. Bored by the attentions of boys of her own age, Joyce began to forget her mum's advice concerning Americans, and one late September evening she was approached by a tall, handsome American sergeant while at the Rex, dancing with Janet. He introduced himself as Sergeant Alan Brodsky and asked if she could jive. She could, and while she thought she was OK at it, after only a couple of numbers with Alan she'd become pretty good; he was a fantastic dancer and teacher. At the end of the night he asked if Joyce would show him around Cambridge the next day because he'd only just arrived. The next day being Saturday, Joyce told Celia she was off to meet Vicky, and met Alan to be his guide.

They had tea at Lyons (Joyce really enjoyed that), walked through the greens and she took him to the University Arms, telling him he had to take a room there, because it was the smartest place that she knew. He agreed, and took a room at the Arms, telling her that it 'sure is nicer than the room I've been given at a tiny house in the south of the town'. As the day ended Alan asked how old she was, and Joyce didn't lie and admitted she was fifteen. Sergeant Alan Brodsky was a gentleman and showed no sign of disappointment at discovering that she was younger than he'd hoped. He told her that they would be 'best chums' if she'd like that.

She did, and for three weeks the pair met regularly to dance, walk, talk and have tea. Joyce learned more about his home state of Minnesota than she could ever hope to (she'd never heard of it until they met), and more about America than even the movies could teach her. And then, without warning or explanation, he was gone.

Joyce went to visit him at the University Arms on Friday after work, just as they had arranged two days earlier, only to be told at the reception that he'd checked out, leaving no forwarding address. She wasn't heartbroken, exactly – they'd never so much as kissed – but for the next week Joyce felt in turns angry, sad and absent-minded, somehow. At work she'd be in the middle of wrapping flowers, cleaning pots or pruning stalks when her mind would wander and she'd think, what had she done? Why had he run away? He'd gone – just upped and went – but why?

Perhaps, she thought, it had been because she'd told him about being hit with a stick by her mother the Monday before they'd last met. A neighbour – Celia wouldn't say who – had knocked on their door while Joyce was at work, and told her mother that she'd seen her daughter out and about on Sunday evening with a black American soldier. She knew it was Joyce because she was wearing her green jacket and black skirt, the neighbour said.

As it happened, Joyce did go out wearing her green jacket and black skirt that evening, but she and Alan (who was not black) had been at the cinema, to see *Monkey Business* with Cary Grant and Ginger Rogers (Alan looks a bit like Cary Grant, Joyce had thought, as they sat in the dark, warm, Empire cinema). She kept telling her mother, 'It can't have been me that the neighbour has seen,' but Celia wouldn't listen and set about her legs with the stick, a piece of bamboo that her father had left outside the back door ready to use in the garden. Joyce's legs were black and blue the next day and they hurt like hell. She had to wear thick socks and a long skirt to work so no one noticed, and when she met Alan she told him about it, half embarrassed, half wanting his sympathy and comfort, which he seemed happy to give. But perhaps he was scared that her mother and father would find out that Joyce had been to his hotel room? Joyce knew her parents wouldn't believe she hadn't been intimate with him.

With her mind not on her work, Joyce kept pricking her fingers on bulbs and roses, barely noticing that she did. But when she cut her neck on a box of bulbs (she held the top one of three, in place with her chin), she really felt the pain, and dropping the boxes sank to the floor. Her supervisor came running over and scolded Joyce about the bulbs flying everywhere, when she saw blood oozing from her neck and hands.

The following day, Joyce felt too awful and weak to go to work, so Celia cycled past Woolies on her way to Barton Road to tell her supervisor. Over the next two days Joyce felt worse and couldn't get out of bed. Celia realized that her daughter was running a temperature and when it wasn't helped by taking aspirin she called their doctor, who gave Joyce a short examination and sent her to the hospital.

'Septicaemia,' he said, 'she really needs to be looked at.' Joyce was rushed to the hospital in an ambulance.

'Thank God for the NHS,' Celia kept saying to the driver as they weaved their way to Mill Road.

Once inside, Joyce, half-delirious, and a distraught Celia, sat waiting impatiently for a doctor to tell them what they were going to do. When the doctor did appear, almost an hour after she'd arrived, Joyce screamed and tried to climb out of the bed. 'Not him, I don't want him nowhere near me, I'd rather die,' she cried loudly.

The doctor stopped, looking confused and half-turned to Celia. Joyce reached out her hand to her mother and said pleadingly, 'Mum, it's 'im, the one who let Trevor die, don't let him near me, please!'

Celia rose from the chair next to the bed, took Joyce's hand and shouted, 'Get out!' at the doctor, who promptly did as he was told.

Joyce was shivering, shaking and crying. Clasping her mother's hand ever tighter, she tried to lift a leg out of the bed, and two nurses who'd appeared at the sound of shouting rushed to keep her where she was.

Eventually a different doctor was found, Joyce submitted to his examination and was taken to an operating theatre where the cut on her neck was scraped clean and bandaged. Afterwards she was given penicillin and slept for almost twenty-four hours straight.

Two days after being admitted to the hospital, Joyce was sent home with Celia, who insisted that she spend her days recuperating in the dining room, which had been rearranged in order that her bed could be set up there. Celia took it on herself to arrange for Joyce's wages be paid up to when she'd left Woolies. 'You're not working there again, I can tell you that much,' she told Joyce, who was too weak to argue.

For three days Joyce lay in the dining room, eating soup and seeing no one, because Celia would turn away everyone who tried to visit. Janet, Vicky and Rita all tried to see her, and Vicky got as far as peering through the window from the side passage, but Celia came in just as Joyce was trying to lift the window in order for them to be able to talk, and chased her friend away.

Late one Thursday afternoon, Joyce heard a knock at their front door, and her mother answered it. Joyce could hear her talking to someone on the doorstep for a few minutes, but couldn't pick out anything either was saying until Celia barked, 'I'm going to call you a liar!'

Another, unfamiliar woman's voice answered loudly, 'How dare you, I am NOT a liar!'

'Right then, just you follow me,' Celia barked again, and Joyce heard footsteps leading to her door. Celia pushed it wide and beckoned for someone to look in. 'Here then, is this my daughter what you saw out on the town again last night with the black American soldier?' A large, frowsy-looking woman with a tight black permed hairdo, and wearing a scruffy looking Astrakhan coat, stepped into the doorway and looked at Joyce, who'd never seen her before, she'd swear.

'Oh, er . . .' the woman looked uncertainly at Joyce.

'I'll ask again,' Celia said firmly, barely able to control her anger, 'did you see this girl out last night with a black American soldier? You can't miss her, 'cos if you did, she had that bloody great bandage on!'

'Well, er, maybe not then, it weren't her, I'm really sorry, missus.'

'You want to say sorry to my daughter an' all, I should think!'

'Yes, sorry, love, I do hope you get better soon . . . I'd better be off, sorry, sorry . . .'

Celia pulled the door firmly to before shouting, 'And don't come round here again making up wicked stories, you old cow!'

The front door was slammed loudly and Joyce giggled for the first time in over a week.

She was smiling when Celia entered her room again, this time with a letter in her hand. 'Who's been writing to you from London, miss?' she asked, curious but also slightly embarrassed. Joyce knew that her mum would never apologize for the beating she'd given her, but she also knew that because of it, her wound, and now having no job, Celia wouldn't give her too much of a hard time about the letter for long.

'Must be my black American soldier, eh?' Joyce smiled. Celia flushed scarlet and left her alone with her post.

It was from Alan. He apologized for leaving Cambridge without saying farewell. Orders, he wrote, had come in that morning sending him to London immediately. Soon he'd be in Europe somewhere, and although he didn't know where, if he had the chance, he'd write again. He signed off after saying that he hoped to find time to return and say goodbye to her properly. Joyce turned the letter over to see if there was anything further on the back of what was essentially a short note, but it was blank. There was no SWALK on the envelope, either. Somehow she knew that the letter was the last she'd hear from him.

When she was recovered enough to work again, Celia brought their neighbour Maud in to meet Joyce and talk about working at a college with her. Or rather, not with her, but in the same building. 'It's bloomin' hard work, dear,' Maud told her, looking her up and down a little sceptically.

'But I'm tougher than I look, missus,' Joyce assured her.

'She is, Maudie,' Celia piped up. 'She's back to making fires and beating the carpets for me when I go out cleaning, you know.'

Maud shrugged her shoulders. 'Alright then, I'll see the

housekeeper tomorra, an' you can help the old lady who needs an assistant. She must be in her eighties, you know, and really don't like going up the stairs no more. So the gentlemen's rooms on the first floor aren't being done at all, and haven't been since the old woman chased her last assistant away.'

'Oh,' Joyce's ears pricked up. 'Why did she chase her off, I mean how did an old woman do that?'

'Well, I don't know the truth of it, but some of the other bedders reckon that the old woman thought her assistant, who was Polish and came here during the war, had been taking stuff what she oughtn't, and I don't mean bread and cakes. Old Annie Hinkley threatened to report 'er, they reckon, and next day the girl didn't turn up. She just stopped coming to work.'

'Well, there's no such worries with my Joyce.' Celia stood up straighter as if to impress the point on Maud. 'She's as honest as the day is long, and won't be no trouble to no one, will you, love?'

Joyce made a face of incredulity and said, ''Course not, I'm a good worker, me.'

A week later, in the freezing fog, Joyce leaned her black Triumph bicycle against the college wall and shivered.

ROSE

Cambridge 1954

Rose Hobbs chain-smoked Weights cigarettes, one after the other all the way down until they almost burned her lips. 'If the cigs don't get me, this cold will, that's for sure,' she joked to her new neighbours, Mr and Mrs Adams, as she plonked the kettle back on top of a slightly lopsided cooker in her scullery (which used to be the coal shed). Rose shuffled back into the kitchen and the spot she'd barely moved from ever since letting the couple into her house.

It was the winter of 1954 and Rose stood against the fire guard, constantly lifting the back of her skirt. 'I think I may have got chilblains,' she lightly complained as the couple sat at the table drinking hot, sweet tea from mismatching mugs.

'That might be from standing in front of that fire,' suggested the nice young woman, named Ann. She was clearly unsure of how personal to be with the bony, severe-looking Rose, whose dishwater brown hair showed red tints occasionally, like the sparks in her smoking fireplace. It was difficult to tell how old Rose was. She could have been anything from thirty to fifty, and in some way reminded Ann of her mother. Rose's clothes were mostly hidden beneath a flowered pinafore wrap-over. Her thick grey socks and brown men's slippers made Ann think of Mrs Mopp from the radio show *It's That Man Again*. Her attitude was much friendlier than her mother usually was though, and for that Ann was glad.

'Well, whatever they are, my legs have started to look like

maps telling a story of where I've been . . . or what's been there, eh?' Rose laughed, showing a gold tooth. 'S'pose it adds a bit of colour!'

The laugh turned into a cough, which Ann waited to subside before saying as gently as she could, 'You ought to get that looked at.'

Rose caught her breath. 'Well, I have precious few luxuries left in me life and I love the heat on me, I can't stand the cold. Love me fags, an' all and have to catch up on 'em 'cos I can't smoke at work.'

Rose now worked as a bedder, and what she thought were chilblains would later develop into varicose veins, a not uncommon health problem among bedmakers of Cambridge colleges. So too was arthritis and housemaid's knee. Bedders, as Rose was always the first to tell everyone, were on their feet or on their knees for long hours. She'd usually then laugh wickedly after saying that and add, 'Mind you, it's better than spending all that time on your back or on your knees, believe you me!'

Rose lived in Queen's Meadow with her two sons, who looked as different to one another as two boys of a similar age could. The Adams had just moved into the other half of the semi-detached council house that Rose had lived in since it had been built. Ann and Fred explained to Rose how happy they were to be there, and how glad they were to have left the damp, cold and unsanitary Nissen hut they'd come from. The hut was always a 'temporary' accommodation, but their move was brought forward after reporting to the council that they'd seen a rat sitting on the end of their baby's cot. 'Oh yes, those Nissen huts are due for demolition soon, I've heard,' said Rose when they told her about it. 'About bloody time, too,' Fred Adams replied with feeling.

Ann had introduced herself to Rose as soon as they'd moved in, and on discovering that Rose worked as a bedder at

the university, she knew that she wanted to be her friend. Rose
was friendly to anyone who treated her well enough, and as
soon as the nice young woman started asking about her job,
she'd told her how much she loved it. 'I'm never gonna leave
there,' she said. 'I don't care if I can't walk, they'll 'ave to carry
me out, to make me leave.'

Rose had begun work at the college in 1951, having been hired
as an assistant to a veteran bedmaker named Vesta ('named
after the little match seller, so me mum told me'), who was to
retire the following year. Because the colleges were once more
taking the same number of students that they had before the
war, the number of staff required to service them had to
increase. Rose had been recommended to Vesta by a neighbour
in Barnwell, so the three women had met at Vesta's house and
she'd approved of Rose, and suggested her to the college
housekeeper. The 'interview' for the job consisted of the housekeeper asking if Rose had ever been in trouble with the police
('No,' she'd lied, knowing that a couple of court fines for soliciting would mean she'd never get the job), and that was it. She
was told that she'd be on half wages while learning the ropes
and started the following week.

    Many of the students that Rose did for had been officers in
the armed forces. Some of them had been invalided out and
were picking up where they'd left off before going into the
services. They were older than new students usually were, and
many were married. Wives were not allowed in college rooms,
though, and so they either had to remain at the family home
and only see their husbands at the end of Cambridge's eight
week terms, or live separately in digs in Cambridge – with
those landladies that would take them, that is, because not all
did. The majority of Cambridge's landladies had a prejudice
against taking in young women, believing them to be too much

trouble and possibly wary of having another, younger woman in their house who might give their husbands funny ideas.

Rose would admit many years after the fact that she had been tempted at times to offer 'comfort' to some students during her first term as a bedder. And not just for the money, either. She had been a slim, attractive brunette in her youth, and always wore make-up to work, was always aware of looking her best when out and about. She knew that men were attracted to her, as much for her flirtatious nature as for her high cheekbones, thin ankles and easy laugh. But she hadn't ever acted 'improperly' as a bedder, knowing that it would mean an immediate sacking if anyone ever found out – and they would, she was sure. She quickly realized that no one could ever keep their trap shut in a place like her college. After only a few weeks as Vesta's assistant, Rose knew well enough that for women like her, being a bedder was a cushy number, and if she kept her head down and did the job then she could be there for years to come. The perks of the job alone made her happy.

Students who knew that she smoked and did so too would offer her their cigarettes. She'd take one for now and one, she'd laugh as she plucked it from their gold and silver cases, 'for Ron', slotting it behind her ear where it was kept in place by the headscarf she wore like a small turban. One day a student misunderstood her quip, and after she had taken a cigarette for 'Ron' he asked what her 'husband did'.

'Eh?' she looked quizzically at the thin young man. 'What 'usband? What 'ave you 'eard?'

'Oh, er . . .' he stepped back defensively as Rose thrust her chin out and leaned on her mop. 'Why, er, er . . .' he stammered. 'Ronald. I mean, of course . . . isn't he your husband?'

At that Rose laughed loudly and said, 'Oh, him. Yeah, he's alright. Was gasping for a fag this morning, though.' At which the packet was produced again and Rose took two. She wasn't going to tell him that 'Ron' was her verbal play on 'later on', and that there was no husband at home.

Because she was chatty, Rose developed relationships with students who responded well to her 'cheek', as she put it. As time passed, she realized that being on good terms – or even simply being on civil, speaking terms – with students held other benefits, too. As well as the cigarettes, Rose often took home bread or cakes that had been left over from breakfast or an evening 'sworee' as she called them. At the end of her first Michaelmas term she was amazed to receive gifts from boys and men whose rooms she'd cleaned and whose beds she'd changed – those whose secrets she kept, the ones for who she disposed of contraceptives and other incriminating evidence of their immoral behaviour, were particularly generous.

Emptying students' bins and tidying their rooms gave Rose clues to the true character of each room's occupant that no amount of talking to them would ever elicit. While there were plenty of students who would always vacate their rooms before she called in the mornings, she knew what subject they were studying, where their families lived and the names of their mothers and occasionally their fathers too, from letters left lying around on their desks and bedside tables. She knew who took what medicine, who hid bottles of booze (and where, of course). Rose knew if they were happy, sad, anxious, over-confident, snobs, proper posh, or jumped-up grammar school boys – and just recently there were increasing numbers of those, it seemed.

Early on during her time at the college, she became very fond of a young man named Stephen, who seemed at ease with Rose from the start, and who not only gave her an extra cigarette for 'Ron', but suggested that she might want one to share with him later, so should take two extra. Within a couple of weeks Rose figured out that Stephen liked a drink. And he didn't mind what time of the day he enjoyed it, either, as she discovered when he offered her a glass of sherry one morning at 9 a.m. She laughed at that, and said maybe later, but she had work to do.

Stephen extended the hand of friendship not only towards Rose, but to everyone at the college, it seemed. His rooms were often the venue of choice for late night student debates fuelled by bottles of red wine, brown ale and clear spirits, so he told her, after Rose complained to him about the extra work gathering bottles. After the first couple of times though Stephen made sure everyone left with an empty, and he'd give the occasional unopened bottle of ale to Rose to take home. Rose had been invited to a couple of Stephen's after-pub 'dos', but had always declined, even after learning that a gardener and a couple of waitresses at halls had made their way to his rooms for a drink or three on different occasions.

Inevitably stories about the parties and invitations found their way to the porter, and one Friday towards the end of the term, he stopped Rose on her way home and spoke to her about Stephen. The porter was friendly enough, and asked if she thought that Stephen might have a drinking problem. Rose made a joke out of it ('Is it 'cos you ain't bin invited, Mr S.?' she laughed), and told him that she was sure Stephen could handle his drink, but she'd keep an eye on him.

The following Monday, Rose warned Stephen that his partying hadn't gone unnoticed and people were 'asking questions about the suitability of his being in rooms'. Stephen subsequently cut down on his daytime drinking – for the rest of that term, at least.

A variety of people at the college – the chaplain and certain directors of study among them – thought that bedders often knew more about their 'boys', as they all called the students, than they ever could. It was commonly held that some homesick students saw the older women as mother figures – and as long as they were only mother figures, that was alright. A couple of porters had noticed that Rose was liked and trusted (mostly) by her boys, and if they had any worries about any of them they'd pull her aside as she was leaving and have a word about them. Rose was no grass, and she'd never tell about some of the things her boys got up to – such as the two who liked to share a bed at night on Staircase H, for instance.

'It's none of my business, is it?' as she'd tell friends in the Red Cow pub on Exchange Street. 'I turn a blind eye, and the boys are always grateful if you know what I mean.' If, however, a boy was a bit too quiet, not sleeping (she could tell), or wouldn't talk to her at all nor look her in the eye, then she'd let the porter know that maybe that boy was having some problems and someone might want to talk to him about them. Stephen's trouble wasn't something that she'd ever talk to anyone in college about, though, as much because if he was silly enough to get drunk in college then they would know anyway, as because she liked him.

Early one morning Stephen was missing from his room and it worried Rose. Twice before he'd let her know that he was staying 'with a friend', and not to worry, but the day before this time, he'd only said his usual, 'Ta-ta, Rose, see you tomorrow,' as she left.

As she stood in the doorway looking at the empty and unslept-in bed, the porter came up behind her and said, 'Rose, Mr Hobbs 'ere has had to go to hospital.'

'Oh no, whatever for?' Rose asked.

'Well, he fell over drunk. Seems he was out on the lash, if you know what I mean?'

'Oh dear, I do. Silly bugger. Never mind, I'd best do his room so it's tidy for when he gets back.'

Before leaving for the day, Rose went back to Stephen's room to see if he'd returned. He was sitting on his bed, the left side of his head covered by a bandage.

'What have you done?' she asked.

'Rose dear, it's just a slight cut, nothing to worry about, but are you in tomorrow?'

'Of course I am, you know I'm in every day.'

'Lovely! Do you think that you could come in a bit early and wash my hair for me?'

'Well, I dunno about that . . . that's a bit much, Stephen, ain't it, really?'

'Please, Rose, you see I've got a date with the nurse who patched me up last night.'

'You what?'

'Yes, I've got a date with the nurse and I can't go with my hair like this . . .' he pulled a blood-caked strand away from the top of his head to show her. Rose laughed. 'She must need her own head seeing to. Alright then, I'll come in a bit early but don't you tell anyone. I don't want the housekeeper to hear about it. She'd have a fit. She doesn't think I should be talking to you, let alone touching your person!'

The next morning as Rose washed Stephen's hair he was clearly feeling hung over, and the headache that he would usually chase away with what he called 'an old family recipe tonic' (it smelled like a compost heap to her) wouldn't shift, he said.

'That'll be the big cut you got the night before last,' Rose told him, reaching round his shoulder for the Vosene shampoo.

'Oh yes! Of course, I forgot . . .' Stephen muttered.

Rose laughed and watched his grin turn to a wince in the mirror above the sink as she firmly pushed his head over it.

The wash took a few minutes, and when Rose had finished clearing the shampoo out of his hair with jugs of warmish water, trying to keep the plaster over his cut dry, he sat back on the stool he'd used to perch over the sink, dried the ends of his hair and said, in as serious a tone as she'd ever heard him use, 'I don't like being here, Rose. My mother and father pushed me to come.'

'Well, that ain't right, is it,' she instantly felt angry on his behalf. 'You shouldn't be pressured into it. It's not like my boys, we had no money and their old man was killed in the war,' she lied, then added, 'But you, Stephen, you've got all the chances in the world, I reckon.'

She finished pouring jugs of water over the un-bandaged part of his head and handed him a towel. 'You dry it, I'm not your bleedin' mother.'

Stephen put the towel over his head and reached for his cigarettes. 'Thank you, lovely Rose, how about a smoke for you, plus ones for Ron and yourself later?'

'You've worried me now, Stephen,' Rose told him, taking the cigarettes and putting two in the pocket of her pinafore. 'You're not getting that depression, are you?'

Stephen laughed with real delight. 'No, Rose, I don't drink because I'm depressed, I drink because I'm bored. Although I suspect that the nursey tonight is going to stop me from being too bored for a while.'

'Well, alright then,' Rose said, not totally convinced. She decided to tell him a story to scare him, though, and to get him to think more about what he was doing.

'During the finals the year afore last, I was asked by Janet Ward on Staircase G to help her get into one of her boy's rooms. "It won't open," she says, "and there's an 'orrible stench." It was first thing in the morning and I followed her up to the room. There was an 'orrible smell, right enough, so we went and got Ernie the maintenance man to help, but he weren't able to open the door and said that there were something drastically wrong. So off he went to tell the porter and fetch a ladder. Once they'd set it up outside, the porter went first, and Ernie after him, through the window. Well, they found the boy dead. He'd taken an overdose they reckoned, and must 'ave been there for a few days. He definitely meant to do it 'cos he'd put furniture up against the door to stop anyone getting in, which is why Janet hadn't been in for all that time. She thought he'd gone away and locked his door to let 'er know he was out.'

Stephen had turned white. 'Do you mean Phelps? But he went home, didn't he? Couldn't hack it, so left. That's what we heard.'

'It were all 'ushed up 'cos the college don't like havin' police in an' the papers finding out about stuff,' Rose told him. 'You know he 'ad just started, an' all. He was another one what din't really want to come to college and was pushed into it. That room really needed to be fumigated.'

Stephen sat on the edge of his single bed and looked up at her from under the edge of the towel on his head, silently smoking.

'You know,' Rose stopped on her way towards the desk, 'most of your lot have never even lived prop'ly at home, 'ave you? What was it, did you come straight from boarding school to university?' Stephen nodded and looked down at his feet. 'Tsk,' she turned and stubbed her cigarette out in the ashtray beside her. 'Bloody hell – no point in 'aving kids if you never bloody see 'em.'

Rose thought about her own two children, and how she'd always wanted them near her when they were little, and tried to give them the attention and care that she'd never had when a child. She'd lived in so many different places as a small child that she couldn't help but feel sympathy with anyone who'd not had a settled home life with a mum at least, and preferably a dad, too.

MAUD

Cambridge 1950–55

Sitting in a tent in the grounds of the college, Maud was having what she thought might just be the best day of her life. There was champagne, music and the young girls all looked like Hollywood stars. It was just like a film, she thought. She sat with her brand new sewing basket inside a tent next to the bar, along with a Red Cross nurse who bandaged a couple of ankles and handed out aspirin, calmed a couple of girls down who'd become hysterical ('Too much booze and not enough food,' she told them both), and spent as much time wandering the grounds looking for casualties as she did seated inside.

Maud had enough time at the beginning of the evening to stand at the entrance to the tent watching everyone passing by, listening to the music (a swing band, a female singer and then the swing band again, she thought she heard). It was a world away from her lonely life at home with Hugh. After a couple of hours people started to arrive asking her for repairs to their costumes. The first couple offered a glass of champagne to Maud, but she refused. 'Oh no, thank you,' she said to one young man who brought a flute glass to her and insisted on wearing his shirt as she replaced two buttons. 'I don't want to get so tipsy that I end up stabbing you with the needle.'

She did, however, accept cheese and grapes that were offered during the evening. 'It's like I've got my own little party going on here,' she told one of the students, while sewing their button back on their suit jacket cuff. She hadn't forgotten her pastilles and made sure she had one every time she ate a new piece of cheese, though the students didn't seem to notice her breath.

Before she knew it, the evening was ending. There were no more requests for her services and she was about to leave, at around five in the morning, when one of the bedders who had been washing the glasses asked her to come with her and the others to stand on the roof of the college. 'We can watch the students going 'ome, it's ever so funny,' she promised.

Most of the women on the roof had spent all evening and night collecting glasses from the lawn. Many of them, unlike Maud, had accepted a couple of glasses of champagne during the evening and were very jolly. 'Just to keep us awake, you know,' one of them said. 'Now, come on, we've got to go to the top and look down across the lawn. It'll be a sight for sore eyes.'

After climbing the narrow stairs up to the spire, the five women stood on the roof and looked across the whole of Cambridge as the sun began to cast a glow across the town. Then they gazed down at scores of students lying on the grass in the college grounds. The women giggled and Maud couldn't help but join in.

After an hour or so of joking and pointing at students who made their unsteady way along the town's cobbled and winding streets, Maud decided to walk back, pushing her bicycle so that she could make the night last for as long as possible.

On reaching home she leaned her bike inside the front garden and put her latch key in the lock of her mother-in-law's house with a deep sigh. But the front door wouldn't open, and there seemed to be something blocking it. Pushing hard she wondered if her mother-in-law had put something against the door as a kind of protest against Maud's staying out all night. Soon she created enough of a gap to be able to squeeze into the hallway. There she discovered what was blocking the door – it was Hugh. His face looked as if it had been slashed and there was blood seeping out of several cuts. She gasped and bent to him, 'Hugh, what on earth happened?'

He lay on the floor silently weeping and didn't answer.

'I need to clean you up,' Maud said as calmly as possible, although she was close to panicking. She ran to the kitchen and grabbed a dishcloth, with which she wiped enough blood from his face to see that the cuts were superficial, and not too deep. 'What happened, Hugh?' she whispered to him.

He looked directly into her eyes for the first time in months and said, 'Help me up the stairs, Maud, please.'

'Of course.' She helped him up on his feet and walked him up the stairs.

'Just put me to bed, I'll be alright,' he told her.

'I need to call the police, Hugh,' she said, as she helped ease him onto his bed. 'You've been attacked.'

Hugh looked away and stammered, 'No, no, don't do that. Bring a bowl of warm water, help me clean myself up. I don't want Mum to see me like this.'

Feeling calmer, Maud obeyed and cleaned his wounds as he sat on the edge of the bed.

'I just want to sleep now. Do you mind leaving me?'

'If you're sure?' She thought she had an idea of what might have happened. There had been a lot of grad bashing going on in town, and nights of the balls were worse than usual. Hugh must have been mistaken for a grad. The rise in the number of attacks lately was the talk of her college, with some people suggesting that it was a son of a bedder from another college who was the worst of them. Maud knew who that was and thought she'd find his mother and give her a piece of her mind.

'Just call if you need anything. You going to be alright?' she asked, and Hugh nodded. 'You sure?'

'Thank you, Maud. I'm sorry you had to see me like this.'

'So am I.' She closed the door quietly behind her and went to her room, exhausted and longing for the oblivion of sleep.

Maud slept in until three that Sunday afternoon, the latest she had ever done so. When she saw Mrs Ingram in the kitchen she explained that Hugh had been hit by a car the night before when on his bike. That, she thought, was a plausible explanation for his injuries. After all, there was no sign of his bike in the yard. Actually, she then wondered, what had happened to it – maybe his attackers had taken it? Whatever, it wasn't important at the moment. 'He's alright, nothing's broken, he was just a bit shaken up,' she continued, 'best leave him to rest.' Mrs Ingram looked duly worried, but agreed with Maud.

That evening Maud knocked at Hugh's door before entering, carrying a tray of food that she had prepared for him. 'It's nothing much. Just a few sarnies and a Battenberg. And a nice cup of tea.'

Hugh sat up in bed wearing his pyjamas. 'That's very thoughtful of you. Thank you.'

Maud put it on his bedside table and Hugh reached over to touch her sleeve. 'Sit down, Maud, please. I want to speak to you. There's something I need to ask you.'

'I'd rather stand.'

Hugh stared at her for a second and then blurted, 'Will you tell Trevor that I was beaten up?'

'Trevor?' Maud was confused.

'Trevor, your porter, at the college. He's my friend, Maud . . . A special friend . . . And he has been for a long time.'

Maud's face grew ashen. 'No, no,' she cried. 'What do you mean? Not that . . .' She suddenly felt sick. 'Is it him that you go fishing with? On those trips to Felixstowe?'

Hugh nodded. 'Yes, only we don't fish, Maud. You know

what I mean, don't you? I thought that you knew anyway . . .' He looked imploringly into her eyes, which were rapidly filling with tears as her heart filled with ice.

Her knowing was a relief for Hugh, but for Maud it was something quite different. At that moment, she realized, she hated him more than she'd hated anyone before in her life. Afraid of what she might say if she spoke, instead Maud threw her head back and walked out of his room, shutting the door firmly behind her.

Maud spent that night lying in her bed, fully clothed, not sleeping but recalling days and nights when she'd thought that her husband was doing one thing when he was clearly doing something quite, quite different. What a fool she'd been. She kept coming back to the sound of her nan's piercing voice in her head telling her that she'd never find a real man to love her; she was too worthless, ugly, stupid and selfish to ever deserve a loving husband. Her nan was right. It was the only conclusion that she could reach, the evidence proved it.

The following morning, a Monday, Maud pulled on her work pinafore over Sunday's clothes and, although she was still furious with him, felt compelled to look in on Hugh. She knocked on the door and opened it slowly. Unsure if he was asleep, she stepped quietly over to the bed. He was lying motionless, his mouth slightly open. There was no sound. The silence became so overpowering that it was like a loud buzzing in her ears.

Hugh had died in his sleep.

Maud didn't scream or cry. For a while she stood there looking at him, unthinking and unfeeling. He's only thirty years old, she thought. It must have been the same heart trouble that had killed his dad. She didn't think that the attack of Saturday night had anything to do with it, after all Hugh only had scratches to his face. Not wanting to upset her mother-in-law, who would sleep for another hour or so, Maud covered Hugh with the sheet and left the room.

She went through her usual morning routine as if in a trance, and then made her way into work on her bicycle. She went to work just as she would have on any Monday, and didn't talk to anyone for the first hour and a half.

Then Trevor came to find her, hurrying across the quad, wiping his eyes, coughing and trying not to run. She saw him from the window of one of her students' rooms as she dusted the books lined up along the sill. Knowing that Mrs Ingram must have telephoned to tell her that she'd found her son dead, Maud dropped her duster where she stood and walked steadily out of the room, down the stairs and, ignoring Trevor who was calling to her, got on her bike to return home.

The post-mortem later revealed that Hugh had received a massive blow to the back of his head, which had caused heavy bleeding on his brain. A short police investigation into the attack drew a blank, and the case was left open. It could have happened when he fell in the kitchen at home, the police told Maud, who had nothing to say in response.

Mrs Ingram cried on hearing the verdict. She was prescribed large amounts of sedatives and didn't leave her room for the following two weeks. Maud made the decision not to tell her about the police investigation into the queer bashing suspicion. Another secret wasn't going to make much difference to her, she thought.

In the weeks following Hugh's death Maud began to hear stories about his past from neighbours and customers, who all thought that she'd known about his double life. One day Maureen, a bedder who worked at the same college, came round to see her. Maureen was particularly close to Trevor, and told her that she'd heard about her husband from him. Feeling

deeply ashamed, Maud said nothing and let Maureen go on.
'Trevor knew your Hugh very, very well, love,' she said in sympathetic tones. Whenever Hugh was on leave from the navy he
visited the public toilets in Cambridge town centre looking for
sex, until he met Trevor.

Maud felt sick, but waved Maureen on. 'They first met the
night of Hugh's supposed first date with you, love, an hour
before you was to meet under the lamp post.' Trevor, she
said, told Hugh that, 'No one suspects that I'm "one of them",'
and that he knew Hugh was, too. 'Takes one to know one,' he
reckoned.

Maureen continued the story of how Hugh and Trevor
went to a nearby toilet after a couple of pints, and then Hugh
left before Trevor, but a group of local boys who'd seen them
enter the toilets lay in wait and chased him. Trevor managed
to give them the slip by going into a college, but two of the
thugs grabbed Hugh – which was where the blood on his shirt
had come from that night, realized Maud. Just as she'd hoped,
Hugh had returned to the Orkneys from that trip home almost
in love – but with Trevor, not Maud.

On his next leave, Hugh went looking for Trevor and
eventually found him. Their relationship developed in parallel
to that of Maud and Hugh. According to Maureen, Trevor
thought it was a good idea for Hugh to marry her, but he
claimed that he told the younger man, 'Make sure you tell her,
though. If she's going to be keeping your secret she needs to
be able to cover for you.' Which was why Maureen and everyone else who knew, thought that she had, too.

In fact, Maud had always felt responsible for the failure of
their marriage. Not that she'd tell Maureen nor anyone else
that. Close to tears, Maud showed Maureen out that wet and
grim afternoon, and then sat to think about the last few years.
She felt again the depression setting in as her hopes of having

a family died. Those nights when she had cried herself to sleep, grieving for the children she would never have, Maud knew that Hugh could hear her through the bedroom wall, but he had never come into her room to comfort her.

She decided, after too many months of crying and silently suffering, to throw herself into working and try to forget about the mistake she had made in marrying the first man who had paid her any attention – just as her nan had warned her she would. While Hugh was 'looking after' her and paying for housekeeping and anything that she asked for, she had thought perhaps that she'd try to save money in order to rent a place and leave him. She wouldn't go back to her nan, even if she was paid to. She had told herself that Hugh was kind and at least didn't beat her.

Still, Maud thought, what a fool I was. She realized that she wasn't the only woman in Cambridge not to know about Hugh's secret life. Clearly, she thought, his mother didn't know, either. Mrs Ingram had tried to help the couple to find a kind of peace between them, and although she meant well she'd only ever talk to Maud and always from a position of support for Hugh. She defended her son's actions by telling Maud that he'd always been like it. One night when Hugh announced that he was going to go fishing, Maud screamed in frustration, and he left the house. Mrs Ingram tried to calm her, 'Maudie love, stop it. Night fishing has always been his thing . . .'

Maud had interrupted her. 'You two must think I'm daft: he's got another woman, hasn't he? He doesn't even have any bloody fishing rods!' She'd thrown herself onto the sofa and cried and Mrs Ingram tried to soothe her.

'He must borrow the equipment, or store it down Bait's Bite. Why would he lie? Some men are loners. He likes his solitude, fishing gives you that. His dad was the same.'

That had been the first time Mrs Ingram had spoken about

Hugh's dad and Maud stopped crying enough to ask, 'What happened to your husband?'

'He died in his sleep. Some sort of heart problem he'd had since he was a child. Sad business. Hugh found him and that was hard. He was only three, just a baby really.' Mrs Ingram continued, 'Hugh became very needy. He followed me everywhere after that. Wouldn't sleep on his own for years after, I had to get in his bed. He was a real mummy's boy and clung to me like I was going to just keel over at any time. Wouldn't leave the house back then. Very sickly child he was, as well.'

No, thought Maud now, she didn't know. Perhaps her 'illness' since his death had something to do with her not knowing then but guessing it now. Perhaps she's trying to avoid the truth about her precious boy, Maud concluded, that's why she won't leave the house, she doesn't want anyone saying 'I know, you know' to her. It was probably for the best, Maud thought, 'cos she won't be able to handle what I've just heard from Maureen.

In the months after Hugh's death, and with her mother-in-law essentially housebound, Maud had to stop working in Grantchester Road, but she was determined to carry on as a bedder (she'd been 'promoted' from assistant after her husband's death). Leaving her cleaning job gave her time to build a proper small side-business out of her dressmaking skills, and for a long time she was the only woman in Ditton Fields offering the service. However, soon she was in competition with Mrs Hamilton who lived three doors up. She had noticed the extra cash Maud was making, and had her own sewing machine plus more time to devote to working on it than Maud could afford. They both made popular dirndl skirts for the local young girls to wear at the dances in town, but Mrs Hamilton could run them up in an hour. Young girls being as impatient as they were, mostly preferred to order their skirts with a few hours' notice and wear them the same evening. So Mrs Hamilton was more popular than Maud, despite her higher prices.

Some of Maud's immediate neighbours, who felt sorry for her, knowing about her poor childhood and sham marriage, were angry with Mrs Hamilton for taking Maud's business from her. Maud felt very uneasy about the atmosphere which she felt responsible for bringing about on the estate, and asked probably her closest neighbour and only real friend, Edith Perry, for advice.

Edith and her family had moved into Ditton Fields in 1951, and the pair were fast friends from the moment Edith came over to introduce herself and her daughter, Audrey, who was only three years old at the time. Audrey was the youngest of four children after three boys, John, Roy and Ron, and as such had earned herself the nickname 'Tiny'. She was the youngest by a good ten years and a very late addition to the Perry family; Edith was forty-three when she gave birth to her. Maud was immediately taken with Tiny and quickly started making outfits for her, which Edith very much approved of, and the two women struck up a friendship that became so close that Audrey soon came to call her Aunty Maud.

Maud explained to Edith how a fast turnaround was more important to a lot of the customers but she had always been slow and methodical with her needlework, and diligent with her machine work. It took a little time, but Edith soon discovered that while the girls bought the same material for their rock-and-roll skirts, Maud could add a little extra to her service which her customers would appreciate. In order to get their skirts to puff out and hold their shape, the girls would wash their lace petticoats and soak them in sugar to make them stiff. Edith told her that she should give them the sugar they needed for the lace, because the girls' parents were not happy with them using their supplies. Thanks to Edith's advice the share of skirt-making levelled out between Maud and Mrs Hamilton, and they would even politely nod to each other in the street.

So a kind of peace came to Maud in the mid-1950s, and she found contentment in working as a bedder and a seamstress. Not that she ever expected her happy state to last forever.

AUDREY PERRY

Audrey Perry was five years old when she first saw the inside of a Cambridge college. Three months after the coronation of Elizabeth II her mother, Edith, began work as a bedder, and within a few weeks her youngest child and only daughter was accompanying her on afternoon trips in order to turn down beds in students' rooms on staircase A. Edith made their trips to college an adventure, telling Audrey that her dad didn't need to know that she'd been there, it was their secret.

Edith had taken the job much against the wishes of her husband, Edward. Audrey was playing by the fire in the back room when her mum told her dad about her decision to take a job as a bedder. He voiced his objections to her working at the university loudly. 'So you're going back into service again, eh?' he almost shouted at her, which made Audrey flinch. Her dad went on, setting out for Edith the servants' duties (as he saw them) that she'd be required to undertake. 'You'll lay up breakfast while they have a bath, clean the bath after them and see to their needs. I don't want you to work at all, but if you have to, what's wrong with working at Pye's on the line or in a shop even? No,' he continued with bitter irony, 'you had to be a bloody bedmaker. It's hard work and you ain't got it in you no more – you're nearly fifty, Edie, not eighteen. They're nothing but a bunch of privileged, lazy buggers, and most of them are bloody thick, got no common sense.'

Edith waited to make sure he'd finished before replying, 'I'll be home in plenty of time to get yours and the kids' dinner ready, and after I've picked up Audrey I'll get your tea on. Don't worry, you won't go hungry.'

She had known what really bothered her husband of more than twenty-five years was that he might have to look after their daughter and get his own meals while she worked. She also knew that his working-class pride wouldn't allow Tiny to be indoctrinated by 'upper-class twits' as he'd taken to calling the students, fellows and even porters at the university. Audrey and Edith were as close as any two females in an otherwise all-male household could be, which made keeping the visits a secret between them more than easy; it was natural.

Edith had been offered the bedmaker position on Maud's recommendation and by 1955, had been bedding for two years, occasionally sneaking Audrey in with her during school holidays. On a couple of occasions, they'd met Mr Horrans, a fellow of the college who Edith cleaned for. Audrey liked him, as much for his appearance as the fact that he greeted her warmly and insisted on shaking her hand. His hair stood out in tufts above his ears, although he was completely bald on top, and he wore large glasses that made him look like an owl, a resemblance enhanced by his eyebrows which were both tufty and pointed at their outer ends.

It was very close to Christmas and Audrey hadn't been into college with her mum for a few weeks. She wanted to see how the place was decorated, so asked her mum how work was and if she'd seen Mr Horrans.

'I have, my love, and it's very sad, so sad,' Edith replied, shaking her head slowly.

'Why, Mum?'

Edith sighed and perched her plump bottom on the stool that was always kept next to the oven. She rooted around in her apron pockets for cigarettes, and Audrey sat at the pink

Formica kitchen table. 'Your dad's gone and pinched my cig-gies again. Bloody bugger,' Edith tutted.

'Go on then, Mum. What?'

Edith ignored Audrey as she searched through the knick-knack drawer, hunting among the odd lengths of string ('might come in handy one day,' her dad always said), fuses, small screwdrivers, nuts and bolts that didn't fit one another, Green Shield stamp books, old postcards from Felixstowe, Scarbor-ough and Blackpool, two-pin electrical plugs and, finally, a crumpled box of Woodbines cigarettes. Edith pulled a bent one from the packet and lit it, inhaling deeply before beginning her story. 'I went to see the old fellow and, as you know, most mornings I see him eating his breakfast with just his birthday suit on, and today was no different. So I told him, not for the first time, "You've got to put your clothes on." He says, "Give me my shirt, Mrs Perry, and help me." I said, "No, get your pants on first," and passed them to him.'

Audrey stifled a giggle and jumped as her father's voice boomed into the kitchen from the parlour. 'You did what?'

Edward had been standing at the kitchen door for long enough to have heard the bit about his wife passing another man his pants, and he looked furious. Audrey jumped up from the table, ran to Edith and buried her head in her lap. Edith was unfazed. 'Trust you to get the wrong end of the stick, you bloody great apeth, Edward. Bloody calm down! He's just the bloody old fellow. Really old. And he's ill, Edward.'

Her husband stepped into the kitchen and stood, glaring at Edith.

She gently lifted Audrey's head and told her, 'Sit down again, Auds.' Turning to Edward she explained, 'I have to get him dressed some mornings. He's got a nurse that comes in to him but sometimes she's not there when I arrive. Anyway,' she turned back to Audrey, 'today I found him in a right state at the end of the day, not in the morning. We were s'posed to be having Christmas mince pies with all the others at the college. They'd come in from Hawkins bakery, and really nice they smelled.' She paused.

'I didn't get to the Halls though, 'cos I saw Horrans coming down the stairs and he'd got a bad tummy and he was . . . Well, you know, all the way down the stairs, all along the corridor, treading in it . . . yeah . . . and the stink . . . I thought the nurse was coming in but she weren't there, and I thought, "What am I gonna do?" Then Maud came along and shouted up the stairs to me I had to come and get a mince pie before they all go, so I shouted back, "Don't come up here!" She said, "What's the matter?" and I said, "Go and get me some disinfectant, quick!" 'cos I'd run out of it. Anyway, Maud and little Mo came back and they helped me clean the stairs and carpet while I cleaned him up.'

'Oh Mum, that's horrible,' Audrey felt like crying.

'It's alright, love, we got it all done soon enough. But when Maud and little Mo said come and have a mince pie, you can imagine how I felt. You couldn't, could you?' Audrey shook her head, and could think of nothing to say.

Her dad did, though. 'Right,' he sounded calm now. 'You ain't working there no more. You've made your point, you've done it for long enough, but you might as well be working in the bloody asylum up in Fulbourn. They'd probably pay you more an' all.'

'Oh, have a bloody heart, for Pete's sake,' Edith sounded as if she was about to lose her temper. 'He's ill. OK, it's a bit embarrassing seeing him naked every day, and I did report it and they said I didn't have to go in there if I didn't want to. But what can you do? You can't go out and leave him when he comes down for breakfast, I have to get him dressed.'

Edward stood up and walked out, shouting after him, 'You

ain't working there no more, and that's final. Fur coat or no bloody fur coat!'

Audrey waited for her dad to slam the front door on his way out (to the pub, she assumed) and said, 'I think Dad's right, Mum. You shouldn't work there. You didn't get your mince pie.'

Edith laughed loudly and told her daughter, 'Do you know what, Audrey, I don't think I could ever eat one ever again. Don't care if they're made at Hawkins or Buckingham Palace!'

Despite Edward's protests Edith continued to work at the college, and two weeks later, on New Year's Eve, she queued up all night outside Eaden Lilley's to buy the fur coat she had been to look at in the window every day for the last two months.

When she got home with it, Audrey buried her face into the plush fur and breathed in a scent of something she couldn't explain, as if it was an animal, but not like the really fluffy rug that her mum's friend Maud had in her front room. Edward ignored the coat. Audrey begged her mum to let her try it on.

'Don't be daft, Audrey, and don't get your dirty bloody paws on it neither!'

Audrey retreated and sat on the foot of the stairs and watched as her mum put the coat on and stood, admiring herself in the mirror by the front door. Still Edward said nothing. With a toss of her head, Edith opened the front door and swept out without saying where she was going. 'Get me some fags if you're near the Co-op!' shouted Edward at the slammed door.

Audrey, her head full of images of movie stars dancing in fur coats, walked to the parlour where Edward sat, smoking and looking out of the window. She asked if they could pretend they were at a dance and to her surprise her dad said yes. He stood to put a 78 on their enormous radiogram record player and the sound of the Glenn Miller band soon poured into the tiny room. Audrey stepped on to her dad's feet and together they waltzed around the front room. She'd never forget that New Year's Eve.

Long after her bedtime Audrey lay awake, waiting to hear her mother's return. Just as she was slipping into darkness, as if from the end of a long corridor, she heard her dad say, 'Hello, love, have a nice time in your new coat?'

Struggling to surface into the cold air of her bedroom, Audrey pulled her sheet and blankets down from her ears and heard her mother's happy laugh, and with it she knew everything was alright. Audrey was asleep by the time Edith looked in on her as she made her way to bed.

A few days into the new term at college, Edith was late getting home. As she hurriedly prepared vegetables for tea, passing potatoes to Audrey to peel next to her at the sink, she said over her shoulder to Edward, who was sitting on a small stool polishing his shoes ready for a night out at the pub, 'Maud was off sick today.'

'So?' Edward responded nonchalantly.

'Well, that's why I'm a bit late.'

'More work for you when she's off, then.' Edward had an edge to his voice.

'I don't mind helping a friend,' Edith snapped back. 'That's what we do. She's done mine enough of late, after all.' Edith had taken a few days off work sick with a bad stomach in the run-up to Christmas, and Maud had covered for her.

'The porter Trevor was really shocked when I told him I'd be doing her staircase for her, and he said it was unheard of that Maud would have a day off. Anyway, I told him that she had some sort of tummy bug and he scoffed. Well, I didn't like his tone, see, he can be a bit catty that one. So I said to him, "Maud ain't no slacker, you know." And do you know what he said?' Edward had stopped paying attention and Edith turned to face him and shouted, 'Are you listening to me?'

Edward smiled and dutifully placed the shoe and the polish on the newspaper at his feet. He nodded his head. 'OK, full attention. Trevor is being horrible about our Maud, yeah, go on. Maud ain't no slacker, go on, what's your point?'

'The point is, Edward, that Trevor told me something today and I didn't like what he was implying. Bin playing on my mind all day it has. He said that she came into the college to do the beds on the day her Hugh died, which must 'ave bin 1950, afore we knew 'er. He said Hugh had pegged it in the middle of the night, but she came in and got their breakfast ready and did all their cleaning, without saying a word to no one.'

Edward looked confused. 'So, what's your point? We know Maud is a bit of a rum 'un and a bloody workaholic, so it doesn't surprise me.'

'I know, but Trevor was really angry, see. Like he felt real hate for her. As if she'd done Trevor wrong or something, you know, as if she gave him that odd limp. I don't know, just 'cos she came in to work on the day her 'usband died, he was really put out. More than once he said, "All the time Hugh Ingram was dead in his own bed and that cow of a wife was carrying on like it's a normal day." I said to him, "It's not like he knew anything about it, so there's no harm done. He was dead, after all. She must have been in shock."' Edith grimaced, and clutched at her side, as if she'd felt a pain. 'It weren't until years after my dad died that I could talk about it, do you remember? It can affect people in different ways, can't it. Although nothing you do is gonna bring 'em back.'

Edward nodded, remembering the deaths of Edith's dad

and his own parents long ago. Edith sat down on the kitchen chair opposite her husband. 'Do you know what that Trevor did then?' she looked concerned and confused at the same time. 'He started crying. I said, "Oh Trevor, I'm sorry, I didn't know you were grieving for someone." Well, that's what it looked like. He told me to shut up and bloody turned his back, sat down and picked up the paper. And without looking at me told me to get back to work!'

'Well, he was embarrassed, weren't he?' Edward himself looked slightly embarrassed at the idea of another man crying in front of his wife. 'But he's a big girl's blouse anyway, you said.'

He slapped his hand on the table and said firmly, 'You better not do that to me if I die before you! Bloody go into work like nothing's happened. I want you to grieve like them Catholic women, wear black for the rest of your life and don't even dare look at another man. Do you get me?' He wasn't joking, Edith could tell, but handled his rising anger as she always did.

'Oh shut up, you're ain't 'alf daft.' She flicked her tea towel in his direction and continued, 'I don't want to ask Maud about it, I don't want to pry. But I didn't like the way he got claws out at her, calling her an old cow like that. That's not respectful. Don't care if he's grieving or not. She's my friend.'

'Huh,' Edward responded, 'Trevor's just saying it like it is. It's simple. People like Maud think that them students are worth more than her own husband. No matter what you think, he was her husband. He was family and they're not, no matter how much she wants them to be, and they'll forget her as soon as they've left to go on and become bosses of the likes of you and me.'

Edith shook her head, 'Maud doesn't have children, remember, and look at her with our Audrey. I do think she looks at them boys as if they're her own. That college is her life. She watches 'em graduate at the Senate House, she used to go down to the Bumps and told me that she was once a seamstress at May Balls too.'

'Sounds like she's their bleeding mascot.'

But Edward didn't dislike Maud, even if it seemed sometimes that he did. He was pleased that she was a friend of Edith's, and that she helped them out on many occasions by babysitting Audrey. He was thankful for those free family holidays she was able to offer them at her caravan in Felixstowe, too.

Edward was to become even more indebted to Maud when a few weeks later she pushed and pulled Edith home from college on her bike. 'I'm sorry,' Edith said as she sat breathing shallowly in the kitchen, having been helped off the bike by Edward and Maud together. 'I just conked out. I don't know what I would have done if Maud hadn't pulled me home on my bike,' she smiled thinly at Maud. 'I just didn't have the insides to pedal, I don't know what's wrong with me.'

As Maud helped Edward get Edith into bed she told them, 'I'll get June's girl Doreen in to do her staircase for the rest of the week at college. She's looking for some work. Edith, you don't need to worry about work, I'll speak to Mrs George, she's a lovely woman and you know she'll be alright with it.'

Edward didn't care a tuppence, he said, he really wasn't bothered with what the college would do without her. His main concern was whether his wife would make it through the night. 'She looks bloody awful,' he told Audrey and Ron when they returned home later that day.

As Edward suspected, Edith's illness was serious. Hospital appointments, tests and consultations during the months that followed her collapse at work revealed that she had bowel cancer. When Edith returned from hearing the prognosis from her doctor and told him, Edward didn't say a word. He stared at the wall until Edith shouted at him, 'Did you 'ear what I said? I've got cancer, Edward. I might not see Audrey grow up. Say something, for Christ's sake.'

'They've got it wrong,' he said quietly.

'They ain't,' Edith moaned. 'You'll have to get used to it. Come 'ere.'

She opened her arms wide, beckoning her husband into her embrace, but his legs had gone and he couldn't move. Holding the back of a kitchen chair he steadied himself, and Edith stepped towards him. She cradled him in her arms as he sobbed. 'You bloody great apeth,' she said softly. 'You've got to be strong, Edward. You've got to be strong for Audrey 'cos she's going to need you more than ever now if the doctors don't get it all out of me. Now,' she gently raised his head away to look into his eyes. 'Please promise me that you won't do to me what Maud did with her Hugh, if I die.'

'What? Leave you here and go to work?' Edward half-sobbed incredulously.

'No, you 'apeth,' Edith smiled. 'Scatter my ashes all over Felixstowe. That Trevor later told me that Hugh's on the pier, in the toilets and in the sea. I don't want to think that my leg is going to be separated from my arm miles away from each other. I want to be completely intact, thank you very much!' Through his tears, Edward laughed.

A few months later, Edith had an operation in hospital. Audrey's oldest brothers John and Roy, who were taking their national service in the RAF, claimed a compassionate leave and on the day of the operation they took Audrey and Ron to the cinema to see *The King and I*. 'It'll take their minds off it,' the older boys said to Edward, who agreed that there was no point in them all being at the hospital.

Halfway through the screening of the musical, though, an announcement came over the speaker system asking, 'Could John or Roy Perry come to the foyer as we have a phone call from Addenbrooke's.' Panicking, Audrey and her brothers ran to the foyer, where Roy grabbed the telephone from the usher.

'She's dead, ain't she?' Audrey cried, as Roy listened to their father on the other end of the line. Edward explained that their mother *had* died on the operating table – not just once, but three times – however they had brought her back to life, and she was now 'stable' and sleeping.

Audrey wasn't allowed to see her mum until she was 'out of danger', as her dad put it, but it was still a bit of a shock to her when she saw her in the hospital a week after the operation. Edith looked as white as the sheets that were turned over her blanket, and she needed help to sit up and talk to Audrey.

Edward was sent by Edith to get a cup of tea and when he'd left the ward she explained to her daughter that the doctors had removed bits of her inside ('me bowel'), then 'cleaned it and put it back'.

Her weak smile brought tears to Audrey's eyes. She tried not to cry, knowing that her mum would then try to make her feel better when it was clear to Audrey that Edith needed all of her strength just to talk. 'Oh Mum,' Audrey's voice almost broke as she took her mum's hand. 'It'll be alright then, won't it?'

'To be honest, love, I don't know,' Edith made a slight movement with her shoulders that was trying to be a shrug. 'But I can't go through this again, I tell you that; but don't tell your dad, he won't be able to hold himself together. It has to be just you and me what knows, alright? We have to make things alright in the house so that if I don't get home for long – now don't you dare cry!'

Audrey sniffed loudly, and angrily wiped her eyes.

Edith continued, 'If I'm not at home for long, we have to get you in shipshape to take over running the house, right?'

Audrey nodded.

'Right, now, shhh! Bet your dad forgets the sugar in me tea!'

Audrey half-giggled, but felt her face flushing as the thought of her mum not being with her forever took a hold of her mind. Edward's return gave her an excuse to leave and find the ladies loo, where she cried and cried, as quietly as she could, in a stall. She was all cried out when she went back to the ward and smiled, being 'brave' just for Mum.

By the time it came for Edith to be taken home from hospital it was clear, the doctors told her, that her cancer had spread throughout her body. Audrey stood in the doorway as Edith asked doctors the question that they never liked to answer: 'How long?'

They hummed and hahed, said it was hard to tell, but when Edith pushed them and asked if she could plan next Christmas one of the doctors, a grey-haired, tall man who looked as if he'd been a general in the army, thought Audrey, shook his head, and then looked at the floor.

'Thank you,' said Edith. 'Goodbye.'

At home, Edith was too weak to do anything strenuous, so Audrey began to do most of the household chores. She was 'helped' by Edith's directions in the first few weeks, but when it became difficult for her mum to walk around, she'd just lie on the sofa, watching Audrey iron, or sweep up and dust the furniture.

One Sunday afternoon when Edith had finished listening to the 2,000th episode of *Mrs Dale's Diary* on the radio, she staggered to the kitchen and stood hunched in the doorway watching her daughter transfer peeled potatoes from the sink to a large saucepan. She took a deep breath before speaking. 'You missed *Mrs Dale's Diary*, Audrey. I was hoping Maud might have come over to hear it, too.'

'What happened?' Audrey asked. She wasn't very interested in the programme, but knew how much her mum loved it.

'It was alright, Bob got married to Jenny Owen. About time an' all.'

'I thought I'd make a start on dinner, Mum.'

'Thanks, love. You're doing alright.' Edith smiled at her daughter who, small as she was, had Edith's pinafore on – its straps tied round her several times to keep it closed. She was not playing at being 'mum', Edith could see, because Audrey understood that she had to *be* 'mum' and keep house for Edward and Ron – until he went to join the RAF, anyway.

Three weeks later, at the beginning of December 1956, Edith passed away. No one in the family cried the day that she fell asleep – which was how it looked to Audrey.

It was the middle of the day, the doctor was round and Audrey heated some soup for her mother, more in hope than expectation, because Edith hadn't been eating for almost a week, only taking sips of water. Edith hadn't spoken properly for a few days either, but she looked over as Audrey came into her bedroom carrying a tray.

Seeing that look Audrey kind of understood that her mum, in that instant, was speaking to her; she was saying 'goodbye'. Edith then closed her eyes and, within seconds it seemed, with Audrey standing stock-still at the end of the bed, the doctor stood up and said simply, 'It's over.'

There was no surprise, which is perhaps why no one cried. Instead there seemed to Audrey to be a collective sigh released, and a feeling of relief rolled over them all, buoying them up as Edward organized Edith's funeral. The service was a small affair but the college sent a wreath with their crest and this touched Edward, who asked Ron, 'Who was there from the college? Was the bursar there? And your mum's housekeeper, Mrs George, was she there?'

The day had been a blur for the family, Audrey thought. Her dad was clearly unsure what to say to people. He had been drinking more heavily as Edith's illness worsened and as she held his hand in the church pew, Audrey thought he struggled to stop himself from breaking down. Her brothers did the meeting and greeting of guests and Audrey didn't leave Edward's side. 'Sorry 'bout your shirt,' she whispered in his ear.

The night before the funeral she had ironed his and Ron's shirts so inexpertly that Edward had shouted at her, 'You've made a pig's ear of it, Audrey.'

She shouted back at him, 'I'm not Mum!'

Her outburst stung Edward, who stopped, knelt before her and said, 'I'm sorry, I'm sorry, I know you're not. I'm sorry.' He looked into the eyes of his blonde, short-haired daughter and hugged her. He promised that he would never shout at her again. After he got to his feet Edward poured himself a large Scotch and reassured Audrey that she would get better at it.

One of the lasting memories that Audrey kept coming back to was of a night, about a month before her mum died, when Audrey showed her the green jumper that she was knitting for her. Audrey had saved her dinner money to buy green wool (Edith's favourite colour), a tray cloth with a printed pattern on it, and some embroidery threads. Edith had loved the embroidery which Audrey gave her on her birthday, and although she had not finished the green jumper she showed it to Edith anyway.

'See how far I've got, Mum.' Audrey held the garment up and said how she was looking forward to seeing her wear it. 'I thought it would bring the green out in your eyes, Mum.'

Edith squeezed her hand and, although too weak to get out of bed, told her, 'I'll wear it like it is.'

Audrey laughed, 'You'll look daft. It's only got one arm, Mum.'

'Don't matter. Put it on me.'

Audrey would never forget watching her mum struggle as she squeezed into the green, armless jumper, smiling weakly. After the funeral, Audrey wrapped the embroidery and half-finished jumper in tissue paper and put them into a box under her bed. She promised herself that she would finish it, one day.

ROSE

Cambridge 1959–63

There were days when Rose daydreamed that some of the boys that she did for were her sons. Well-spoken, smartly dressed, always respectful, even the naughty ones, those boys never really gave her any trouble. They were so unlike her children that she felt as if she was living in another world when at work, and one that compared very harshly with what awaited her at home.

Clark and Maurice couldn't have been any more different to her students than they were from each other. Clark had red hair, was stocky and thought to be 'a bit backward' by people who knew him. 'The trouble is, he don't like school,' Rose would tell teachers and truant officers when they called to talk to her about him, which was often. 'I can't force him to go. You've seen the size of him. I shout at him, I open the curtains, I even threw a bucket of cold water over him one morning! But he'd rather be sat on the bank down Fen Ditton fishing than in a classroom.'

In contrast, Maurice was tall with blonde curly hair. He passed his eleven-plus exam and was accepted at Soham Grammar School in 1959. It was quite a trek for him, but he caught a bus from Newmarket Road Cemetery every morning and soon he was missing the bus home because he'd stay behind to play sports, and have to hitch back. He played for the school football and cricket teams, and did a bit of boxing, too – he figured that might be handy in dealing with Clark, who could get violent if the mood took him, as it often had.

By the time he was thirteen, Rose was aware that Clark was building himself a reputation as a bit of a hard nut, and was fighting other kids for pocket money, conkers and the leadership of a gang. She wouldn't have been surprised if his gang – who thought they were Teddy Boys and nicked their dad's donkey jackets when they could (he took one of his gang's stolen jackets) – were going out and beating up grads, but she didn't want to think about it. If her Clark set about one of her boys she didn't know what she'd do. Shop him to the coppers, she thought. That'd teach him a thing or two.

'He's a nasty one, my Clark,' Rose told one of her students one morning, who she was trying to warn off cycling across Midsummer Common at night. Two students had been pushed off their bikes into cowpats the night before, and one of them had been daft enough to challenge the boys who'd done it. The student ended up with a broken collarbone. Rose had heard from the porter that he'd described his attackers to the police as looking like workmen with big boots, trousers hitched up to show them off, and grease in their hair. 'Full of anger he is, my Clark,' Rose continued. 'An' he wants to fight anyone who in't like him – anyone like you, partic'ly.' Her student looked suitably alarmed at the prospect.

'My Maurice is like me though,' she went on, trying to assure him that not all town boys were like Clark. 'He's a hard worker and does seven paper rounds. He gets more for his Sunday one, and I don't have to get him up for it neither, he's out before I am. Mind you, he's cheeky like me, too. Him and that Terry he goes to Soham with, go to the back of the Co-op on Whitehill Road and collect all the empties, then go to the front of the shop and get the money back on them. Little bugger, ain't he.'

Rose's varicose veins had become so bad that she had to stop cycling to work and instead caught the early morning 'bedders bus' (it was a tram before the war, she recalled Vesta telling her) that stopped at every college in Cambridge. She'd been offered an operation to repair them in the winter of 1958, but knew that if she did then she would miss work, so said she'd wait until the summer.

The housekeeper, knowing how Rose was suffering with her veins (and knees, too), moved her to staircase H and gave her two staircases to another bedder. Working on H meant she only had to do for two fellows and a BA student. They each had coal fires that required cleaning out and rebuilding, and a scuttle of coal left in their rooms every day, though. Still, she thought, it's hard work but not like it was for old Vesta. She told me that she used to get up on a Sunday morning and go there for three shillings pay, working seven days a week from seven until ten in the morning. Blow that, it's not for me. I got to have a Sunday off.

Rose attended the Pentecostal Mission on Newmarket Road every Sunday. The parson, Sid as she called him, seemed to be a great fan of hers even though she'd tell him after services, 'You know I ain't religious, Sid, but it helps. Thank you.' Then she'd head straight to the Seven Stars pub for her first Sunday drink. She was, she claimed, 'Welcome in all them pubs along there, they all know me.' The landlords and barmaids of the pubs that lined the Newmarket Road from the Seven Stars to the cemetery bus stop would see her every Sunday as she made her way home. She'd have a glass of port in every other one, mixing that with a half of mild in the others. It took her mind off her legs, she'd say.

The housekeeper of the college where Rose had worked for almost a decade, allocated her one of the first vacuum cleaners they'd bought. The other bedders had to come to her in order to use it, or else stick with the carpet sweepers they all had, which were hard to run over the Turkish carpets and bare floorboards. Having the vacuum cleaner not only made Rose's work easier, but it made her feel important, somehow. Working for the fellows also made Rose feel as if she was a notch above the average bedder, but working for the two old men had its own set of worries. One morning when she was cleaning the fireplace for one of her fellows, she watched him put bread on a fork to toast over the fire that she was setting, when she said, 'Oy–oy–oy! You can't eat that bit of bread, look at the fur on it!'

He turned to Rose and amazed her by saying, 'But that's how I like it.'

'Oh,' she responded, 'but you'll die eating it.'

He laughed then, and so did she, and they became firm friends.

When Maurice reached his middle teen years Rose managed to persuade the junior bursar at the college to give him a job. She had taken on extra work as a dishwasher in the kitchen three nights a week, for the dinner shift. Maurice was taken on as a waiter on the same days that she was there. He was one of a half-dozen local teenagers who were paid to serve, clean and run errands on formal hall days.

They were not considered to be 'proper' waiters by the older, experienced and proud servants at table. In the late-1950s a generation gap had appeared in British society, with working class teenage boys on one side with their Elvis and Tony Curtis-inspired haircuts and James Dean attitude they picked up from films like *Rebel Without a Cause*, and the upper class sons of veterans of a world war, who had inherited their parents' sense of decorum and deference, on the other. That class gap lasted well into the 1960s, and it was inevitable that Maurice and the other young lads at the formal hall dos would annoy the older ones in any number of ways, not least when, at the end of their shift, the lads would jump into what was known as the meat lift, a dumb waiter that rose from the kitchen into the dining hall. To them it was simply a short cut out of the college. The chef would shout and bawl at the 'young 'ooligans' if he caught any of them in the lift, though, usually telling them that they were 'sacked' as they ran across the quad to the gates. But the same boys would be back the following week, the junior bursar having no idea of what the chef had done (plus, the chef had no authority to sack waiting staff anyway).

Maurice was a hard worker usually, and the head waiter gave him extra work waiting at table, although only on the first course. All went well until one night when Maurice spilled boiling hot soup on one of Rose's 'boys' named Graham, who was, she always said, putting on a voice that was supposed to mimic his, 'verrry posh'. The soup accident wasn't Maurice's fault strictly speaking, although an experienced waiter would anticipate the person they were serving not moving to the left, as was customary to allow soup to be ladled into their waiting bowls. Maurice had been shown how to virtually throw it at the bowls as the diners leant left, but on this occasion Graham failed to move and the hot liquid landed in his lap as the ladle caught his shoulder. Graham leapt to his feet shouting, and chased Maurice out of the dining room, through the kitchen and into the college grounds. He couldn't catch him, though, and so Maurice waited for ten minutes before returning to the kitchens, where he stayed to load plates and didn't go into the hall again that night.

That occasion earned Maurice a reputation among Graham's cohort for being entertaining, and not long after the soup incident he was invited to a college party, held near the river. Rose was partly proud and partly jealous when he told her. 'You've barely been there a month, and I've never been invited to no proper college parties all the years I've been there!' she said. 'Well, I don't count the Senate House graduation, nor the two times I was took in a punt by one of my boys,' she added.

Maurice laughed and told her that she should try dunking hot tea on them if they didn't get out of bed quick enough in the morning. 'That might get you invited to all sorts of places, Mum.'

'That'd get me to the 'ospital, more like,' she replied, ''cos I'd have to 'old the student's hand. So was the river party really good, then? You didn't get up to no trouble, did you? Them college boys can be a right bunch an' all, I tell you.'

'No, Mum, there were just very nice boys and girls drinking wine. Bloody 'orrible stuff it was. Wished I'd taken some of Uncle Bob's 'ome-brew with me. Still, nice to see 'ow the other 'alf live, innit?'

'That's all well and good, but you be careful with them if you get invited again. Some of those boys are funny and get into all sorts of trouble. There's a rower has fits now 'cos he got bashed on the head by some local lads on Midsummer. Sometimes he just sort of slumps over, with his eyes open, but can't see nothing.' She lit a cigarette from the gas flame on the cooker, and turned back to her son.

'All that grad bashing is rotten. Some might say it's their own fault, you know, 'cos they walk around with them boards on their heads and their long gowns like they're showing off. And they are privileged and that, but there's no reason for anyone to bash them up. It's a 'orrible thing to do to anyone, what they did to that rower. They lay in wait and then pounced on 'im and a mate. Gave them a right pasting they did, before legging it, leaving him for dead. He says that when he has his fits he sometimes wishes he were dead.'

'Was it night-time, Mum, when he got hit? Weren't the

proctor's bulldogs out there nannying them back to their colleges?'

'It were, and you know them bulldogs go out round town, but this were over by the Fort St George, a bit further out than usual, silly bugger. Poor boy. What must his parents be feeling? They send them away to college and think they're going to be safe and then . . . I'd 'ate for one of you or your brother to be responsible for that sort of thing. You don't, do you?'

'No, Mum! I ain't gonna run away if one of their lot starts something, but I don't go in for all that fighting. Might rip my new jacket what you nicely did up for me.'

Rose smiled. She knew that Maurice wasn't the fighting kind, even if he knew how to look after himself. No, Clark was more than likely to be one of the townies who went grad bashing, she knew that, but didn't really want to confront her son with the accusation. He was becoming more unpredictable with age, and at sixteen was already a good few inches bigger up and across than her. She also knew that the previous Bonfire Night Clark had worked out how to land bangers in cowpats near to where students were standing, making sure that they got sprayed when it went off.

Mind you, the students had started it. It became something of a tradition on every 5 November for students to throw fireworks at townies. The rugby players and rowers from different colleges would team up and run through the market place, throwing bangers and letting fly at any townies who got in their way. It wasn't always a matter of townies starting fights with the gowns, by any means. Fights between town and gown had been happening in the streets and on the commons of the city for centuries, and during the Second World War there were times when students had sided with townies in fights with American airmen.

The most memorable occasion was in 1943 at the market place, where the 5 November bonfire had been built, and after that Bonfire Night became a regular date for US airmen and Cambridge townies, plus a few students, to go to battle with each other. When things became very nasty in the 1950s – with bicycle chains and knives being used – the local police, American military police and college bulldogs had to team up in order to keep the sides apart. By the early 1960s, thankfully, the number of US airmen in the region had declined to such an extent that there were never any in uniform to be seen at the bonfire. So it was just the juvenile delinquents of the town who got into fights with the gown and mortar board wearing students, with fireworks, cowpats and the occasional knife and cricket bat as weapons. Rose didn't know whose side to be on, and so stayed away from the bonfire and fireworks celebrations. That way she wouldn't have to witness either of her sons fighting with any of her boys from college.

AUDREY

Following Edith's awful death in 1956, Maud became the only constant woman in Audrey's life, and so when Audrey was aged twelve in 1960 and Maud asked if she'd like a part-time job on Saturdays, helping her prepare the college fellows' breakfasts, Audrey said 'Yes' without a second thought.

Audrey had loved the college rooms that she'd been to with her mum and Maud. They were always warm in deep mid-winter, while the stone corridors and dark stairwells were cool in high summer. She'd smelled expensive aftershave and run her hand over expensive silk and cashmere clothes as she helped tidy students and masters' rooms, all of which were totally unlike anything she'd ever experienced. Sometimes she'd got to eat cake, bread and all manner of fruits that were left for her by the bedders, who knew she'd be in with her mum (and who'd been given the food by the boys in the rooms that they did for). The college was a world away from the one Audrey usually inhabited and she'd loved being able to escape into it when a small girl, especially when she hadn't had to do too much work and could sit and read a book instead.

So after agreeing to the Saturday job, Audrey said, 'I can't tell Dad though . . .'

Maud knew that was wise – she also knew that Edward wouldn't notice Audrey was missing on any given Saturday morning, because he was always nursing the worst hangover of the week, having drunk a good portion of his Friday pay packet the night before. 'Well, I can't tell the college either,' she said conspiratorially to Audrey, 'they might not like it if they cotton on to it being a regular thing. It's fine every now and then to bring your kids in, but best if it's our secret. I need the company and you need some pocket money, so it's a good arrangement.'

Audrey smiled at the memory of having often done the same with her mum as a small child.

'What are you smirking at?' asked Maud with a smile of her own.

'Oh, not much, just that some of my mates asked yesterday if you was Dad's girlfriend – you know, 'cos I call you my aunty and we're not blood related.'

Maud looked shocked. 'Your dad! Not on my nelly.'

'What?' Audrey giggled. 'He ain't that bad, is he? He's actually quite handsome, my dad.' Maud shook her head, and then looked sad, thought Audrey. 'But, I know,' she continued, 'it's his temper, ain't it?'

'No, you're right, love,' Maud placed a consoling hand on Audrey's arm, 'he ain't bad looking. But Audrey, I wouldn't even dare look at a man at my age. I'm thirty-six. You don't get married when you're as old as me. And I doubt any man would look at me, anyway. Not with these lovely brown pegs in my mouth.' She smiled to show her unfortunate gums and teeth, badly worn and discoloured from the years of neglect. 'Mind you,' she continued cheerily, 'they'll fall out when they're good and ready. But no, I'm alright, love. I reckon you live longer if you avoid men. Nothing but trouble if you ask me.'

Audrey took one of the encyclopaedias that sat on Maud's sideboard down and thumped it onto an armchair saying, 'I like boys though.'

'Blimey,' said a mock-shocked Maud, 'you better not let your dad hear you say that. I'm sure he's determined to keep you locked up forever, I reckon.' She was sitting at a small, round table with a deck of cards, and turned her attention to them.

'How often can you play patience and not get impatient, Aunty Maud?' Audrey asked in wonder.

'It keeps my mind busy, Audrey. And in some strange way it helps with my rheumatism.' Maud twisted the new copper magnetic bracelet around her wrist. 'Tea's not gonna be ready for another half hour, it's slow-cooked beef bourguignon. I'm experimenting I am, Bertha at work told me how to cook it.'

'Sounds nice,' Audrey said politely.

Several weeks into her 'job' as Maud's assistant, Audrey was standing in the gyp room staring at the dirty plates and cup that had been left there from the previous night. 'You wash and I'll dry,' Maud told her.

'I always have to dry,' Audrey replied sulkily.

'You don't have to come if you don't like it, Audrey. I don't want you to feel like I'm forcing you,' Maud told her sternly. It was as if Audrey had grown moodier after each Saturday, Maud thought, and she was growing tired of her sullen moods. Perhaps it was getting too much for the girl, after all she travelled from the other side of town to school, was running the house at home for her dad, and now had to get up early on Saturday mornings to do more work.

'No, no. I don't. I'm sorry, Aunty Maud,' Audrey's sad voice interrupted Maud's thoughts. 'I'm saving really hard. Come on let's get started.' Audrey passed Maud her pink marigolds and told her, 'I'm just tired – and hungry, Aunty Maud.'

'Oh,' Maud started. 'That reminds me. Remember I told you about Professor B. never eating anything in the mornings, and I told him, "You'll get ill if you don't eat proper?" Well, he's only gone and bloody died!'

'What!' Audrey exclaimed. 'You can't die from not eating breakfast, can you?'

'No, course not. He died of a heart attack. Only young he was, maybe forty-three.'

'That ain't young, that's how old my mum was when she had me.'

'Well, it's young to me. Anyway, one of the porters found him. We've got to clear out his room, pack his things up.'

'Lovely.' Audrey looked queasy at the thought.

'Sorry, love,' Maud told her, 'don't know why they can't do it. All they do all day is bloody sit on their backsides listening to the wireless, reading the papers. Don't seem fair.'

'It's alright. I don't mind,' Audrey replied. By now she was putting the plates and cups away in the cupboards. 'You know, Aunty Maud, I think that's probably the best way to go? He didn't know, did he? Not like my mum, slow and drawn out. We had to watch her die really. It was cruel to have an illness like she had.'

Maud couldn't avoid thinking about her husband's death, and she quickly steered Audrey back to the subject of the fellow that had been found dead. 'There was talk of him having a baby with one of the female students from Girton, you know, but I don't know how much of that is true. People talk, don't they?'

Audrey thought that Maud certainly did. In the past year Maud had moved into a new flat and Audrey noticed that she seemed to be forever gossiping about people at the college and even more about her new neighbours. It was beginning to get on Audrey's nerves and she much preferred it when Maud was quiet, so she usually buried herself in a book when she went to visit, which was often because her dad wouldn't turn the rented television down so she could read at home. Maud didn't have a telly, only a radio.

While they were finishing up in the gyp room, and as if it had just struck her, Maud began another of her stories, this time about a neighbour and not a fellow. ''Ere, I forgot to tell you about the Willis girl,' she began – the Willis family lived next door to Maud. 'There was a knock at my door from old man Willis in the early hours of the morning. I could see the nurse's bike propped up against their gate and he was in a right old panic he was. He wanted me to go to number sixteen and ask for some nappies, told me not to tell them why, just to borrow them. So I went and got some, took 'em back to the Willises and it turns out that their big daughter wasn't big 'cos she was eating all them cakes from Hawkins. No, she was pregnant! And she didn't even know, so naturally nor did her mum and dad neither.'

Audrey knew that Jennifer Willis had been out with Jim, a good friend of her brother Ron, and hoped he wasn't the father. She liked Jim. Maud continued in a whisper, as she always did, even though there was only ever the two of them in the gyp room and the bedrooms were further down the corridor. 'She's been sent away now, and no one's to know. A couple that can't have kids will adopt the little 'un. That poor Jennifer won't see it again. I bet she only did it once an' all. That's all it takes, Audrey.'

Audrey felt faint. She disliked the idea of talking about such things with her Aunty Maud and disliked even more the thought of Jim being with that girl. She could feel herself getting angry, and tears pricked her eyes. Unaware that Audrey was upset, Maud hurried her assistant along. 'Come on, we'll get the bathrooms done and the fires made before we do Prof. B.'s room.' Audrey reluctantly followed her into the bathroom and Maud went straight into another tale of terrible things other people had done, still not noticing Audrey's discomfort at hearing about their sex lives, if that's what it was to be (and it more often was than wasn't, with Maud). ''Course, that Jennifer's story is different from fat Marlene's, do you remember fat Marlene, Auds? She worked with me and your mum, and lives down Whitehill Road near the Co-op. Your mum must have mentioned her, she used to help her sometimes with that fellow who had trouble remembering who he was. Anyway, fat Marlene had a baby boy about ten years ago, and ever so brainy he is. Goes to Priory. Very nice boy, lovely looking.'

Maud handed Audrey the Ajax and Brillo pads, and perched herself on the side of the deep bath, ready to turn on the taps to rinse after Audrey had scrubbed, and continued. 'She got pregnant by a student.' Audrey sighed deeply, and thought she really didn't want to hear any more, but Maud went on. 'She told Bertha that it was one of the grads. The one with real black hair she said, and her boy had the same hair. Now, I don't remember the student. Marlene must have been about forty so she must have thought that she wouldn't get caught out, you know like your mum did with you. But she did, and do you know, her husband stayed with her! He knew that boy weren't his. Bertha said because she was married she could get away with doing something like that, but if you're not married . . . So don't you be getting into trouble, Auds. 'Cos it's a hard secret to keep something like that. Living a lie is a hard secret to keep.'

'I wish you hadn't told me,' Audrey said quietly.

'Well, you ain't going to say nothing.'

Audrey knew she now had to keep the Willis girl's secret from Jim and her Ron, and she knew fat Marlene's son because she often saw him with his mum when she went to the Co-op. Audrey felt burdened with all the stories Maud shared with her.

'Maybe you're right, maybe I shouldn't have told you,' Maud said reluctantly. 'I forget that you're still a kid really. You see, I think you're wiser than your years. Probably 'cos you lost your mum so young. I sometimes think that you've been here before. An old soul you are, Audrey.'

The girl continued to scrub, using both hands on the well-worn wooden brush, thinking that she certainly felt older than twelve, or imagined that she did.

'Ron's neighbour on Gold Street said the same thing to me the last time I was over there with Dad,' Audrey said without turning her head. 'Been here before 'cos I did something bad before, perhaps.' She leaned back on her haunches as Maud turned on the taps, then rose as the suds washed away, and washed her red hands under the cold tap using a large green bar of fairy soap.

'Oh, Auds,' Maud sighed at her. 'Maybe you should really be with friends your own age to keep you young, rather than always being with your dad and me. We're just fuddy-duddies.'

'It's alright.' Audrey didn't want to lose her job, she was desperate to save enough money for a wig stand she had seen on a visit to Selfridges months ago. 'I'm a good worker, ain't I?' Audrey's voice carried more than a hint of anger, challenge and resentment in it, and Maud looked away, down into the bathtub.

Audrey remembered why she was here, on a sunny Saturday morning, cleaning bathrooms and fireplaces, when all of her friends were out shopping or watching boys play football. She thought that even if it took a few years she was determined to save for that wig holder. She'd been obsessed with the idea of becoming a hairdresser ever since she could remember, and since she couldn't practise on anyone, had taken to buying wigs (many from junk shops) that she could style and experiment with whenever she could find the money and the wigs at the right price. A wig stand would allow her to put her motley collection of hairpieces on it and sit it in front of a mirror to work on, just as if she was in a salon. Her dad had promised her another trip to London in the summer, and she told Maud about it now.

'I'll take you there too, one day, Aunty Maud. We'll go to the beauty hall where there's hundreds of perfumes, and you can try them all if you want to. It makes our Boots look like a corner-shop chemist.'

Maud smiled because Audrey still looked like a little boy, with her short blonde hair and body as straight and skinny as a board. She just wasn't developing into a young woman at the same rate as her classmates, the older woman knew. Maud couldn't imagine Audrey experimenting with hairstyles or wearing the wigs she had almost obsessively bought, nor wearing perfume. Audrey, she thought, was far too much of a tomboy for any of that.

'Are you laughing at me?' Audrey asked.

'Not at all, Tiny!' Maud replied. 'I think you just might be starting to grow into a lady – well, in your head at least.'

'Me!' Audrey laughed. 'I don't think I could ever be a lady, but I know I'm going to train to be a hairdresser in a couple of years. You know, get a trade. I want my own business one day. Them ladies that work in Selfridges they all "talk like this",' Audrey held her head in the air and pinched her nose. '"Would modom like to try this fragrance?"' She laughed and mimicked spraying perfume on Maud. 'But Ron says I could never be refined like them, 'cos I sound too much like a foghorn.'

The contrast between the college bathroom and the marbled halls of the big London shop made Audrey determined that her hand-scouring work would be rewarded with whatever she wanted to buy when she got to the capital city.

Maud sat quite still on the corner of the bath and looked like she had disappeared into another world. Audrey worried that she may have offended her with her moodiness, and forced herself to be more upbeat. 'Come on then, Maud,' she said with as much of a song as she could, 'enough about Selfridges, and Fat Marlene and Jennifer's unwanted babies – let's go and sort out that dead man's shoes.'

Maud laughed nervously. 'Oh Audrey, please, please keep your voice down. I don't want to wake the other fellows yet, 'specially not today. I don't fancy seeing them. We'll get their breakfasts ready first and then we'll go in his room, I don't really want to go through his things at all, to be honest . . .'

By lunchtime, though, Audrey and Maud were satisfied that they had done a good morning's work, and Audrey was chuffed with the clothes Maud had let her sort in Professor B.'s room. 'Dad's going to love this hat and jacket, Maud, you sure it's alright?'

''Course it is. The porter won't notice and I'm sure the prof's wife won't have a record of his belongings; after all she didn't keep a track of his goings on with the Girton girl did she? Poor woman.'

Audrey took Maud's hand as they left the college, and smiled at her. Maud smiled back. 'Come on then,' she said to the girl, 'let's you and me have a treat and get a hot chocolate at Eaden Lilley's, shall we?'

'Coo, yeah why not,' Audrey squeezed Maud's hand and they almost skipped to their bicycles.

ANN

Cambridge 1948-62

Ann always considered that the main reason for a girl to marry was so that she could have children. So she and Fred set about making a family with happy hearts and plenty of enthusiasm. Living at her mother-in-law's house made Ann feel shy at first, but before long she and Fred could be heard giggling at all hours of the night – as his mother put it when complaining about not being able to sleep one morning at breakfast. 'Sorry, missus,' Ann said quietly, her face going a deep shade of red. Fred, who felt no such sense of embarrassment, piped up happily, 'We're tryin' to start a family, Mum!' Mrs Adams blanched, choked on the sip of tea she'd just taken and left the kitchen, coughing.

When Ann could say that she was actually pregnant, her mother-in-law was delighted. It changed everything as far as the expectant grandmother was concerned, and Ann went from being 'Cinderella' (which is what she used to tell Bet, complaining about having to do all the fireplaces in the house) to being a princess, and being waited on all day and evening. Ann enjoyed the early months of her pregnancy, although her husband didn't. Fred got himself into a terrible state. She'd never heard of it before, but he – so the doctor told them – suffered a phantom pregnancy; he showed all the same symptoms as his wife, including morning sickness, food cravings and strange stirrings in his stomach, which even bloated a bit as Ann's bump grew.

Being pregnant somehow buoyed Ann's mood through some troubling times for her extended family. Ann was deeply saddened by the news of Johnny's death, which arrived just after New Year. 'He didn't get to spend one Christmas with us,' she cried to Bet, who broke the news to her well after the fact – and even after his funeral.

Bet was almost as angry as she was sad about his passing. 'There's no plaque, no stone,' Bet said, adding, 'there's nothing to say he was ever here. Barrel went looking for me at work yesterday.' Only Grace and Jack had attended the brief ceremony at the Fulbourn Hospital where he'd died and been buried. Following Johnny's funeral Jack became a 'broken man', said Bet, who saw him far more often than Ann, who wasn't able to cycle from Waterbeach into Cambridge any more. 'He's barely eating or drinking, an' he stopped playing his piano and banjo. He hardly talks to anyone, least of all Mum.' Ann dried her tears, and Bet did the same, and they sat silently for a few minutes, almost as if in tribute to the little brother that they'd never got to know.

It was Bet who broke the quiet. 'How's the pregnant dad, then?' she half-smiled and sniffed.

Ann laughed and cried again. 'He's having morning sickness, still!'

With that, both women laughed away their sadness and got on with planning what they'd need for when Ann brought the new baby home.

Ann gave birth at Mill Road Maternity Hospital in March 1949. As was normal, so Ann was told, she was alone with the midwife for most of the labour. At first Ann tried to make a joke of things, telling the nurse that, 'Fred really should be in here with me. He's having the contractions too, you know.' The nurse at the newly nationalized hospital shook her head dismissively. 'You know it's not allowed,' she told her. 'He'll be fine. We've seen it before, and as soon as the baby's born his pain will go away.'

She was right, of course. After sitting for hours, sweating or pacing up and down the Maternity Ward corridor, Fred felt no pain, only elation when told that he had a daughter. He was so proud that he ran around the ward telling everyone the exact words the nurse had told him – 'She's healthy and bonny!' – all the while grinning like a skull.

'What are we going to call her?' he asked Ann, as soon as he'd been allowed to see the new mother and daughter. 'Glenis,' said Ann firmly. 'After Glynis Johns but I want it with an "e" in the middle. Glenis Catherine. That's what we're going to call her. Catherine after your mum, Kate.' Fred thought for a moment, before agreeing. 'Yes, I like that. It's different.' He didn't think to ask if Grace might be upset at her first grand-daughter not being named after her, and didn't need to ask Ann if it might be a good idea, because he knew his wife would not even want to discuss it.

Ann was a little apprehensive about what Grace's reaction would be to the naming of Glenis, but was amazed at how absolutely thrilled she was to have become a grandmother. Jack shared the delight, as Ann expected him to. But that her mother was made immensely happy by the arrival of Glenis was almost a physical shock to her, and she couldn't help won-dering if the death of Johnny had anything to do with the wide grin that Grace seemed to have stuck on her face when she met Glenis.

With the arrival of Ann's daughter, Jack and Grace threw themselves into becoming model grandparents. 'I don't recog-nize Mum,' Rene told Ann, two weeks after the birth. 'She's so happy, she's singing all the time and can't stop talking about your Glenis. And Dad's laughing and playing the piano, the banjo and the accordion again. He's even got himself a type-writer and is teaching himself to type. It's changed them, Nance.'

While the new grandparents were in such a good mood, Bet thought that it might be time to get their youngest sister home for good. 'We need to make a plan for Joy,' she told Ann and Rene when they were all together. Their little sister had remained in various special boarding schools ever since the war, and although they'd had her with them for school holidays, none of them could honestly say that they knew her – only that they loved her, unconditionally, whatever she was like. 'But Bet,' Ann interrupted her, 'Joy isn't old enough to leave school yet, she's only eleven. Let's leave her in Gorleston until she's fifteen, hey? Mum would only try and get her into a job if she was living back here permanent like, wouldn't she? God forbid, but she'd take her to Royston and try to get the same housekeeper to take her on as she did to me.'

Bet opened her mouth to argue, but Rene leapt in before she could say a word. 'No, Bet, Nance is right. You know how much I loved Johnny and couldn't persuade Mum to let me look after him, and while I'd love to have Joy live with us, we'd have a hell of a job getting Mum to agree, and the only reason she might is if she thought Joy could earn a bit of money. Plus, I'll be leaving school in a bit and there'd be no one to spend any time with her, would there?' Bet had no argument that would work with her sisters and knew that she'd have even less chance of getting Grace to accept Joy living at home as there was no special school for her to attend in the area.

In the following years, Bet added two daughters to her family, Sheila and Christine (Chrissy). Ann had two more daughters, Dorothy – for Lamour – who arrived almost exactly a year after Glenis, and Shirley – Temple – two years after that.

Rene got a job at Pye's electrical factory on Church Road in Chesterton, on the television set production line. Despite their growing family, Ann and Fred continued to live in Waterbeach with his parents as they worked their way up the council housing list.

Fred still refused to let Ann go out to work, and his earnings didn't rise in line with the number of new mouths they had to feed. There would have been another child between Dorothy and Shirley, but in the fifth month of pregnancy Ann contracted chicken pox and measles from Dorothy and miscarried. She would later say that the loss 'was quite lucky, really.'

When a year later she discovered that she was to have Shirley, Ann cried, 'How do I stop getting pregnant, Bet?' much to her sister's surprise. Ann had never asked anyone about birth control, had no idea of how a condom worked and thought the rhythm method was a dance step. Once Bet had explained a few facts of life to her, Ann felt almost cheated about having had so many pregnancies. 'I only wanted two,' she told her.

Having three children helped Ann and Fred move up the council housing list, though, and they were finally offered a place of their own in Cambridge in 1952. It wasn't exactly a house, being an ex-Second World War Nissen hut constructed of corrugated iron over a wooden frame and flat roof, but at least it was in the town, had two bedrooms, a kitchen and sitting room, and a garden that showed signs of once having been a vegetable patch. It was supposed to be a temporary home until they could move into a three-bedroom council house in Cherry Hinton that was being 'freshened up' for them.

Fred and Ann never really argued, at least not for long and never seriously. Fred was a proud dad and an involved one, too. He loved changing nappies, feeding the babies and taking them out for walks, to the playground and along the river when the weather allowed. His mum also loved the kids, and before they moved from Waterbeach the kids must have thought they had two mums. Naturally the parenting was done Kate's way when they were in her house, but Ann wasn't unhappy about that. After all, she thought, she's done it before, and I 'aven't. So when the young Adams family moved into a new area, Ann was comfortable having three small children, Fred was eager to show them off to new neighbours, and life seemed to be getting better for them.

They couldn't afford a car, so Fred bought a tandem bicycle and fitted it with extra child seats in front of both sets of handlebars and a baby seat over the rear mudguard. All five of them could get to Grace's on it for Sunday dinner when the weather wasn't too bad. Sometimes they'd cycle over to Queen's Meadow in the Barnwell area, so close as to be called Cherry Hinton, to look at the houses that the council were working on and wonder which one they'd be getting. There was a big green space in the middle with houses facing onto it, and it was lovely and quiet. Which was more than could be said for the Scotland Road residence of Grace and Jack at that time.

They both loved being grandparents and welcomed their children's children as often as they could. But when Joy moved in with them after leaving school, as her daughters predicted, Grace seemed determined to find work for her as soon as she could and get her out of the house. For six months Grace asked everywhere she went about a job for Joy with little luck. Sometimes she dragged her daughter to meet shopkeepers, market stall holders and one time a concierge at a hotel. While everyone was pleasant enough to Joy, as soon as they realized she didn't have great eyesight, they said that they'd let Grace know if or when something came up. Which it never did.

Joy tried to adapt to living with her mother, but she was

really only happy when she could help with Ann or Bet's children who'd be dropped off for her to look after. Which was quite handy once Fred gave in and let Ann work part time. Ann became a cleaner at three houses in the town centre. When she went to work she could leave Dorothy and Shirley with Joy while Glenis was at school.

One evening in 1954 when Bet and Ann were sitting in Ann's newly decorated kitchen in Queen's Meadow, Bet was telling her about how badly Joy and Grace were getting on. 'Mum's getting angry with her 'cos she can't find her a job. It's not through lack of trying, she keeps dragging her around and Joy is getting right fed up. She's sure that Mum's embarrassed by her, you know, 'cos of her eye and that.'

'But that's why she won't get a job, isn't it?' Ann sympathized. 'If she ain't got great eyesight she might make mistakes, poor thing.'

Bet was desperate for Ann to understand how hard it was for Joy to be back home, and decided to tell her straight. 'But the problem is, Nance, Mum doesn't know her. Never bothered to get to know her, did she? We always looked after her when she came home in the holidays. Yesterday when me and Barrel were visiting with the girls, we saw something right bad. Joy had some cigarettes in her bag, Woodbines I think, and Mum saw them. Well, she shouldn't have been looking in her bag but that's not the point, the point is Mum saw them and knocked her sideways with a slap.'

Ann was shocked, she had seen her mum and Bet occasionally have stand-up rows that fell into slaps, but that was because Bet stood up to Grace and challenged her. She began to think hard about why her mum would hit Joy. 'Mum didn't want Joy spending her money on cigs,' Bet went on, 'but that's not all, though. Me and Barrel, we think that Joy is scared to eat, you know, 'cos she's not bringing any money in. You've seen how skinny she is. This week Mum sent to get her a job at our laundry, and they tried her out but asked her to use those heavy old irons. She only lasted a day, she was so exhausted. It's too much for a small girl like her.'

'It's ignorance,' Ann said. 'Mum doesn't know how to cope with her disability. It scares her. Our Joy, she's different from us. She's not as sheltered for a start, she's had to live away from home, from us, and she felt like an orphan – she told me that, once. Joy might be timid around Mum but I reckon she could hold her own. That's going to help her in the future. She's had to cope with living away, I think she'll be alright.'

'Well, that's as may be,' Bet agreed, 'but I can't stand by and watch, and Barrel said she can't live there any more, it's not good for her. So we're going to have her move in with us. My Sheila and Chrissy love her, and I think if she's away from Mum and gets herself a job, it'll do wonders for her confidence and she may make some friends.'

Nodding in agreement, Ann spoke as if she'd just had an idea. 'Here, I reckon she'd be alright as an assistant for a bedder, like Jane Granger was doing a while back.' Bet laughed at her sister's continuing obsession with the colleges, but Ann continued, 'Actually my neighbour Rose is a bedder, why don't I ask her if there's anything going?'

Bet looked sceptical, but nodded her assent, and gratefully Ann continued, 'Yes, I'll see what Rose says, let's hope there's something for Joy. You know, that's really good of you and Barrel. I reckon our Joy would love that.' She wished that she had been able to offer Joy the chance to live with her, but that would have meant Glenis sharing her room, and Ann wanted her eldest to have her own room. Ann had never had a room of her own, so when they finally moved to the council house, she'd told Fred, 'Dot and Shirl can share, but Glen needs her own room. She's the eldest. It's only right.'

Ann visited Joy a week after she moved in with the Reynolds, and it was clear that for the first time Joy felt like she was part of a family. 'I don't want to do bedding, as it'd only be for a few hours a day,' she said apologetically to her big sister. 'It's good of you to have got me the chance of something, but I need a full-time job. You know I like cooking so I should go for something like that.' Which is what she did, with G. P. Hawkins on Parsonage Street, where she made short pastry and cakes. The pay wasn't great, but she loved the job and stayed for many years, which made Ann and Bet happy.

When the time came for Derek to do National Service, Jack and Grace decided to move from Chesterton to Fisher's Lane in Cherry Hinton so they'd be closer to their grandchildren.

Ann really liked living on the green, and along with the other mums (which sometimes also included Rose) she'd stand at the gate at the end of the day and call the kids in for tea, just as their dads got home. Her children played in the orchard and fields that surrounded the estate and had a much more active time than she'd ever managed when she was their age. During the summer holidays, on warm evenings, the families of Queen's Meadow would sit around small bonfires built on the green out of wood they collected from the orchard, and any broken furniture or rubbish that would burn. It reminded Ann of VE Day and the fun that she had dancing and singing along with what seemed like the whole of Cambridge.

Ann watched her children grow up and was content, if not completely happy, to keep house, wash, cook, clean and raise them the best way she knew how. Fred's job at the building firm could be for life, if he wanted it, but pretty much any job was safe if a man was any good at it, he reasoned. As the fifties wore on, the Adams family, like many other working-class people they knew, for the first time began to forget the privations of wartime, and found that there were lots of new things to spend their newly earned money on. It was true, thought Ann, just like old Macmillan the prime minister had said, 'we've never had it so good'.

Fred loved having three daughters, but he really, really wanted a son, and when Ann became pregnant again, they both hoped for a boy and were delighted when Kenneth arrived in 1956. 'He's named after Kenneth More,' Ann told her family. 'It's Fred's idea. I would have liked Errol but Fred weren't having any of it.' Fred hadn't suffered any sympathetic pregnancies since Glenis, and he cared for the girls when Ann went to hospital for the delivery of their fourth child. She was admitted a few days in advance, the midwife having suggested it 'just in case', without making explicit reference to the miscarriage.

When Ann and Kenny had been home a few days Fred told her that Shirley had been hit on the back of her head by a swing while out playing at the park with her sisters. She wasn't knocked out, but a big bump developed, and her dad put her to bed telling her she'd be alright in the morning. Ann was inclined to agree with him. They weren't to know the terrible consequences of the bump on Shirley's head.

JOYCE

Cambridge 1953–62

It took Joyce a couple of weeks in her new job as a bedder to feel that she was entitled to walk into the rooms of the two students she'd met on her first day and shout, 'Come on, get out of bed, I want to do your rooms.'

She would inevitably hear, 'Oh Joyce, don't be like that,' from one of them and, 'No! Please let us have five more minutes!' from the other. To her they became known as the 'Terrible Twins', not that they were related – or really all that terrible. They were good friends and seemed to enjoy sharing their sitting and gyp rooms, and were very happy to have someone even younger than they to talk to. 'We're so glad that they gave you to us, dear Joyce,' Terrence told her after the first week. 'Yes,' Oscar added, 'the old girl was frightful and left the rooms feeling as dirty as they'd been before she came in.'

Joyce was pleased. Not exactly flattered, but proud to be appreciated for her work. The Twins didn't flirt with her, but they spoke to her as if she was an equal. 'Morning,' they'd call to her on arrival when eventually they emerged from their rooms, and then ask, 'What have you been up to?' They would tell her when they expected to return and what mornings they were at lectures. Several times they told her, 'It's smashing the way you do our beds,' which was hospital style, which she learned to do when she joined the TA at the age of fifteen.

In her second week some other students left their sitting room in a mess, with dirty glasses and empty bottles everywhere. Joyce banged her way around the room, making enough noise to bring them out of their bedrooms. Clearly angry, she asked them in a very cold voice to, 'Clear up your empties when you're done, please.' After that, whenever anyone on her staircase had any kind of evening do which resulted in glasses and plates left in the sitting room, the students would be up as she arrived, apologizing and saying, 'We've left a mess you know, so sorry . . .' Joyce didn't mind as much then, because at least they'd noticed that she was a person like them, and she encouraged conversations with as many of the students as possible. If one of them let Joyce know they had to be at an early lecture and their breakfast plates were left unwashed, she didn't mind doing it for them. It wasn't part of her official duties, but she'd do it for any who were decent to her.

In fact, the students spoke to her far more than any of the other bedders. From the beginning Joyce took her tea breaks apart from the others, and when she'd got to know them well enough, she'd have her breaks in the Twins' gyp room. The other bedders would gather in the kitchens of the halls for their break to smoke, gossip and – she was convinced – make up stories about her and her Terrible Twins. She didn't care, they were all old women who should know better, just like so many of the old women that her mother knew, like the old bag who'd accused Joyce of seeing a black American airman. They were jealous of her, Joyce thought, envious of her youth at least, if not her looks and popularity with most of her students – who she called 'my boys', just like Maud did.

Some of the students were less than polite to her at first, though, and a couple seemed shocked that she was so young and tried to order her around as if (she assumed) they thought she was their maid. When one posh boy asked her to fetch some cigarettes for him, she tartly told him, 'What did your last servant die of? I'm not here to do your fetching and carrying. Either get them yourself or find a servant who will.' She left his room unfinished and walked out. He complained to Mrs Atkins, but was told in no uncertain terms that he was in the wrong, not Joyce.

Things didn't improve much with that student over the coming weeks, and Joyce was often confronted by his still being in bed when she arrived, refusing to get up. He never seemed to wash himself, judging by how he smelled to Joyce, and he left his dirty crockery all over the place. After three weeks she threatened to not do his room at all. When that had no effect, she didn't clean for him. Unfortunately for her, Mrs Atkins chose that exact day to visit the student and she blew up at Joyce because she hadn't done her job.

Once Joyce had explained to her that every time she went in he was either lying in bed or in his pyjamas, that he didn't clean the bathroom and always left his dirty things all over the sitting and gyp room, plus he never cleaned the oven, the housekeeper calmed down. She returned to the student's room, gave him a rollicking and told him if he didn't keep his room tidier that he would have to leave college and get rooms outside. Then she went back to Joyce and told her not to do his room for a week.

A week later Mrs Atkins returned to the student's room and found a complete mess. He did not return to the college rooms the following term.

Joyce and her Terrible Twins became more friendly as the term progressed, and soon they were playing pranks on her. Oscar had an interest in magic, and liked to do conjuring and card tricks. He had inherited some props from an uncle who'd been a member of the Magic Circle, among them a glass and bottle that both looked as if they contained liquid, but didn't.

The first time that Joyce found the glass in his bed, hidden under the blankets, she almost screamed as it tumbled from between the sheets and looked as if it was spilling onto the floor. A couple of days later she was surprised by a bottle of gin (she thought), rolling from between the sheets and yet not pouring anything out of its unstopped top. Both times Oscar and Terrence were waiting in the living room to hear the sound of her surprise – at which they rushed into the room full of mock concern.

Joyce couldn't help laughing as she told her mum about the joke, at which Celia looked surprised. 'What!?' she asked, her face full of concern. 'Ain't these two proper toffs? They don't sound stuck-up like the others. They sound more like one of the boys round here.'

'No Mum,' Joyce informed her, 'They don't talk la-di-da, I think they're from a grammar school. But they're nothing like the boys round here.'

The Twins were rugby players, good enough to play for their college, if not the university. Joyce had no interest in the game and had never as much as seen a match, which she told them one day when they were comparing bruised arms after a particularly hard session the day before. Astounded, Terrence insisted that she had to come to their next game, to be played that Saturday at the university ground on Grange Road. Joyce went, but had to leave at half-time because she simply couldn't watch her boys getting tackled, barged and grappled with by their opponents. She wasn't the only female at the game, but she was definitely the only woman there under thirty who was not romantically involved with any of the players.

She didn't ever dream about going out with either of the Twins or any other student on a date, and none ever asked her. Joyce took at least three of her weekly tea breaks alone, which was how she liked it. She was never lonely and simply wanted her quiet time. She wanted only to get on with her work when at the college.

During her third term as a bedder, some of the other, older bedders had come to realize that Joyce wasn't stuck-up, ill-mannered or think she was 'better' than them because she didn't go down to join them for tea. A couple began to visit her during their tea break and sit with her, sometimes talking, but just as often not saying anything, but enjoying a companionable quiet.

One of the older bedders, Brenda, enjoyed telling Joyce about her students and they shared a common attitude towards them of curious interest. Brenda, like Joyce, would wait for students to talk to them rather than make any approach and, again like Joyce, had become friendly with the occupants of the rooms that she did for, most of whom were post-graduate students and younger fellows.

Joyce learned from Brenda that every new academic year, which began in October, the names of new students and occupants of each room would be posted on the board at the front of the halls at least a week before they were due to arrive. Brenda liked seeing the names and guessing at what kind of man they'd be. Last year, she told Joyce one break time, 'I saw a Mr Thomas on the board, and I thought, he must be Welsh I should think, you know,' she laughed. 'But when I went in the room he was a coloured man. He was a post-grad I presume, 'cos he must have been in his thirties. He was from Sierra Leone, he said, and he was ever so nice and ever so friendly. He said, "Have a cup of tea," so we did.'

'Did he talk English alright then?' Joyce asked.

'Oh yes,' Brenda replied emphatically. 'He spoke lovely, and we became quite friendly. One day near the end of term I told him, "I don't know if I'll be in tomorrow," I said, "'cos I'm going to have my teeth out," and he said, "I do wish I could bear the pain for you." I thought, Yes, so do I.'

'That's nice of him though, Brenda.'

'It was. I was gonna have my teeth out 'cos I'd already lost the top set and I thought I might as well have the bottom lot out.'

Brenda paused, and Joyce asked her, 'Why?'

'I don't know, I just thought that they wanted coming out. My sister said they made my breath smell. The thing was, though, the dentist told me not to 'cos they were all alright!'

Joyce laughed and told her, 'Good thing an' all, I reckon. What did the man from Sierra Leone say?'

'He was happy for me, he said. And do you know, when he left he said he had some saucepans, one or two odd things and his gown with an overcoat that he didn't want back in Sierra Leone 'cos it's hot there. He said he could leave it to his friends but then he said, "You have it." The overcoat did fit my hubby, so we had it cleaned and he kept it.'

'What about the other stuff?'

'Well, I didn't know what to do with his gown,' Brenda said, lowering her voice to a near-whisper. 'There's a fella that comes in to polish the floors, have you seen him? He's not here very often, he's a sort of cleaner. Anyway I told him about this gown, and he said, "I'll get rid of it for you and we'll go halves." So he took it and we went halves – but I couldn't tell you how much he got for it!'

Joyce learned before the end of her first year as a bedder how generous her Twins could be when they bought her a box of chocolates and a bouquet of flowers for her birthday (they'd asked the housekeeper when it was, apparently). At Christmas she'd received gifts of chocolates and pairs of stockings. At the end of the year, as students left the college having finished their studies they asked Joyce if she wanted any of their kitchen stuff, or glassware because they were leaving it behind. Joyce was surprised at how sad she felt at saying goodbye to the Twins, both of whom asked for her address so that they could 'stay in touch', and each gave her envelopes with £25 inside, which was more than a month's wages for Joyce. She gave them her details thinking she'd never hear from them again, and was surprised on receiving letters a few days after the end of term from both sets of the Twins' parents. The letters were written by their mothers, both thanking Joyce for 'looking after' their son. Both boys, wrote their mothers, were always talking about 'our bedder'. Reading the letter made Joyce feel sad, and at the same time glad because she was appreciated by the mothers. For the next few years the Twins stayed in touch by letter. Terrence became a surgeon and moved to Australia, where he married and had a baby. Oscar visited Joyce in Cambridge three years after graduating, informing her that he had become a GP in Buckinghamshire. They lost touch after a while, but Joyce always remembered them fondly.

Joyce worked as a bedder for two years, during which time she spent most of her weekends on manoeuvres with the territorial army, having been encouraged to join up by her dad. Not only did the TA teach her how to drive, they taught her in five- and ten-tonne trucks. She also got to go to Scotland for the first time ever for a weekend of marching and war games. Her social life revolved as much around shining hobnailed boots as it did applying lipstick in the toilets at the Embassy. Her old school friends Janet, Vicky and Rita were in the same TA regiment, and they bunked together when away on operations, teamed together when doing medic or driving exercises and were as close as any four young women could be. They all had boyfriends – all of them also in the TA – and went out dancing or to the cinema as couples. Celia was almost as happy that Joyce was involved with the military as her dad was.

At the end of her second year as a bedder, Joyce decided that she would leave along with the students in June, simply because she wanted to earn more money. So she applied to a language school for work as a kitchen hand and got it. That job lasted a few hot, hand-scouring, back-breaking months, before Joyce took the opportunity of making more money on the production line at Pye's electronics factory.

The work at Pye's was well paid, but dull and repetitive. There was a certain camaraderie among the women who worked the line, and there was a lot of joking and flirting with the male foremen and drivers, which entertained Joyce, so she settled there for a couple of years. But nobody seemed to last much longer than that at the factory, and she left in order to take a job around the corner, at Chesterton Hospital. She was employed as a cleaner but also worked as a general assistant, aiding nurses and doctors where needed, and walking the tea and sweet trollies through the wards. The job allowed Joyce to talk with patients as well as staff, and she soon developed a friendship with many of them.

One of the more severely injured male patients in the hospital couldn't speak nor move, but Joyce made contact with him. The nurses, and particularly the matron of the ward in which the patient lay, hadn't managed to make any sustained, useful or comprehensible communication with him. Unlike the majority of the patients in the long-term, disabled ward who were elderly, this man wasn't; he was probably in his early thirties, Joyce thought, and suffered his injuries in the war. Whenever she was cleaning his ward or taking the trollies through, Joyce would talk to him as if he was just like anyone else, and after a few weeks she realized that he was winking at her, from

which she deduced that the man was capable of communi-
cating using eye contact. She told him to blink three times for
yes, twice for no, and move his head sideways when he wanted
her to go away.

One day as she walked the sweet trolley through his ward,
Joyce stopped it for him and asked if he wanted anything. He
blinked three times, and she ran through what was available;
'Sweets?' she asked. He blinked twice. 'Mints?' Two blinks. 'Box
of chocolates?' Three blinks. Joyce put them on his side table,
but he jerked his head at her. She asked, 'Do you want one
now?' he blinked twice, and jerked his head towards her – and
she understood; he wants me to have them! The matron
watched from across the ward as the 'conversation' was going
on and, as Joyce made her way past her, tutted loudly. Joyce
didn't care, and figured that the matron simply didn't like it 'cos
she hadn't thought of the eye contact business with him.

Joyce worked at the hospital until 1960 when her mother
was taken ill. Leaving the hospital meant she was able to care
for Celia as well as earn, taking on Celia's job for her until she
was able to return to work. Joyce also left the TA. As well as
her mother's illness her brother Douglas had returned home.

He had been in the regular army since 1955 and seen service
at Suez, and had been part of General Foot's bodyguard team
in Cyprus, but now Douglas was suffering from shell shock –
not that anyone recognized the symptoms as that. He couldn't
sleep, but when he did terrible nightmares would wake him,
and he would be screaming and thrashing his arms. Celia had
received a black eye one morning when taking Douglas a cup
of tea in bed. He would only sit in the corner of the room with
sightlines clear to the door and window, and hated leaving the
house, and so couldn't get a job. He was seeing a doctor to help
with his problems, though, and they all hoped he'd soon be
back to normal.

More than once over the next couple of years Joyce would think how lucky she was that at least her dad was robust. If she mentioned it to him, he'd laugh and remind her that nothing could get him. He had been in the navy as a young man and was struck by lightning while at sea, working on the radio. He'd not been injured then, even though he smelled burning for a few seconds. (Remarkably, years later his bike was struck by lightning as he rode it over Elizabeth Way bridge in Cambridge, and he was fine, but there were burn marks on his seat.)

Joyce also considered herself lucky because just before she left the TA she met Ken, a former navy man. The pair became a couple pretty soon after meeting, and they got on well. There was no arguing between them, Ken was attentive and punctual, generous when he could afford to be, and he could jive, too, which pleased Joyce, who loved to dance. When she had the time, she'd spend all Saturday mornings bathing her petticoats in sugared water to make them stiff enough for that night's jive session at the Embassy.

Until 1962, Joyce spent her mornings cleaning the house of Celia's professor, then she'd go home in time to cook dinner for everyone: toad in the hole or chops, mince, a casserole, onion and bacon suet roll in a cloth, anything that would make meat and two veg. On weekends, for afters she'd make treacle pudding or spotted dick, and on a Sunday sometimes it would be Yorkshire pudding with jam. It depended wholly on what she could afford to buy and make. If there'd been beef or bacon over the weekend, Joyce would have dripping and bread for breakfast before work on a Monday (and a tin of Batchelors soup for lunch when she had to).

When Celia was strong enough to return to work, Joyce and Ken – who had rejoined the navy earlier in the year – were married. She was twenty-six, which was old for the time (all of her old pals had married at least four years previously), and they had to marry because Joyce had become pregnant. Of course it was an accident, and Joyce was grateful for her parents' reaction on hearing the news. They were perfectly calm about it – Celia might actually have been relieved, Joyce thought, since she had begun to ask pointedly when she and Ken were ever going to tie the knot. Although Joyce was worried what her brother would say – Douglas had recently taken a job at Sainsbury's in town, had no girlfriend and probably never would, his family thought – he was very good about it, and said, 'It happens to lots of people, you're not the first and you won't be the last.'

The ceremony was at the registry office, and two weeks later Ken was back at sea.

AUDREY

Cambridge 1962–63

The winter of 1962 was cold, harsh and haunted by a freezing fog that blanketed Cambridge for days at a time. When it cleared, the yellow gloom was first replaced by hard white frost, and then layers of snow. It made Audrey happy to have her job as Maud's assistant at college, because she could spend Saturday mornings away from the cold in the fellows' sitting room, where they always got a fire blazing first thing. She sat with her little legs slung over the arm of the large, blood-red Chesterfield armchair next to the warmth, reading a copy of *Punch* she'd found by the hearth. Not that she could enjoy too much time at leisure.

'You can't get comfortable,' Maud reminded her, from the drinks cabinet where she was dusting bottles. 'You're going to have to get up in a minute and help me with the fires in the rooms, Audrey. What's wrong with you today? You haven't lifted a finger.'

'The girls from school are all going to the minors today,' Audrey moaned, 'and Dad said I couldn't go. He said, "Put a load of teenage boys and girls in a dark room, what do you think they're going to do? You are not going there to be groped by some randy little upstart."'

'Well,' Maud countered, 'he might have a point.'

'Maud, please, give me some credit. I'm worth more than a grope on the back seat of the pictures. I want to see a film with my girlfriends. I might just go and risk it. Bugger him.'

Maud ambled over to the Chesterfield and sat, smoothing out her overall with her misshapen hands. She looked at the fourteen-year-old girl and told her, 'Your dad's got his spies everywhere, love, namely your brothers. He told me the last time I saw him that he don't trust anyone around you. You're growing up into a very pretty young woman and he's just protecting you. So don't be daft about going behind his back, he'll go for you if you do. We've been lucky so far lying to him about you working with me 'cos we get here so early, and you stay over mine on a Friday night.'

'Well, I'll be leaving school next year, when I'm fifteen, you know, so he won't be able to tell me what to do any more, will he? I could move in with Ron – or you, Maud.'

The older woman laughed, 'I doubt that very much. You can't live with me, it's alright you sleeping round mine once a week, but let me tell you, I lived with my nan in one room, just about, and it was hell. You're not living with me, Tiny, bide your time he'll come round eventually. You're his little girl.'

Audrey sighed, resigned to the truth of what Maud had said. 'I know, but I feel like I'm ready now, ready for work, ready to go out and have some fun. Be a teenager!'

Maud nodded, even though she had no memories of having a carefree time as a teenager herself.

Audrey stood and announced, 'You know, Aunt Maud, I see what Dad means about this job. Why can't they build their own fires? It's not like they do a lot, is it? They read books, go to lectures or give lectures and have seminars or whatever you call them. They eat, and eat a lot, don't they, in their grand halls.'

Maud laughed. 'You know that's not all they do, love. They make discoveries here, do lots of research, and make history. You should remind your dad about that the next time he has a go. You've got to look at it like this; if we weren't keeping them warm and getting their breakfast ready, and that's the most important meal of the day, they might not be able to make discoveries. So the likes of us are quite important.'

'Really, Aunt Maud, we help make history?' Audrey looked doubtful.

'Well, how are we going to cure cancer and all them other diseases if we ain't got our professors looking into it? How are we going to change the world and people's attitudes? You have more power when you have an education, and don't you forget it. That's why I kept them encyclopaedias for you. I'm not saying that the likes of us could do any of this – after all, we're not from moneyed families like them, and you'd be a fish out of water here, but different breeding for different reasons, right?'

Maud straightened her overall again as she rose from the chair. She held her shoulders back and stood upright. 'I'm on your dad's side when it comes to protecting you, but, just like he gets to you he can really get to me, sometimes. He would wind up your mum all the time with his bitterness about the upper classes, but it's them that pay our wages, ain't it?' She pointed her index finger directly at Audrey and shook it as she continued, 'Wouldn't have a job would we, if they weren't here, and we should never forget that.'

'Alright, alright,' Audrey said, trying to calm Maud down. She remembered only too well the heated conversations she had overheard between her mum and dad that were all about working at the colleges.

They smiled at each other and Maud showed the gaps where at least seven teeth had disappeared in the last year. 'Let's get the coal out of the bunker so we can get off early, shall we?'

Audrey led the way out to the coalbunker in the yard, putting her overcoat on as she did so. She picked up the shovel, shaking snow from it in the process, while Maud carried the bucket behind her. After a couple of digs in the bunker, Audrey noticed something unfamiliar in the coal, and she bent over to get a closer look at what looked like pieces of coloured paper.

'What are these?' For an instant she thought that she was seeing things, but as she pulled one of the papers from the heap of coal, she realized that she wasn't. Audrey was shovelling up five-pound notes. Thin paper ones, lots of them. She called out to Maud, 'Aunty, there's money, lots of money in here!'

Maud stepped closer and saw that there were bundles of notes tumbling out from the coal bunker. Excitedly she half-shouted, 'Get 'em out! Get 'em out!'

Together they pulled out all of the piles of money and carried them back inside to the sitting room, where they sat on the floor exhausted and thrilled from the adrenaline.

After a few minutes, Audrey said, 'Someone must have stashed them in there, Maud. Do we tell the porter, or what?' Audrey's 'or what' came out slyly, temptingly, and had enough of a hint of conspiracy about it that Maud's first instinct – to report their find – was put aside.

'Let me think, girl, let me think!' she ordered.

Audrey sat, holding her breath as Maud deliberated for what seemed like an age before saying, 'We've got to put them in my shopping bag and take them back to my house. You alright with that?'

To which Audrey simply nodded.

'Right,' continued Maud firmly, 'if no one claims it, we'll keep it.'

On their way home (the cold didn't seem to bite quite as hard following their discovery), Maud worked out a justification for their keeping the money and not telling the porter. 'Do you know what?' she said to Audrey, expecting no answer. 'If I told the other staff, do you know who would have taken the money? Them porters, that's who would have had it, and they wouldn't have told the fellows or the master. You can't trust any of them.'

'Well, it was in your staircase bunker, Maud,' Audrey agreed, 'and I reckon it must have been there a good few years. So by rights it's yours. It was hidden well in with the coal. So it was meant to be hidden, weren't it?'

'I'm not going to feel guilty', Maud went on, sounding almost convinced of that herself. 'It'll do you the world of good to get some new hairdressing things on your next trip to London. The rest of it I'm going to put in my Post Office account, and save for a rainy day.'

Maud had no intention of spending the money, and planned on saving it for something much better, she thought, than a rainy day. They had counted more than £100 from the coal bunker that day in 1962, and although they were all old, pre-war notes, they were still legal. Her savings were growing very nicely ever since she had been surprised to hear after the death of Professor B., from a heart attack, that he had bequeathed her the sum of £250. When she got the news, Maud had been shocked because she thought that he had taken a dislike to her due to her not really talking with him much. She almost felt guilty about gossiping to Audrey about his extra-marital affairs, but, of course, she told herself, she had only told Audrey and not any other bedders. Still, that £250 sat in her account, earning interest, and this extra would be added to it and it'd grow (so the bank manager had told her), without much bother. One day, Maud thought, it'll come in very handy for someone.

It would be a year before they'd dare remove the bag from Maud's wardrobe where it lay buried under a pile of old shoes and coats. Finding the money and saying nothing about it proved difficult for Audrey. An honest girl by nature, she tried hard to justify keeping it without telling anyone, including her dad. She didn't tell him, though, as much because she was ashamed of taking it and not saying anything immediately, as she knew that if she told Edward, he'd likely tell her to keep it ('Those rich buggers have got enough money,' she knew he'd say). He'd also ask for a share of it, and she'd gladly give all of it to her dad, except that he'd only spend it down the pub. That was where almost all of his money had seemed to go since Edith had died.

A few months later, Audrey wished that Maud had given her at least some of the money when she learned that the Beatles were going to perform in Cambridge, at the Regal cinema. She loved 'Please, Please Me' and persuaded Edward to buy the record for her, and she'd almost worn out the grooves (Dad said) ever since. Finding eight shillings and sixpence for the show was going to be difficult unless Audrey took it from her hairdressing fund (which she'd managed to keep secret from Edward by hiding it under her bed in a sewing box). As her friends grew more and more excited by the forthcoming show and began to wave their tickets around at school, Audrey knew she'd have to be there too, and so she took it from under her bed. She told Edward that Maud had treated her to the ticket for the first, early show at 6.15, which he accepted, telling her, 'Make sure you're home by nine.'

As soon as school finished that Tuesday, Audrey went straight to the Regal to stand in line and hope to see the Beatles arrive. They weren't the main act that night – the Americans were, Chris Montez, who'd had a hit with 'Let's Dance' last year, and Tommy Roe, whose song 'Sheila' Audrey liked – but it seemed that the gang of fifty or so girls who waited impatiently alongside the cinema were only there to see the Liverpudlians. Audrey didn't get to see them before the show started, and it took what seemed like an interminable wait in her seat for the Beatles to play. She restlessly sat through performances by a Shadows-like guitar act called the Terry Young Six, an old rock-and-roll group called the Viscounts (she vaguely remembered their 'Who Put the Bomp' song), and a blonde woman who did impressions and sang with Mrs Mills on the telly, until the Beatles finally got to the stage.

When they did, the theatre became eerily quiet just for as long as it took for John to say 'Evenin' folks' and put the harmonica to his lips, and when the first bars of 'Love Me Do' rang out, Audrey, and everyone close to her, began to jump up and down in their seats and shout, scream and sing along. She didn't know which Beatle she loved best, but Paul kept looking at her she was sure, and from that night on he'd be her favourite.

They only played six songs – 'Please, Please Me' was the best as far as Audrey was concerned – and couldn't play any more, because men came on and started clearing up the stage, even before Ringo had climbed from behind his drum kit. The DJ Tony Marsh walked out with his dinner jacket and Brylcreemed hair, smiling as if he had a back pain or felt sick, and said something that Audrey simply didn't hear.

She was dazed, deaf and felt lighter than air. Must be not having had any tea, she thought as she sat, dumb and unmoving in her slightly wobbly seat. Tommy Roe came and went before Audrey could move, and when Tony Marsh came out again, she got up and left. Walking home she felt as if the world had changed. The smells and lights of Cambridge streets were sharp, almost dazzling. She didn't feel the cold until she got home and stood in front of the fire in the parlour.

It was only a concert, but it was also something more, Audrey knew. She hadn't felt excited or really happy, as if she was ready to do something – anything – since her mum had died, and now she did. She wanted to hang on to whatever it was she was feeling for as long as possible. But how?

By changing things, she thought, and getting a job that'll lead to me becoming a hairdresser, like I want to be. Maud will have to do the bedding on her own, but she'll manage.

The following Friday evening, Audrey visited Maud, but she didn't go with her to college for work the next day. She told her that she couldn't do it any more, and was surprised when Maud agreed with her.

'It'll help to get me moved to a smaller staircase anyway, I reckon,' she told a grateful Audrey.

That Saturday Audrey visited every hairdresser's shop in Cambridge asking if they needed any one to sweep up, clean, wash hair and learn the business.

At Raymond's, on the top floor of the Joshua Taylor department store, on the corner of Sidney Street and Market Street, she met with a positive response. Impressed by the style and size of the salon, Audrey could hardly wait to get started.

The following week the manageress welcomed Audrey to the job and told her that she might be able to get an apprenticeship with them in a year or so, if she worked hard enough. Audrey didn't need telling twice, and set about her job with pleasure.

By the summer of 1963, Audrey felt as if she was fulfilling her dream of becoming a hairdresser. Most of her school friends were training at different jobs or working in large stores around the town. Audrey loved every minute at Raymond's.

'We have to buy white carnations and dye them blue with hair dye when the boss comes in,' she told Maud on one of her aunt's frequent visits to the salon. 'We fill up all the vases with them, it looks stunning.'

'Is that Mr Teasie-Weasie your big boss, Audrey?' Maud

asked, as Audrey was about to lower the hairdryer over her head.

'Yes, Aunty Maud, but please don't call me Audrey. I've told you, when I'm at work I'm Tessa.'

'I don't get it. Why can't they just call you Audrey number two?'

Audrey laughed, and explained again. 'One more time! There are a hundred of us here and there was already an Audrey when I arrived, well, her name isn't really Audrey it's Barbara, but there was a Barbara here when she started so she became Audrey. So my trade name is Tessa.'

'You don't look anything like a Tessa, though,' grumbled Maud. 'Why can't this Audrey change her name now that there's a real one?'

'Oh Maud, it's not like making a bed. Your students can't tell who has made their bed, can they?'

Maud looked up quickly at Audrey. 'Damn cheek,' she told her, 'they'd soon know if I haven't made it. They'd be asking what had happened. The other bedders can't make a bed like me, my boys always tell me that.'

'Alright,' Audrey soothed the older woman. 'But if I start doing someone's hair and they had asked for the other Audrey, well, Gina and Michael wouldn't be best pleased.'

Gina and Michael Wilson were the salon managers, and Audrey did not want to do anything that would upset them and give them reason to let her go (which is how they'd explained Janice's sacking the week previous). There was always another girl waiting to start training at Raymond's.

'It doesn't matter, it's not like I'm not used to being called other names, is it, Maud; you still occasionally call me Tiny and the boys and their mates are still calling me that, too. Look at me – I don't think I warrant it any more, do you? Tessa is just fine. Please remember.'

Now fifteen years old, Audrey had blossomed into an attractive young woman. She was always dressed in a black miniskirt and a white blouse, and with her short blonde hair she was the epitome of fashion. Naturally, this made Edward even stricter with her, and he would not let her go out after work or with her friends at the weekend.

'You been saving your wages?' Maud asked as Audrey handed her a cup of tea.

'Don't be daft,' the girl responded, 'most of my wages go on bus fare. But my pay will start going up with my age and experience. I reckon I'll be on one pound, eleven and six by the time I'm seventeen. I have to start saving for my own salon as soon as possible of course, it's the only way you make anything. It's like Dad says, I shouldn't be selling myself for next to nothing.'

'One day you'll have your own business. I can see it.' A dreamy look came over her face as Maud stared into the middle distance, seeing visions of what she imagined Audrey's future to be. 'You'll have "Audrey, Hair Stylist" above a shop,' she told her, 'and I'll help you get it when you're qualified.' She didn't want to mention to Audrey that she was saving for the girl's future, not just yet anyway. She wanted her to complete the training and was so proud of her working at Raymond's.

So was her dad, and as he told Maud, 'He's got horses that Teasie-Weasie fella has, up in Newmarket.' Edward told Audrey, 'Your mum would have liked him as well, I have no doubt. He worked his way up in his dad's barber shop and he can demand stupid money for a hairdo. Good for him, I say, if people are prepared to pay for it.'

Edward approved when his daughter said that she didn't want to go back to school after the summer. She had been offered an apprenticeship at Raymond's whereas some girls had to pay £200 a year to be trained by them. It wasn't long before she was doing more than putting customers under dryers and making them tea, too. She was washing hair, and assigned to watch and learn from a couple of older cutters by November 1963, when the Beatles returned to Cambridge. This time Audrey had no problems affording the ticket, because she won one in the salon's sweepstake.

There were some 2,000 girls waiting before the show to try and get a look – or even a touch – of the band before the concert, and Audrey joined the queue early, knowing she might miss something otherwise. But when she found herself being shoved every which way by girls as they pushed against policemen, who were trying to keep them off the road outside the Regal, she took herself off away from the crowd and to the Civic café, where she had a cup of tea with a couple of friends. Like them, Audrey had ordered 'She Loves You' from the record department in the basement of Miller's Music, across the road from Joshua Taylor's, at least two months before it was released – even before they knew what it was going to be called, it was simply 'the new record by the Beatles'. She'd played it at least twice every day since getting it in August, alternating it with the other Beatles 45s, 'Love Me Do', 'Please, Please Me' and 'From Me to You', and their first long player, *Please, Please Me*. She was waiting for their second LP, *With the Beatles*, which was about to come out. They were all looking forward to getting their copies of a new Beatles 45 the Friday after the concert, and had their orders in.

That single, 'I Want to Hold Your Hand', wasn't played that night, but ten songs that they all knew were performed – only it was very difficult to hear any of them because of the constant screaming and shouting from the audience. Audrey was sure that Paul was always looking at her again, but the music and the night was spoiled by all the hysterics of the girls – some of them looked as if they were barely twelve years old,

she thought, with irritation. At the end of the night, Audrey
was very glad she'd seen them again, but she didn't have the
same floaty feeling afterwards like she had in March. Still,
she thought, I'm older now, more mature. A look at her reflection in the shop windows she passed on her way home showed
the truth of that: her hair was backcombed into a trademark
Raymond beehive, her kitten-heel stilettos and tight pencil
skirt made a perfect line from the short, flared wool jacket with
three large buttons. She knew that she could easily pass for
eighteen.

MAUD

By the time that Audrey was established at the salon, Maud looked forward to her regular hair appointments with 'Tessa' enormously. Maud had moved to a different part of town in 1960, and since Audrey had left the colleges for hairdressing, they didn't get to see each other as often as they used to.

Maud hadn't regretted moving house, only that it took her further away from Audrey. She had been offered a two-bedroom flat in the brand new section of the Arbury estate called King's Hedges, and as Hugh's mother had died she could see no real reason to remain in her three-bedroom house in Ditton Fields.

Maud had no money worries, as she still had Hugh's pension. Her work as a bedder had become a matter of routine, and while she didn't get as close to the boys as many of the others at her college, she had no reason to complain about the way she was treated by either the college or the students. As the move neared, she became almost excited at the idea of starting again, and saw it as an adventure – which is what the twelve-year-old Audrey had said it would be. Maud decided to take very few things from the house in Ditton Fields to the flat in Campkin Court. She would buy new furniture, all modern and in bright colours, with Formica tops and glass doors. She'd had enough of the dark brown Edwardian and Victorian sideboards, cupboards and ball-footed, heavy table that she'd inherited from the Ingrams. Naturally, the Singer sewing machine that Hugh had bought her (and which she'd paid him back for) would make the journey across town with her, as would the dressmaking basket she bought for that first – and last – May Ball in 1950.

When the housekeeper asked if she'd like to attend the next Ball, in 1951, Maud told her that she'd rather not. 'I didn't really like seeing them all drunk like that.' Which wasn't true, but she couldn't tell anyone the real reason why; that she didn't want to be reminded of the attack on Hugh that happened the same night. She was ashamed that she was dazzled by the lights, dancing and fun being had by all at the May Ball while her husband was being bashed up. She never went to another in all the time that she continued to work for the college.

Maud ordered most things for her new flat from the Littlewoods catalogue, which she and Audrey spent hours looking through, selecting everything from tea towels to a record player. 'I'm really enjoying this,' she told Audrey after they'd just decided to get a new alarm clock. It looked like something from outer space, with silver spikes for legs and little black balls at the end of them.

'But can you afford it, Aunty Maud?' Audrey asked as she completed the order form for her (she did them all because Maud said her handwriting was clearer).

''Course I can,' Maud said with feeling, 'I would never get it all otherwise. I've got a little put away in the Post Office, I'm alright, Tiny.' In fact, she had quite a lot of money saved having had nothing to spend it on before now.

On the day of the move, Maud had Edward and a friend of his put all of the Ingrams' old furniture into her front garden for anyone to take as they liked. To her surprise, a large man with a horse and cart arrived just after 11 a.m. and loaded the whole lot onto his wagon. The rag and bone man took everything, including crockery and cutlery, and Maud didn't mind at all, at least it was gone.

The previous day she had taken all of her late mother-in-law's clothes to the Red Cross. She had removed Hugh's clothes the day after his funeral, although not to a charity. Instead she'd put them into his old navy duffle bag and left them on the desk at her college porter's lodge with no explanation. At the time she had taken great pleasure in doing so, although she would later come to regret it.

The only things she took with her from Ditton Fields that had once belonged to her late husband were the *Encyclopaedias Britannica*, and they were for Audrey. Maud encouraged her to read as much as possible when she was with her. 'If you were a boy, Audrey, you'd probably have been allowed to go to grammar school like Marjorie Mizen's youngest son,' Maud told her and Audrey laughed.

'You mean Alan?' she replied with a snort. 'Alan Seymour? He boxes at the Henley Road boxing club with some of the boys from my school. I can think of other boys I'd rather be like.'

Maud looked crestfallen at that, and Audrey joked, 'Blimey, Aunty Maud, do you know his great-grandmother as well?'

'Cheeky bugger,' Maud perked up. 'She was a bedder too, but no, I never met her. Both his mum and his Nana Bertha are, you know, and that's how it is at the colleges, daughters, nieces and sisters.'

Maud had encouraged Audrey to choose a job that she wanted to do, and thought that if she could help Tiny through life avoiding the mistakes that she'd made, then she would have something to be quietly proud of. Maud hated the idea that Audrey might end up in a loveless marriage like she'd had.

It was a Saturday morning in 1965, after her shift at the

college, and Maud was looking forward to catching up with
Audrey. As soon as she was settled, she asked her about her
love life, which she'd been doing since the girl had begun to go
out dancing.

Most of the time, Audrey didn't mind. She could get away
with denying that she'd dated any boys, and only saw them to
dance and drink with. Nothing serious had gone on (or not as
far as Audrey was concerned; she knew Maud might think
differently about what she got up to during the slow dances at
the Dorothy and the long, quiet walks home at 1 a.m.).

But at the salon, where there were lots of interested parties
listening in, Audrey knew she needed to get Maud talking and
thinking about something else. 'But how are your boys, Aunty
Maud, how's that blind boy, Simon, doing? Is his dog still there
an' all?'

'Oh yes, he's ever so nice. I don't know how he does it, you
know. He doesn't let me get things for him when I'm in his
room. Did I tell you he gave me a tenner at Christmas?' Maud's
eyes sought Audrey's in the mirror, and the girl looked back
quizzically.

'I said, "You do know what you've given me, don't you?" and
he says, "I most certainly do and you're worth every bit of it."
And I thought for a bit and then said, "But 'ow do you know
what you've give me?" And he says straight back, "Barney" –
that's his guide dog – "got it out of my wallet for me." Well, I
laughed at that, and said, "No, really Simon, this is too much,
it's . . ." and he said quick as a flash, "A tenner, Mrs Ingram. I
know." Blow me, I thought, his dog must be clever!'

Audrey laughed at that and said, 'No Aunty, a tenner will
feel different to a fiver or a pound note, won't it? It's bigger, for
a start.'

'Oh yes, I s'pose you're right. Anyway, he made me keep it,
and of course I look after him as best I can, you know. But that

dog of his, he's a right life saver. Simon told me the other day how he was walking up Regent Street with Barney leading him, and I've seen Simon walking about and he don't half move fast, I tell you. Anyway, Simon says, "Barney suddenly stopped, so I had to as well, but couldn't think why. I could hear the traffic to my left and nothing in front. I couldn't get him to move forward at all, and he sat there, solid as a rock. Then a nice gentleman spoke to me and said what a good dog I had, and would I like to be helped around the very large hole that covered the pavement! If I'd dragged Barney on I would have done who knows what harm to myself and him."' Maud paused and Audrey looked suitably impressed. 'He's lovely though, that Simon, and of course this is the third year I've looked after him, which the college don't usually like doing. But 'cos of his blindness they let him have the same room, and Barney with him. He must be right clever, my Simon.'

'And what about that other boy who took you punting, Maud, how's he?'

'What, Matthew? He's alright, got himself a girlfriend, though – I burst in on them in a state of undress the other morning – I din't know where to look! So I left and came back to his rooms last, and he was waiting for me. "Oh Maudie," he says, he always calls me that and I don't mind, he's proper handsome an' all, "Maudie, I'm terribly sorry about you catching me giving Miss Sellers an examination." I said, "You what? That din't look like no 'zamination to me!" He smiled and said, "Oh but it was, you know. I'm in second year medicine and Miss Sellers was complaining of a having a bad chest, so I was, er, listening to it" – and do you know, he managed to keep a straight face!'

'Ha ha,' said Audrey, 'I bet he's doing vet training, not medicine, eh Aunty?'

'He's lovely really though, so I won't say nothing. Now if I was to catch that 'orrible Gervaise doing something sim'lar I'd be straight down to the porter's lodge, I tell you.'

'Oh dear, is he still being 'orrible to you?'

'He never says nothing nice, never a "Good morning, how are you today," it's just "Clean under the bed, don't move my books, where's my bloody Bakelite tea set." Little sod. I threw that old set out when he left it by the sink in the gyp room at the end of last term. We're told to chuck anything like that if it's left behind when they're gone, an' so I did. He was upset, though, and told me he wouldn't care if I'd kept them, but I told 'im, "I wouldn't want that old rubbish," and ever since he's been as surly as anything with me. Still, not for long, eh, he'll be off somewhere else next year.'

Maud turned her head both ways, admiring the cut that Audrey had given her. 'Oh, that looks lovely, Aud dear.'

'Glad you like it, Aunty, now do you think it's alright if we change your regular Saturday morning appointment for one at the end of the day from now on, please?'

Maud agreed hesitantly, and Audrey explained that they didn't have time to chat properly on a Saturday morning, but there wouldn't be the same pressure at the end of the day to get her out of the chair so another customer could take it.

From then on Maud spent Saturdays after her shift at the college wandering around town, looking in shop windows. She had never given herself time to do this before and took to sitting on a seat opposite the entrance of the Sainsbury's store on Sidney Street or outside the Post Office, watching people go about their business. She sat, staring at people, imagining what their lives were like, until it was time for her appointment with Audrey.

After a year or so, though, Maud began to miss appointments with Audrey, usually without telling her beforehand. When she'd missed three appointments in a row, Audrey rang her college on a Friday and asked to pass a message to Maud, for her to visit Audrey that evening.

'Another cup of tea?' Audrey asked as Maud settled in the kitchen that evening. She nodded, thinking that the tea making would give her time to think about what to say to her Tiny.

'I'll do your hair if you like seeing as you've come all this way,' Audrey suggested as she put the kettle on. 'I've got all my kit.'

'No, no, it's OK, I'm not really in the mood.'

Audrey leaned against the cooker and looked quizzically at Maud.

'What's up, Maud? Come on, out with it. I know something's bothering you. You've not been coming to the salon. Is something wrong?' Maud looked away from Audrey, who turned on the gas ring under the kettle and tried again. 'Come on, Maud. You can tell me. Is it 'cos you didn't get Charlie, is that it? The last time I saw you, you said there was talk of him going to your college?'

Audrey meant Prince Charles, who was going to be coming to the university.

'No, that was just talk,' Maud said dismissively, 'he didn't come to ours. No, it's not that. He got Flo Moore from White-hill Road. They picked her specially for him and she's a nice lady. Look, I know you're a fighter, Audrey. It's me that's not. I've had enough. I stood at the bus stop at five-and-twenty to six yesterday morning in all that snow and I said out loud, "I can't do this any more."'

'Something else must have happened to make you do that, Maud, you don't just pack in your job without a by your leave.'

Maud sighed. 'I'm just tired, Audrey. Tired. My joints hurt, my rheumatism hasn't got any better you know. Look at my hands . . . and my knees are not far behind. But yes, I suppose something did happen. The new assistant housekeeper doesn't like me much. She's told me off a few times, says I keep forgetting to put things away or that I'm taking too long with the Hoover when others need it. And I s'pose it's been grinding me down. She's always having a go, but never when anyone else is around, until pay day, when she shouted at me in front of everyone.'

'How dare she? I'll go up there and give her a piece of my mind!' Audrey was indignant on her aunt's behalf.

'No, no,' Maud patted Audrey's hand. 'It's alright, love, some of the other bedders had a word with her after she shouted at me. We were all queuing for our wages and when she called me over she near screamed at me, said I'd left a window open and that it was irresponsible. Said there could of been an intruder come in or anything. But I don't remember leaving it open, Audrey, really I don't.' She shook her head slowly.

'You probably didn't, Maud, she sounds like a right bully.'

'That's what the other bedders told her, "Don't bully Maud, how do you know it was her left the window open?" they asked, and she went quiet then.'

'Right,' Audrey tried to sound decisive, 'you're going to have to stand up to her.' But she knew that was impossible for Maud, who she'd never seen argue with anyone. Audrey had had only ever seen her lose her temper once before, and that was when she was defending 'her boys' against a woman at the hairdresser's who said all the students were on drugs. Audrey knew that she would never stand up to this woman.

'Thanks, love,' Maud said, as if Audrey had helped in some way. 'Best if I leave though. I'll be alright, I can sleep in, can't I, if I quit work? Maybe I'll start going to the caravan more. I'll have time on me hands and I might like it.'

Audrey reached across the table and pushed Maud's head up so that she could see her eyes, which were fixed on the floor.

'Are you really sure, Maud? You love your boys. What about Simon?'

'He's gone, love, left to go to America, he said. Anyway, it's too late. On my way home Friday I stopped at the pay phone and called the housekeeper and said I wouldn't be in again, so not to expect me. Maybe I should have left a long time ago. But Audrey, I need you to write a letter for me, to explain like.'

In all the time that she'd known her, Audrey had never seen Maud write anything longer or more difficult than a shopping list. 'Yes, of course I will.'

She fetched a writing pad and pen. 'We'll just tell them you're not well and explain that you'll be back in a couple of weeks, maybe get the doctor to write a note too, shall we?'

Maud burst into tears.

'Oh Maud, it's alright you know, you're gonna be alright.' Audrey felt like crying too.

Maud shook her head and it was a few minutes before she could say, 'I've bottled it up for so long. I think I'm just relieved to be gone from there, there are too many reminders for me lately. I've had enough of pretending, Audrey.'

After asking what she meant, over the next hour Audrey heard the story of Maud's life and all about Hugh. Audrey wasn't shocked by the revelation about him, and in fact she had known for a couple of years about his being a 'poofter'. She had heard it was a long-standing joke at the Post Office that workers on the late shifts should be careful out walking near the public loos as they might get mistaken for an Ingram; they all knew what he was up to.

Maud continued to explain how after Hugh had died she started to feel guilty, that she should have taken him to hospital that morning and they might have saved his life. She also told Audrey about Trevor from the college and how she had made a mistake in giving him Hugh's clothes. 'He wore them every day after I left them there, to torment me I think. Not when he was working, though. When I was clocking in he would be clocking out and there he would stand at the gate wearing Hugh's hat or his jacket, something anyway, there was always something of his, and it'd give me a fright sometimes seeing him in the mist, looking just like my Hugh, and him not saying a word.

'But I never said a word to him, neither. Then, one day out of the blue, about five years ago, I was off work with the flu that had been going round the college and the next day Bertha Mizen came round with a letter from him. She said Trevor had hung himself at home, and he left that note addressed to me. Bertha hadn't opened it, she just handed it to me and told me what had happened. I asked her not to tell anyone about the letter and trusted her: I still do. For a week or so everyone at the college was told that Trevor was off sick, but after the inquest, it was hard to hide what had happened. They were all talking about him committing suicide saying he couldn't live with being a poof. No mention of Hugh though, thank God. I've still got that letter, Audrey, I kept it hidden in my sewing basket, and never opened it.' At that Maud buried her face in her hands and wept.

'It's alright, Maud, you're going to be alright,' Audrey tried to soothe her, 'just burn that letter, or better still let me burn it, it's been years that you've been carrying it around. What's it going to tell you that you don't already know? Hey?'

Maud nodded and felt a surge of something that seemed like a release. She continued to cry as Audrey cradled her in her arms, holding back her own tears.

The college accepted Maud's resignation and sent her flowers and cards from the staff and students. Audrey read a letter to her from the college explaining that she would always be welcome back and to expect invitations to the staff Christmas dinners. Audrey also told her, 'They said you can go on the trip to Great Yarmouth in the summer if you want.'

'I won't bother,' Maud smiled, 'but that's nice of them ain't it? They have been good to me I s'pose.'

Two days later Maud visited a doctor who told her she had suffered a nervous breakdown, and their remedy was that she take 'a little holiday'. Audrey wished it had been a real break, away somewhere in the sun, perhaps. Maud never wanted to go far from home, but it still didn't seem fair to Audrey that her aunt was prescribed pills and took her 'rest', as she called it, at the psychiatric hospital in Fulbourn. It wasn't to be her last 'holiday' there, though.

ANN

The first few years after the arrival of a fourth child in the Adams house made everyone happy. The girls loved having a little brother and Fred was besotted with his son. He wanted to take him to watch Cambridge United play football at the Abbey Stadium before Kenneth was three weeks old, but sense prevailed (and it took at least six months until he became a United supporter). The family's sense of contentment was upset however, when Shirley's bump on the head from a swing turned out to have horrible after-effects. It didn't happen immediately after the accident, but several months later Shirley suffered a small fit unlike anything that Ann had ever seen before. She didn't fall to the floor shaking and twitching, but her eyes glazed over and she slumped in the kitchen chair she was sitting on and, although she looked awake, she couldn't speak to answer her mum, who kept asking what was wrong.

'It was as if she'd become a waxwork,' as Ann tried to explain it to Fred, 'for about three minutes it was like there was no one in her body.' Which was how Ann explained it to the doctor after it happened again, a week later. He sent them to the hospital, where Shirley spent a whole day being looked at, prodded, questioned and examined. When finally they were allowed to leave, Ann told Fred, 'They said she might keep having small seizures – "petty mal" they called it – or she might not. They're not able to say. We should've taken her straight to the doctors after the accident, they said.'

Fred felt terrible and Ann tried to share the guilt for not taking the accident more seriously. It soon became clear that Shirley would have a seizure at least once a month and although they were not that bad, her parents had to make sure she was not left alone for too long, in case she had a fit and fell, hitting her head.

Her school were told and they tried to make sure Shirley was watched as much as possible. Glenis was instructed to look after her when she could, too, which meant that she missed a lot of after-school sports activities which she had really taken to, in order to get Shirley home at the end of the day. After a while everyone accepted that Shirley would have a 'petty mal', go quiet and feel exhausted for a couple of hours after it, so needed a lot of rest. Her schooling suffered, and she was moved into a small class with children who were having difficulty keeping up with the others. Soon enough the Adams family adapted to the new kind of normal life in which their Shirl sometimes went 'funny'. They coped well enough and never complained.

Early in the new decade though, the family were devastated by another illness that affected the youngest Adams child. It had been an ordinary Saturday afternoon, and the by now thirteen-year-old Glenis was seated at the kitchen table when Ann came into the kitchen carrying a limp-looking Kenneth, who had the measles, in her arms. She put his almost lifeless body on the table and said, 'Call an ambulance, Glen, Kenny's not good.' Ann's voice remained calm but Glenis could see the panic in every movement her mum made, as she frantically started to pat his whole body with a towel that she'd wet under the tap. It didn't seem to lower the heat radiating from his body, though.

'Go, go to phone box, take some pennies from the jar. Go on Glen, go.'

Glenis did as instructed, ran to the phone box on the corner, dialled 999 and asked for an ambulance – then she redialled but received no answer at the other end and so rushed back to the house almost in tears. 'You've got to call the doctor they said,' Glenis blurted as soon as she opened the kitchen door, 'they won't come unless the doctor says so.'

'Did you try Dr Silverstein at the surgery?' Ann was still trying to stay calm.

'I did but there's no answer. What do I do now, Mum?' she begged

Being a Saturday, Fred had taken Shirley and Dot to the football thinking that Kenny only had the measles and would be alright. Glenis stood at the door looking on in shock at how ill her little brother was, and waited for further instructions.

'Try again, just keep trying until someone answers,' Ann told her. Glenis ran back to the phone box and after several more attempts finally got through to the doctor and begged for him to come and see her brother. Finally, the doctor arrived, took one look at Kenny and told them both, 'We haven't got time to wait for an ambulance. I'll take him in my car.'

For months, six-year-old Kenny lay in intensive care at Brookfields Hospital. He had contracted meningitis. During that time Fred seemed lost, and Ann was in bits and hardly said a word to any of them. There was an unusual sense of calmness and quiet about the house. What was most unusual for the girls was their parents not speaking to each other. They were used to their mum and dad's closeness, which was never expressed in shows of physical affection in front of the children, but rather in their sharing household jobs such as washing up together, tidying up, and always talking about things together. They would be in the garden together gardening or tending the vegetables and they'd be chatting away. It was sweet to watch, but now they were rarely seen in the same room together. Thankfully, Grace and Jack came in every day to cook for them and help Glenis get Dorothy and Shirley off to school. 'This will change them, whatever the outcome,' Nana Pilcher told Glenis one morning before school. It already has, thought Glenis.

When he was allowed to return home, Kenny was no longer the sweet little boy who loved to kick a football around with his dad, or the little brother who followed his sisters around everywhere; he was permanently brain damaged and had severe epilepsy. His condition meant that the family had to adjust in many ways, and the house became uncomfortable; Ken had to have his own room and special bed, which meant that they needed another bedroom. Fred, who had changed his employment from bricklayer to binman after Kenny was born, applied to the council for a larger house, and was rewarded with one pretty quickly, sited a half mile from Queen's Meadow, in Fisher's Lane.

It didn't take long for the family to settle into their new house, but they found it much harder to settle into the kind of contented unit that they had been before Kenny's illness. Brain damage had altered his behaviour and loosened his self-control. Fred had decorated the house before they'd moved in, but Kenny soon redecorated it by writing 'open' and 'close' on every door, window and drawer, as well as on his toys and the walls. As soon as Ann had put something away he got it out again. He had become grumpy and inconsolable, was restless and uncontrollable by anyone, Fred included. The adults' relationship suffered badly and they argued over the best way to deal with their son.

One Sunday afternoon, Glenis sat on the stairs listening to

Fred and Ann arguing. Their voices grew louder and Fred began to shout. When she heard the sound of things being thrown about Glenis became genuinely scared, so she ran to the phone box in order to call the police. They came to the house but Ann told them it was nothing, 'Just a domestic.' They left and Ann warned Glenis never, ever to do that again. 'We keep it in the family, you understand?'

Finally, in 1963 Ann made the decision to send Kenny to a day school in Cambridge for handicapped children, the Lady Adrian in Courtney Way. She also arranged for Shirley, who was now ten years old, to be schooled there. 'It makes perfect sense,' she told her. 'You can travel with Kenny on the bus. Me or Glen will walk you both to the top of the road for the special bus that'll take you there. When you're there you can keep an eye on him. You know, make sure he comes to no harm. We don't want him to feel like he's being sent away.'

'But what about my friends?' Shirley pleaded with her mother. 'I'm not handicapped like Kenny, Mum. I just have a few fits.'

'Well, they said you can go and I want it that way.'

So Shirley and Ken were sent to the Lady Adrian, just as Glenis was preparing to leave school. Aged fifteen, she'd arranged a hairdressing apprenticeship at Rust's Hairdressers but, unfortunately, the cost of getting to the job and the clothes and equipment she needed to keep it up proved too much. Instead, Glenis took a job in the offices of the Co-op where she worked for a year, until applying for and getting a job she really wanted, at Boots the chemist. By then Dorothy was working in the shoe department of a store on Burleigh Street.

Ann and Fred still had two kids to be kept in food, clothes and shoes then, and they were struggling financially. Fred kept at his day job as a binman, and he and Ann had taken to working together as night cleaners at the Pye factory. From six until nine in the evening Fred worked the heavy cleaning machinery while Ann cleaned the canteen. They were also preparing for another move. This time to Mowbray Road, which was closer to town and Bet's house, allowing the sisters to care for each other's children more if possible. However, although Kenny was getting good school reports and was well behaved at the Lady Adrian, who said that he enjoyed learning, he grew more and more difficult to handle when at home. So when Shirley was about to leave school and looking for work, Ann knew she would not be able to cope with Kenny's high energy and seizures on her own. So she and Fred found a special school in Lowestoft for Kenny to board at, which would be paid for jointly by the department of education and NHS.

'He'll be back in the holidays and we'll visit him at the weekends, he's not being shut away,' she told the family when explaining the arrangements. 'It's very difficult for him, you know. Every time Kenny gets excited he has a fit, you see that. We have to have an ambulance out every time he kicks a football, and every time he has a fit his brain becomes more damaged. At this school he'll be watched all the time.' After taking the decision, Ann suffered some sleepless nights during which she'd punish herself for doing to Kenny what her own mother had done to Joy and then Johnny. During daylight hours though, Ann reconciled her conscience with the thought that her son was much older than Joy and Johnny had been when they were sent away, plus he genuinely seemed to be happier with other boys around and being constantly cared for.

When Kenny was settled in Suffolk, Ann had more time to find paid work (and hoped to lose herself in being busy), and for the first time in their long marriage, Fred told her that, 'You can get a job now up one o' them colleges, and maybe even take our Shirl with you.' Which is when Ann mentioned to Rose that she'd like to get a job as a bedder.

While sounding out Rose, Ann and Fred were still finding it hard to make ends meet. Ann was loath to throw things away that she thought could be mended – often to the embarrassment of her daughters, who began to despair of ever seeing her wear anything that didn't have patches and stitches in it. Nothing was ever done with in Ann's home until it had been completely used up. One day Glenis entered the house and wrinkled her nose at a terrible smell of burning rubber. Poking her head into the front room she found Ann stoking the fireplace, in which a pair of old boots were smouldering. 'What are you doing, Mum, it stinks in here!'

'Hello, love.' Ann smiled up at her daughter and turned back to poking the smoking boots. 'They had a hole in 'em. Waste not want not, eh?'

Fred had discovered the benefits of other people's discarded possessions and he often brought home some of them, regarding it as one of the perks of his job. He and his team of refuse collectors would split the 'valuables' from the bins they emptied. The first time Fred returned with something, he gave Ann his wage packet along with a stunning-looking brooch. 'What do you think, Annie?' he smiled.

'It don't look valuable,' she told him, holding it up to the light, 'but it's pretty costume jewellery.' She smiled and wore it pinned to her pinafore that night as they cleaned.

A month later Fred presented her with a diamond-studded cross and Ann was chuffed to get £10 for it at the pawn shop. With the money she was able to buy Glenis a record player for her birthday. 'The things people throw away, I don't get it. Must have money to burn,' she never tired of saying to Fred as he handed his 'treasure' to her.

When Rose told her that she'd arranged for the housekeeper at her college to talk to Ann about a job as a bedder, Ann was so pleased that she gave her old neighbour three different necklaces from her bin collection. Rose took them saying she'd give them to her granddaughters, 'If Maurice ever gets around to having any.'

Ann's quiet nature and can-do attitude impressed the college housekeeper well enough, and almost forty years after she'd first dreamed of being a part of the university, Ann Adams found herself standing in the sitting room on the third floor of staircase H, with an electric vacuum cleaner in one hand and a bucket filled with dusters and cleaning materials in the other. To her they were just as good as a sceptre and a mitre. The 'boys' she met that day were all very well spoken, polite and tried to keep out of her way as she set about giving their rooms the best clean they'd ever had. Ann worked so hard on her first day that she only managed to get half the rooms done in the time allotted. At 12.30 Rose went looking for her in the gyp room on the ground floor, and found it empty. She climbed to the first floor, and called for Ann. She found her on her hands and knees vacuuming under a bed in the furthest bedroom from the staircase. The rest of the room was tidy and the surfaces gleamed.

'Whatever are you doin', Ann?' Rose asked in astonishment, pulling the plug to the vacuum cleaner out of the wall. 'You should of finished this lot ages ago.' Ann looked up at her, sweat running down her face, which was red with the effort she'd put into her work. 'But there's so much to do, Rose!' she exclaimed. 'These poor boys, their rooms are filthy, there's rings round their baths, washing up in the sinks, dirty cups and glasses all over the place, and their desks are a right muddle.'

'Oh no, Ann, you din't . . .' Rose looked over at the desk under the window, seeing it neatly arranged with piles of papers stacked alongside each other, pens standing upright in a pot and books closed and stacked with the largest at the bottom of the pile.

'Yes, Rose, you should have seen that desk, it was a right mess, with papers all higgledy-piggledy and books left lying open and all ways up, but it looks lovely now, don't it?'

Rose sighed deeply. 'Ann, you don't touch their papers, din't no one tell you that?'

Ann nodded, 'Well, the housekeeper did, but I couldn't leave it like that, could I? You should of seen it.'

'No! Now Ann, you 'ave to leave their work alone, it might look a right muck-up to you, but they all know exactly where everything is, or so they say. Now the chap what has this room will be mad as hell, I reckon. Come on, we'd better go see the Mrs and tell her you made a mistake, before the boy in here does.'

'But what about the rest of the rooms, Rose? I ain't done the floor below yet.'

'Orright, I'll 'elp you, but it'll 'ave to be a surface clean 'cos we ain't got time and we 'ave to be out of 'ere by one o'clock.'

Ann got better at finishing on time pretty quickly, but she would still occasionally be found finishing something in a room by the occupants on their return from lectures. Her reputation as an honest, modest and damned hard worker was made in the space of her first eight-week term, and as it came to a close, she received a number of gifts from students and fellows who she cleaned for. 'I don't expect gifts, but look at this present,' she said to Fred when he got home one day in late December. 'Just look at this one,' Ann said, getting up from the kitchen table. She wrapped an Indian silk scarf around her neck and did a twirl. 'What do you think? Where am I going to wear it?'

Fred looked confused. 'Where'd you get that?'

'From the wife of one of the professors,' Ann gazed almost shyly at the scarf as it hung along her arm. The professor was leaving the college and she had only looked after him for a few months. Ann was very touched by the gift and the note that came with it, thanking her for being so kind to him. That wasn't all, either. 'And he left me some money in the porter's lodge in an envelope. It's more than I earn in a week, Fred. I went straight to put it in the bank.'

It was another instalment towards what Ann was determined would be a house of their own one day. Her plan was not to have a mortgage, but to buy it with cash. 'If you can't afford to buy something outright, don't buy it all,' she told everyone. 'It's my motto.' Her fund had begun with a £100 win on the pools the week before she started work as a bedder. 'It's a good sign, eh, Fred?' she said. They gave £1 each to the children and banked the rest. It proved to be a very good sign, and that first Christmas as a proper employee of the college Ann attended a carol service in the chapel and gave thanks for how her life had turned out.

Ann was glad that her mother, who'd died peacefully in her sleep a few years earlier, had made the decision to move them all to Cambridge during the war. It seemed like a long time ago now, but the place still looked almost exactly the same as it had when she first saw the turrets, towers, gates and wide, tree-lined avenues that crossed the greens.

Ann and Fred bought a house at the end of the 1970s, and they brought Kenny home to live with them there. His fits continued until he was well into his forties, when a drug was found that could prevent them. In the early 1990s they all moved to a bungalow in Cherry Hinton, near to Queen's Meadow. Ann continued to work as a bedder until the mid-1990s, when she had to retire due to heart problems. Aware that she might not have long to live, and having been saving for Kenny's future since the 1970s, in 1994 she arranged for her son to be looked after at a special care home nearby. He visited his parents every weekend until, sadly, Ann died shortly after undergoing heart surgery in 1996, at the age of sixty-nine. Fred lived on for only another seven years following the death of his beloved wife.

Once married, Bet became a mother to four children, who she looked after full time. In what spare time she could find, Bet sewed and made dresses for her children and nieces. On retiring from his work as a stoker in the 1980s, Barrel did volunteer work as a driver for the local hospital, until his death in 1987. Bet passed away a decade later.

Rene married and had three children; she now lives in Milton, just north of Cambridge. Joy lived in Norfolk when a young mother to two children, but returned to Cambridge following her divorce from their father. She worked as a volunteer among old people in Cambridge, where she still lives in happy retirement.

In the 1970s, Shirley moved to Plymouth to live with her husband. She returned to Cambridge in 1981 following their divorce, and with her mother's help and encouragement, later became a bedder. It was her failure to arrive for work at college one morning which alerted her family to the sad fact that she had died, in 2008. Her college almost seemed to miss her as much as her family continue to do.

AUDREY

By the time she was seventeen, Audrey had finished her apprenticeship and was now working full-time at Raymond's, the hairdressers. She was pleased that Edward began to treat her as if she was an adult. She was finally allowed to go out to clubs around Cambridge, and although her father always said she had to be in by midnight, he would always lend her a few bob if she was short. And, often, Audrey would arrive home after the appointed hour. 'Better late than never,' she'd say, to which he'd smile and make what became a stock reply, 'Better never late!'

In the mid-1960s it seemed as if there was a dance every night. Audrey, her friends from work and a couple of old school pals would regularly go to the Victoria, the Corn Exchange or the Guildhall, where there'd be live bands performing. Some nights they simply walked about the town, watching people go in and out of different pubs. They could tell the students who'd dare to go out without wearing their gowns, and witnessed many a chase through the market place as young men ran from older, bowler-hat-wearing bulldogs who had the authority to march them back to their colleges. One night, she found herself being used as a shield against bulldogs when a student grabbed her arm and pulled her into an alley by the Dorothy, where he started kissing her. After the shock wore off, Audrey thought that he was a terrible kisser, so she shoved him away and told him to get lost. Which he did, without a word.

Audrey particularly liked seeing people who went into the Criterion in Market Passage. It was a huge old pub, with a front bar usually populated by an older, local crowd of men who, on Saturday nights, took their wives to show off their new beehive hairdos. Audrey sometimes recognized customers as they passed her on their way in, some would smile at her as she and her friends chatted across the way from the Cri. Every kind of fashion was worn by the younger blokes who drank there. Mods and rockers wouldn't exactly mix, but they'd tolerate each other's presence in the back bars. After closing time, though, they'd invariably have a fight outside. Drunken brawls were the late night activity of choice for Cambridge local lads who didn't have enough money (or had drunk too much beer) to get into the nightclubs which stayed open until after midnight. There were a few beatniks ('fakeniks', she'd heard some of the rockers call them) around, most of them post-grad students who liked their duffel coats, pipes and trad jazz records they sipped mild beer and smoked roll-ups, Ron told her. Beatniks would avoid confrontations outside the Cri and make their way to someone's flat or house in order to smoke away the rest of a Saturday night, or so Ron said. Ron couldn't decide if he was a mod or a rocker, so mixed with both.

After people watching, Audrey and her mates would make their way directly to a club for a couple of hours of dancing on a night out, and didn't go into pubs. Nice girls certainly didn't go into the Cri alone, and seeing it at closing time once was enough for her not to want to visit the place without someone to protect her. A boyfriend that she was serious about, perhaps, if she had one.

Some of her friends met boys soon after leaving school, and quickly settled down, even though they'd only just turned eighteen. Audrey wasn't keen on getting too serious with anyone too soon, and had no plans to start a family until after she had her own salon. She had boyfriends, but none were serious. One of the more regular ones, Dave, played in a band and they dated often enough that she decided to introduce her dad to him, at one of his gigs.

That night, a Friday, she returned from work with aching feet, sat down on her mum's favourite old stool and kicked her shoes off. She shouted to Edward, who was in the hallway, combing his hair in front of the mirror. 'His band are called Joker's Wild and they're quite good.'

'Do they play anything I might know?' Edward called back.

'Yep, they'll play some old rock-and-roll songs like that "Why Do Fools Fall in Love", and they also really like the Four Seasons, you know, "Big Girls Don't Cry"?'

'Right-o, I'll get me brothel creepers on then, shall I . . .'

'Now Dad, behave yourself, you were never a Ted.'

She heard him laugh, and seconds later he came into the kitchen looking smarter than she'd seen him in a while. 'It'll make a change stepping out with you,' he told her warmly. Edward's health had been worrying Audrey. He was out every night at the pub with his mates, and she thought he wasn't going to get any better if he carried on drinking like he did. At least tonight she would be able to keep an eye on him.

After Audrey had changed and put her hair into a style that looked something like Brigitte Bardot's, she walked her dad up to the Racehorse on the corner of Wadloes Road. Having seated Edward at the bar ('I'll be happy here, love, go off with your pals,' he told her), she joined her friends close to the front of the stage and they all danced, never taking their eyes off the band who roared through a thirty-minute performance. When they finished, Audrey, gasping and sweating, made her way back through the crowd to where Edward was sitting. As she got closer to him she noticed he was looking unsteady, and just before she could grab him, her dad slid off the bar stool in a collapse. Dave came over as soon as he realized what was happening, and they sat with Edward until the ambulance arrived, reassuring him that everything was going to be OK. Edward tried to make a joke out of it, telling Dave that his band weren't that bad, really, but he was clearly in pain and near to unconsciousness.

Audrey travelled to the hospital with her dad and made sure he was settled before making her way home, alone. Dave and the rest of the band had gone on to a house party, but she really didn't feel like joining them.

The next day at the hospital Edward told Audrey that he had stomach ulcers. 'They said I've got to change my "habits",' he said as dismissively as he could. Then he snorted. 'I'm too old to change.'

'Well, if you don't you'll be dead, Dad,' Audrey said as calmly as she could, before giving her voice an edge and adding, 'So you better stop drinking for a start!'

They both knew that as much as she might nag him and he'd agree just for a quiet life, that would never happen. All she could hope for was that he'd take heed of the doctor's advice and at least cut down on drinking, smoking and eating badly. Which he did, for a while.

Over the next few months, as Edward tried to get better and pretended to drink less, Audrey and Dave split up (he had to go to London in order make a living out of playing music) and she met a new bloke called Barry Woolard. A bus conductor, he'd made her laugh and asked her out just as she reached her stop one day after work. Ex-army, he lived at home with his mother – his dad had died in the war – but was more mature than most blokes she met. He could certainly hold his beer, as she discovered after a couple of nights out together. She felt safe, happy and like she could be herself around him, though.

If she'd thought hard enough about why she liked Barry so much, she'd probably discover that it was because he was a lot like her dad.

She liked him enough that within a year they were engaged and Audrey put their name down on the council list for a house. A year after that, they were married.

It had taken a while but by the time of the wedding Audrey knew that, like her dad, Barry was more than just a drinker, he was a heavy drinker. It hadn't put her off, even after she'd returned from their honeymoon at Maud's caravan in Felixstowe with a black eye. Edward wasn't impressed when he saw that and wanted to give his new son-in-law the same, but Audrey reassured him, 'Don't worry, Dad, he came off a lot worse.'

Audrey had arranged for them to rent a small house on Milford Street, which they moved into after their honeymoon in Felixstowe. 'I like it here, it's close to the pub and that's no bad thing,' she'd told her Aunty Maud on her first visit.

While they'd argue sometimes before they were married, it seemed as if having the ring on her finger made Barry bolder about being physical with Audrey. Not that their arguments were strictly one-sided, and they still had a giggle together most of the time. Barry had never learnt to drive and Audrey teased him that it was a 'good job you don't drive, 'cos you'd never know where to find the car. You struggle to find your bike, as it is.' Which wasn't that funny, since Barry's bike wasn't his, but belonged to the GPO and every time he misplaced it they stopped money from his wages for a replacement.

He'd started working for the Post Office the year before they were married because the pay was better than on the buses, and they were both keen to start a family. That wasn't to prove easy, though. 'We could have had a lot more fun before we married if we'd known about your blocked tubes!' Barry half-joked following a hospital visit a year after they'd married. Audrey said nothing, feeling too disappointed to speak, afraid that she'd cry if she did. As it turned out, she would become pregnant soon enough.

The first year of their marriage was also complicated because Edward moved into their home with them. Audrey had to look after him because his health had worsened. He developed lung cancer and was unable to care for himself. That very dark cloud had a thin silver lining, though, in that the council gave them a two-bedroomed flat on Wadloes Road, so at least they had more space.

It was something of a relief for Audrey to get to work these days. She had discovered that she was pretty good at organizing people and running things. She understood, without being taught, how to plan ahead and make sure everything ran smoothly. She wasn't afraid of upsetting people if they deserved it (as she saw it), and was promoted to positions of responsibility at the salon despite having had a couple of run-ins with suppliers.

She was often disappointed when she had to close Raymond's at the time that the boss told her to. Work allowed her to occupy her mind with something other than worry for Edward, or about Barry's drinking. So she took on as many extra jobs doing people's hair at their home in the evenings as she could. Audrey saved the extra money she made, and by 1968 she was able to buy her own hairdressers.

Despite having had the vague but determined plan to open her own salon, Audrey hadn't done any real planning for it, but as is often the way in life, she happened on an opportunity that she took eagerly and almost without thinking. She'd gone to the launderette on Newmarket Road one morning and noticed that the shop next door for was for sale. She went home and told Barry and her dad about it, and they pooled their finances, determined that she should become her own boss. Audrey refused the money Aunty Maud offered her, though. She'd only recently left her job as a bedder, and it 'don't seem right taking her money now she's not quite right in the head, and anyway she taught me to stand on me own two feet,' she told Barry, who wasn't as keen on refusing the money.

The next day, she and Barry went back to the shop and asked to speak to the owner of the laundrette, who also owned the place next door, and the deal was done there and then. Just as Maud had predicted, Audrey's name was soon up above the shop at 125 Newmarket Road, along with 'Hair Stylist Tel. 54871'.

Inevitably, as Edward's illness worsened, she knew that she would have to nurse him at home as he became increasingly incapable of doing much for himself. Nine months after putting up the sign with her name on it, Edward was still insistent that Audrey go to work, that he'd be fine at home, alone. But soon she started to get desperate phone calls from him.

At first when he called, or tried to, her two staff thought it was a dirty phone call because nobody spoke, and all they could hear was heavy breathing. They put the receiver down, but it rang again and they heard the same breathing, so it was put down again. On the third ring, Audrey somehow knew that it was her dad, and that he needed help. She ran out of the salon to catch a bus home, where she found him collapsed on the floor in the hallway with the telephone in his hand. She called the doctor who came round with an injection of morphine, after which Edward slept. The next day Edward insisted that she go to work, so she did. Three days later the same thing happened, and again a few times after that. It became too

much for her to run the salon and care for Edward, so Audrey
sold the business barely twelve months after she'd opened it.

Edward died within weeks of Audrey taking on his care
full time. While she grieved for him she was dealt another
terrible blow. Only weeks after Edward's funeral she and Barry
returned to the Newmarket Road cemetery to say goodbye to
her Aunty Maud. After giving up work as a bedder, Maud had
drifted into a strange kind of life, spending almost as much
time in the Fulbourn psychiatric ward as she did at home.
Audrey tried to see her as much as she could, but with work,
her dad and Maud's illness (she'd stare vacantly at Audrey
when she visited in Fulbourn, barely able to speak), somehow
they didn't see one another for weeks on end. It was an
enormous shock though when Audrey heard that Maud had
died at home, alone, after taking too many sleeping pills. The
coroner ruled her death an open verdict because the number of
pills that she'd taken was not excessive, and she may have taken
too many while her mind was 'unbalanced', they said. Maud
lay undiscovered for three days, which really upset Audrey.
When she heard that, she cried non-stop for a day and a half.

There were only a few people at Maud's funeral, among
them bedders who'd worked with her, including Bertha Mizen,
in the cold chapel. The size of the congregation for Maud
was considerably smaller than it had been at Edward's funeral.
Her dad had known so many people, mostly from the various
public houses that he patronized in his forty years of drinking.
Barry had known some of the mourners at Edward's wake
(which was held at the Racehorse, naturally). 'Auds love,' he'd
told her late into the evening as the singing, drinking and
toasting of Edward carried on some hours after they'd left the
cemetery, 'there mush be all the landlords and drinkers of
Newmarket Road in 'ere. What a man your old dad was. I loved

him . . .' Audrey had left then, hoping to not have to go to another funeral for a while, but here she was only weeks later.

Standing in the car park as a light drizzle wet her hair, Audrey approached Bertha and told her, 'You can come back to mine if you like, Mrs Mizen, I can make some sandwiches.'

'No, you're alright, Audrey, I just wanted to pay my respects. I'd known her since she was a little 'un, and it weren't all that long ago, neither. Dear little thing she was. And only forty-nine when she passed. Tsk.'

'She spoke highly of you, Mrs Mizen. She liked you a lot.' The women looked consolingly at one another. 'Yes, she was a dear thing she was, my Aunty Maud.' In her head she could hear her mum telling her, 'No point in crying, Audrey,' so she choked back the tears. 'Like a mum to me, after my mum died,' Audrey told Bertha.

'She would have liked to hear you say that, I'm sure.' Bertha touched Audrey's arm gently. 'She had such a bad start in life, no mum and just her nan. And to think her life ended just like her mum's did.'

'Yes, Maud told me her mum had been in Fulbourn,' Audrey said.

'Yes,' Bertha was warming to the tale, Audrey could see. 'Her mum had a breakdown after her husband's ship sank. They gave her electric shock treatment I heard, but I think that made her worse. She killed herself there, 'pparently. And then poor Maud with Hugh, tsk. Old Mrs Ingram, she was a bit loopy, never let Hugh out of the house when he was a boy, kept him locked in his room they say. I was worried when Maud went to live there, I have to tell you. Poor Maud.'

'Yes,' Audrey agreed sadly. 'I didn't go and see her as much as I should have. I know I should of, but what with my dad being ill as well, it was hard to get out of our house. I never knew how unhappy she really was . . .'

'Don't give yourself a hard time, she wouldn't want that.' Bertha held out a pink handkerchief to Audrey, who shook her head and wiped her eyes with her fingertips. 'I've got to go,' the older woman continued, 'but do pop in and see me at the college for a cuppa and a chat any time, love. I remember you as a young 'un coming in with Maud on a Saturday morning.' Bertha smiled, patted Audrey's arm again and turned to walk home. As Barry drove the car slowly past her on their way out, Audrey wound down the window and called out, 'Thank you, Mrs Mizen, and I'll come and see you soon for a cuppa.'

As much to keep herself busy as for the money, Audrey returned to hairdressing, but couldn't bring herself to work for anyone else, so she had people come to her new home in Thorleye Road where she set up a 'salon' in the front room. She had regular customers and they recommended her to friends, and so she worked most days of the week. She kept up a steady stream of customers, even after becoming pregnant for the first time, in 1971 – which was a very pleasant surprise, as she kept telling everyone.

She had to carry on working because Barry was on strike at the GPO, and the industrial action lasted several weeks. Barry didn't mind that scores of women were descending on his home during the day; he was pleased that they were paying and told Audrey to stop doing favours for friends and start charging them too, since now more than ever they needed her to contribute to the housekeeping. Which was a bit of a cheek, since she always did.

Sometimes she thought she was stupid for obediently handing over all of her income to Barry, emptying her purse to let him hand back just enough to do the food shopping. The failure of the salon, and the repayment of the loan she'd taken in order to get it, meant that Barry had taken full control of the family finances. He paid the rent and bills, making sure that he always had enough for him to go out and have a pint or several, of course. Even during the strike she'd seen him crawl home from the Drill Hall, where they'd had all they could eat (her) and drink (him) for just £5. It was because of his drinking that the landlords changed that particular Friday night policy sharpish, she was sure.

They survived the strike, and after it was over Audrey continued to work from home as her belly grew bigger. But she still ended up with the same amount of 'spending money', regardless of how much she'd taken from her customers. Barry wanted to make sure that she didn't have any extra for herself.

'What are you going to spend it on anyway?' he sneered at her. 'It's not like you're going to go out, is it?'

Actually, Audrey longed to be able to put on a nice outfit and go out with her old friends or the neighbours, maybe to see a film or just for a catch-up drink. But Barry forbade it.

'You are not going anywhere unless I'm there with you,' he insisted whenever she asked if she could have a few new pence extra for a night out.

Maybe it was the pregnancy, or the loss of her dad and Maud, but Audrey no longer seemed to have the fight in her that she had had in the early days of their marriage. Although there was one occasion, when she was heavily pregnant but found it in herself to go against his wishes in the strongest way she could think of.

She had told Barry she was going out, to the pictures with a friend, and he sat on the bed watching her get ready. 'What do you think you look like? It's embarrassing the way you look; you're fat and ugly, look at you,' he insulted her as she applied her make-up.

It was far from true and he knew it. He was worried that she was going to meet somebody else if she went out without him, even while heavily pregnant. When Audrey ignored him, Barry snapped.

'You're not going out,' he told her heatedly.

She laughed at him. 'You can't stop me, Barry.'

'We'll fucking see about that,' he shouted, and stormed out of the bedroom, slamming the door after him. Audrey heard the lock click.

'Don't you dare!' she screamed and threw a lipstick at the door.

'You're not fuckin' going nowhere,' Barry yelled through the locked door at her, and stomped down the stairs.

Audrey didn't have to think for long about what to do, and she finished getting ready. Then she opened the bedroom window as wide as it would go and squeezed through it, feet first. The garage roof was only a six-foot drop below, so she clung to the sill and pushed gently away from the wall to land with bent knees on the flat roof. From there she climbed down onto the bins and was away before Barry knew anything about it.

She knew what would be waiting for her when she returned, that by then Barry would have had several pints, which meant that he might – even in her condition – take a swing at her. But she was not going to let him rule her life, she told herself that night, and so she marched through the back door and into the sitting room where he lay sprawled on the couch. He was amazed to see her as he hadn't realized she'd been out.

She launched into him, shouting that if he thought she'd be at his bloody beck and call and only do what he wanted her to, he'd better be ready for a fight, because she wasn't going to take it.

Barry was clearly mystified. 'No other bloody woman disobeys their old man! Why do you?'

She pushed him back onto the couch as he tried to get up

and confront her. ''Cos I ain't no other bloody woman, that's bloody why! I ain't having no man tell me what to do!'

For the next couple of weeks they barely spoke to each other, and on Fridays Barry refused to give her any money at all, telling her to get the shopping out of what she earned if she was so bloody independent. Which was why, on a Friday evening three weeks later, almost at full term, Audrey sat in the snug of a pub and sighed. She was with two old friends (they'd insisted she join them and they'd pay for a couple of rounds of drinks), and explaining that this would be the last evening out that she'd have with them for a while. She'd decided it was best to go along with what he wanted her to do for a while.

'It's easier this way,' she told them, adding unnecessarily, 'after all I am pregnant. What can I do? He's insecure. So it's best that I just go out with him.'

The following night, Audrey and Barry went to the Drill Hall Post Office social club, where at least she could chat with the other wives while Barry and his mates propped up the bar.

Following the birth of Nadine, which was surprisingly easy and quick, Audrey and Barry got along well. She didn't go out without him, but then they didn't go out much at all, since they couldn't afford to. Instead they'd sit in front of the telly (rented for £2 a week), barely talking and occasionally laughing at the same jokes or films they watched. The weeks that Barry had been on strike had badly affected them and they needed to start trying to save some money in case he had to come out again, Barry warned. For nine months after the birth, Audrey did hairdressing in their front room, tended the baby, and put a bit away whenever she could (without telling Barry). Then she became pregnant again.

ROSE

Rose was in her early forties and had been a bedder for more than fifteen years when two tragic accidents led to her leaving the college. After a successful operation on her varicose veins, and with the introduction into the college of various labour-saving devices (one of which was as simple as a cart on wheels used to carry the dirty linen to the laundry), Rose moved back to working on two staircases (and cycling to work again), although she kept her original B staircase and the fellows on it. It was the middle of the 1960s, and while Cambridge had seen the Beatles and Rolling Stones perform at the Regal cinema, various boutiques open up selling new women's fashions and the old Dorothy dancehall evolve into the Dorothy nightclub, life in college went on much as it always had. Except that there were an increasing number of incidents of students taking drugs and acting strangely.

On more than one occasion Rose had entered a student bedroom early in the morning and found the detritus of the previous night's activities. Where once there had been empty or half-empty bottles of alcohol left lying around, now there were little piles of tobacco, small medicinal bottles with lysergic acid diethylamide written on the label, and loose, small blue pills on side tables. One morning she found a bottle of pills that was exactly the same as the diazepam her doctor had recently prescribed for her nerves in the rooms of a nice young boy who didn't seem nervous at all, to her. When she asked him about

them – 'Mr Alexander, are those pills for your nerves, then?'
he seemed confused about what she meant, until she said,
'Dies-a-pam?'

'Oh,' a smirk of realization spread across his face, 'my
mother's little helpers!'

'What?' Rose was shocked. 'Has your mum been for a visit
then? She must have been scandalized seeing the state of your
rooms last night!'

Alexander laughed so hard that he couldn't answer, and
annoyed at his rudeness Rose turned and left the room.

She knew that all manner of drugs were being taken by
young people, including her son Clark, who had stolen some
of her tablets from the bedside table. Still, she thought, it
might do Clark the sort of good it did for her if they calm him
down a bit, maybe. But when she also found Dexamyl tablets
in his trouser pockets that were not in a bottle, she thought
that he must be mixing them all up and that it couldn't do him
much good. Not that she saw a lot of Clark at the time.

Now aged nineteen he had recently begun working on a
vegetable stall in the market place and seemed to really enjoy
it, even if he did have to be up and at work at the crack of
dawn. Sometimes he was up and out before she was. Plenty
of nights he'd stayed over at his boss's place (he said) so he
wouldn't be late for work. The stall must have been successful,
thought Rose, because they paid Clark enough that he had
managed to buy himself a second-hand, four-year-old Mini.
He also paid Rose half a quid a week for his keep and didn't
eat much at all.

On weekends, Clark would take three or four mates in
his Mini to nightclubs in other cities, sometimes to London,
other times to Norwich, Ipswich or even as far as Leicester or
Nottingham. The drive took hours but the dancing and the
new scene was always worth it, he told Rose. He was kept

awake by the amphetamine tablets which, he said, was the reason for having them. 'You wouldn't want me to fall asleep at the wheel and crash, would you, Mum?' he asked reasonably.

No, she'd agreed, maybe it's best that he keep taking them if they were legal.

'They are, Mum, don't worry,' he'd told her. But while they were legal, she knew they usually required a prescription before a person could get them. Clark didn't have prescriptions as far as she was aware.

In fact, she learned later, his pills came from a friend who worked in a chemist's shop. He was stealing them for Clark to sell, and they were splitting the proceeds. The income from the sale of the pills meant that Clark could afford new clothes, petrol and the car. The shop was run by an ancient pharmacist who trusted Clark's pal to do the stock taking, so nothing was missed. The arrangement worked perfectly for several months. Clark was so confident about the arrangement that on a Friday he'd drop by the chemist's back door during his dinner break to collect the weekend stash. Everything went perfectly until one fateful Friday in November 1965, when Clark picked up a bag of pills and told his friend that after the Dorothy club that night they were heading north, about thirty miles, to an all-night party 'at some rich bloke's place'.

Clark drove his friend and two girls that they'd invited along to the house, arriving just before 1 a.m. having got lost in a slowly falling fog. While there, Clark made a good few quid selling blues, purple hearts and black bombers to a bunch of farmers' sons and village boys who were not as smart as Clark had hoped. Still, they paid top price for his pills. The party wasn't great though, and men outnumbered women so much that Clark's female guests felt uncomfortable and asked to leave after only a couple of hours.

The girls climbed into the back seats with the men in the

front, and they set off just before 3.15. The fog had fallen heavily by that time, although there were brief spots of totally clear road so that it seemed as if the little Mini was an aircraft travelling through clouds. One minute its front lights were illuminating the tops of hedges and trees along the roadside for several feet ahead, and then a blank grey wall would appear and swallow them, rendering the lights little more use than a candle in a gale. Clark was a confident driver at the best of times, but after a few pills he was over-confident. There hadn't been enough good music at the party for him to dance and work any of the amphetamines out of his body, and so he drove too fast into those banks of fog, unaware and unafraid of whatever might be hidden in them.

The police told Rose that he hadn't felt a thing. He hadn't seen the lorry that he drove into the side of and which peeled the roof of the Mini backwards like the lid of a sardine can. Because he hadn't seen the lorry, he couldn't have felt fear as death approached, she thought. That was some consolation, as was the fact that while the two boys in the front had died instantly, the two girls in the back had escaped with their lives. They would be scarred physically and emotionally by the accident, but at least their mothers got to see, hold and talk with them again. Their mothers got to see their child grow up, have children and families. Clark would never do any of that. At his funeral Rose reminded herself that she always said he'd never make it to a ripe old age, that he was too full of life and his body couldn't last with all that energy he had. But it didn't make her feel any better.

As the vicar went on about 'we leave this world as we entered it', she couldn't help but remember Clark's innocent expression when he was telling her that the pills would prevent a car crash. Now she was certain that they had been the reason that she had to bury her eldest child when he was not even twenty years old.

That early winter was a terrible time for Rose, and the week after Clark's death she learned from another bedder that one of her boys at college had gone missing. Phil, an engineering student who liked motorbikes and beer in almost equal measure, hadn't been seen all week, and his bed hadn't been slept in.

Desperate to not mope around at home following Clark's funeral, Rose returned to work the following week, and was told that she couldn't do Phil's room. Initially she thought he had left college because someone had reported him for having a motorbike in his room. Rose didn't mind that he used to have newspaper on the floor with all his bits of motorbike on them, even though she knew it was breaking college rules to do so (he shouldn't have a motorbike within thirty miles of the place, so having one, albeit in pieces, in his room was very wrong). She was saddened if that had been the case, because she would have liked to have said goodbye to him. She and Phil got on well, and always had a good chat in the mornings. He'd told her that he was not totally happy at Cambridge and she knew he drank too much on weekends, and had mentioned as much to the porter who let Phil's director of studies know. In recent weeks, Phil didn't seem to have been drinking as much, or at least Rose wasn't taking so many empty bottles back to the off-licence from his room. Still, she thought, if he's left, maybe he'll send me a card to say goodbye.

However, when later that day Rose was asked to go to the housekeeper's office and found a policewoman waiting for her, she had the same sinking feeling she'd felt when a policeman and woman had knocked at her door early that horrible Saturday morning two weeks earlier.

'Have a seat, Rose,' the housekeeper said to her. 'The WPC wanted to talk to you about Phil on your staircase, you knew him quite well, didn't you?'

'What do you mean "knew"? We have a chat and a laugh most mornings. What's happened, he's not in any trouble is he?' Rose looked anxiously at the WPC.

'Rose, did you think Phil was very unhappy here?' asked the WPC.

'What? No, I mean, a bit, but nothing terribly bad, why?'

The policewoman explained that they'd found Phil's body that morning. 'It seems the boy had been walking over Jesus Green on the previous Saturday night,' she explained, 'and must have wanted to go to the toilet. Rather than going behind a tree or bush, though, we think he went to the footbridge by the cricket pavilion and fell into the water. His body was washed down river and we found him today. His flies were undone.'

The news was too much for Rose and she broke down and cried hard. She wasn't just crying for Phil, of course, but also for Clark and his friend, and all the boys that she'd known at the college who had never grown up, the ones who committed suicide or met with terrible accidents. She covered her face with her hands, leant forwards onto the housekeeper's desk and sobbed until she was dry.

Rose left without doing any work that day, and never returned.

The college forwarded a letter to her a week later, from Phil's mother. In it she thanked Rose for looking after him. But I bloody didn't, did I? Rose thought to herself, not really. I wasn't there that week, was I?

Inside the letter was a thimble that had been found in Phil's room and sent to Rose as a keepsake. She recalled that he was always sewing buttons on shirts, not just his own, but those of other students on his staircase who needed it doing, too. As tears came to her eyes, Rose again determined that she wouldn't go back to her staircase. There were now too many bad memories for her there. Not just of Phil but also of Clark. His chemist shop pal's mother also worked at the college, and seeing her reminded Rose of the accident. It was too hard to take, so she sent in her notice by letter.

Less than a month later, Rose was on her bike at 6 a.m. in a freezing fog that left icicles in her hair, riding in tandem with a couple of old friends named Doll Gentle and Plummy Smith, to start as a bedder at the college where they worked. Aware that Rose was out of work, the women had spoken to their housekeeper, Mrs Moyer, about taking her on to work with them. After a very brief meeting in the housekeeper's office, Rose was hired and began work a couple of weeks before Christmas 1965. Her work was pretty much the same as it had been at her previous college, and because they all looked the same, sometimes she forgot where she was and thought she was back on staircase B, and might see Phil at any time.

But meeting new people proved to be reviving for her. She had one fellow named Jocelyn who she'd always describe as being 'kindness itself, and wonderful to look after', as well as twelve undergraduates who shared a gyp room between them, which was in a constant state of chaos and mess. It didn't take her long to find the chapel, designed by Christopher Wren, which she loved to sit in for a bit of peace and quiet at the end of her shift. While there she'd think about Clark and what might have been for a while, until the nagging worries about what she was going to do when Maurice left home took over.

The bitter winter of early 1966, although not quite as bad as it had been in 1962, added to Rose's troubles. Large amounts of snow prevented her from cycling every day, and the buses wouldn't run, so often she'd walk and push her bike to work, hoping that by the time she finished the roads would be clear enough to cycle home.

Rose felt more tired than she'd ever done before. At first she put it down to the increased workload – carrying coal to make up seven or eight fires a day was exhausting – but when she started to get pains in her lower abdomen, she decided that it was time to see a doctor. He sent her straight to Addenbrooke's, who admitted her for an emergency hysterectomy. She had enough time to telephone Maurice at his workplace, a garage on Newmarket Road and he told her friend Ann that evening. She went straight to visit Rose.

It was usual practice in those days for women to be advised to take three months off from work following such an operation. The hospital had suggested that Rose go to a convalescent home in Hunstanton to recover, but she had refused, not wanting to leave Maurice on his own. Not that she felt as if she'd be any use to anyone anywhere at present, as Rose explained to Ann. 'They said I won't be able to pick a cup and saucer up, and they were right, Ann. I can't do nothing. They've cut me up and I've got clips and God knows what in there,' she pointed to her stomach. Sighing, Rose reached for her cigarettes and lit up.

'I'm a bit stressed, an' all, 'cos I won't be at work at the end of term and so I won't get my usual end of term tips, will I?' At the end of every term the money Rose received in tips went towards paying her bills or she would put some away for Maurice. 'You know they've put the rent up when I started getting family allowance for Maurice, don't you?' Rose went on. 'So I took the ten bob from the family allowance straight down to the rent office when it arrived, and said, "There you go!"'

Rose relied on those tips more than she liked to admit. The students would leave it on the coffee table under something like a pot, a cup or a book. Sometimes Rose would be given a little ornament or something similar, but she preferred to get the cash. 'How about if I ask Doll or Plummy to get them for you?' suggested Ann.

'No, don't worry, if they've taken on my work then they deserve the tips themselves.'

Ann changed the subject. 'Fred said I can get a job at the colleges, Rose, if I want to, now the kids are older.'

'Well, I should think so an' all. It's a good job, and they'll look after you too. There's a pension, trips out and the perks. You'll have to tell them you won't be able to work on the conferences in the summer, though,' Rose remembered. 'You know, in the school holidays.'

'Oh right, yes,' Ann said brightly.

'Yeah,' Rose shifted slightly in her bed, 'I'll have a word soon as I get on me feet again, if you want? Or I'll get Dolly to ask around. Don't worry, we'll find you something.'

'Thanks,' said Ann with feeling.

Rose raised a smile, shook her cigarette packet and asked, 'Ann, love, do me a favour and bring me some more fags tomorrow would you?'

JOYCE

Joyce and Ken's marriage wasn't the stuff of romance novels or soppy movies. They were both happy to have carried on as they were before the 'accident' that prompted the ceremony. Ken was away at sea as much as ever, and sent wages back for his new wife. Joyce continued to work as a cleaner until she became too big with their first son, and then she stopped until baby Trevor (named after the brother she sadly lost) was six months old and her mother could care for him – Celia and she slotted their cleaning work in to suit each other's schedule. Ken was home on extended leave only four times in the first couple of years because he was stationed in the Middle East, and two weeks' leave didn't really give him enough time to get home quickly and cheaply. Flying was out of the question, which meant taking a ship or trains, boats and buses, and at least four days out of his precious fourteen of freedom from duty. He'd write, but Ken's letters were usually prosaic, regular affairs, never written with any kind of romance or even much love, it seemed to Joyce. Still, life went on pretty much as usual for her and the baby, and they'd moved in with Celia and Charles because it was cheap and convenient, plus his grandparents loved Trevor.

When Ken did make it home they'd have a couple of days of 'smooching' as Joyce put it, and then he would be out most nights at the pub, and in no time it seemed he was gone again.

When Trevor was two years old Joyce was pregnant again, and nine months later Trevor had a little brother, named Kevin.

With the arrival of a second child came the offer of a two-bedroom council house which was barely a year old. It was sited at the edge of a new development in the process of being built in the north-west area of the town, called King's Hedges. Kevin was ten months when they moved into the new house, and a few months later Ken arrived for a surprise fortnight leave.

As usual he had arrived home unannounced, having not written to tell her he was on his way, nor left a message anywhere that had a telephone where they knew her. He was his usual self, she thought, for the first week of his leave, playing football with Trevor in the fields out back of the house – although for no more than fifteen minutes at a time – and she and he went to the pictures to see a Western film called *Apache Rifles*. 'This is good, innit?' he said with eyes widening as Linda Lawson walked across the screen. 'Cor yeah,' she agreed, as her favourite cowboy Audie Murphy rode up to the blonde actress on screen.

All was well until one night after tea when, with the boys in bed, Ken turned to her and said, 'Oh by the way, I shall be going tomorrow and I shan't be coming back.'

'Pardon?'

'I'm leaving ya.'

Just like that.

Bang.

The next thing Joyce knew she was standing in a field. She'd walked out in a daze and didn't know where she was going, but after a good long walk, she came to in a field with the thought, I've left the kids with him!

She ran home.

Ken nodded at her as she entered the back door and asked, 'You alright?'

'What do you think? I'm going to bed.'

He nodded again. 'OK, I'll be up there in a minute.'

Joyce started. 'You don't think I'm sleeping with you, do you?'

She made her way upstairs to Trevor's room, gently moved him across the bed and lay down next to him, fully clothed.

The next morning, the memory of which would never leave her, Joyce stood at the door as Ken was about to walk off down the road with his kit bag slung over his shoulder. He looked her in the eye and told her that he didn't love them, they were nothing more than pieces of driftwood on the beach to him. With anger flaring, she said, 'Right, you can tell that boy why you're leaving,' and pointed at Trevor, who was trying to push past her to get to his father.

'He won't understand,' Ken said dismissively.

'Oh yes, he will, you tell him why you're leaving. He'll want two sides to the story, so you give him your side.'

With a sigh, Ken bent down and spoke directly to his four-and-a-half-year-old son. Then he straightened up, turned and walked off.

As he moved away, Joyce let Trevor out and he ran after Ken, crying, 'Daddy, Daddy, come back . . .'

They heard nothing from him ever again. There were no birthday or Christmas cards, nothing. When he was older, Trevor took to keeping a cricket bat behind the front door and said that he'd use it on his dad if he ever turned up again. When Kevin asked why his dad didn't live with them – he was about four or five years old at the time – Trevor said, 'I'll tell you why, but I don't want to hear about him ever again.' He told Kevin that, 'Dad said he didn't have any love for us any more and he was going away.'

Ken's parents, the boys' grandparents, also cut off all contact and sent no cards at birthdays or Christmas. Despite the fact that they lived barely thirty miles away in the Fen town of March, they chose to never see their grandsons again. Joyce would have been happy for the boys to visit and even stay over with Ken's mum and dad, but they never as much as wrote a letter saying how sorry they were about everything. It was as if she and their grandsons had ceased to exist.

It was left up to Joyce to initiate divorce proceedings, which she did nine months after he'd left them, citing desertion as the reason. She had heard that Ken had gone off to live with another woman, but she didn't know for sure if that was so, and didn't really care either way. When the divorce was granted she was awarded £5 a week maintenance money from Ken. It was automatically taken from his wages and sent to Joyce as a postal order, which she'd put into her Post Office account. Out of that she'd give a pound each to the boys.

Being a single mother of two young boys is not easy, and Joyce knew that she'd need all of her strength and attention for her sons if they were not to grow up getting into trouble all the time. She was hugely thankful that her own father took it upon himself to spend as many weekends with them as he could, and instilled in them both a respect and interest in the military which resulted in them joining the scouts and then, when old enough, the army cadets.

They were amazingly well behaved at school and when playing out in the neighbourhood. Trevor and Kevin always showed respect for their mother, tried to help out at home as much as they could and loved their grandparents – when Celia was taken so ill that she couldn't work and Joyce took on her cleaning work as well as her own, the boys would go to Celia's house and cheer her up. When Celia was too ill to look after the boys, Joyce took them with her to the houses that she cleaned. At one house they played with the sons of her boss, who were the same age, so she could get on with her work without interruption.

Even when they entered their teenage years, Trevor and Kevin gave Joyce no cause for concern, and she never had the mortifying sight of policemen bringing either of them home. She'd seen so many of their neighbours' sons being helped out of the light-blue-and-white Austin panda cars by policemen on Saturday evenings, that she fully expected her boys to appear in the back of one, too. But they were never sent home from school, kept behind as punishment for cheek or unruly behaviour, and she never had a visit from the truant officer. She might not have been lucky in love, Joyce often thought to herself, but she was blessed with her boys.

Both of them understood from an early age that because they didn't have a dad, then their mother had to work and couldn't afford to buy them everything that their friends had. Still, when they were little Joyce would save up some money in order that once a month they'd be treated to a bit of dinner at the Civic Restaurant then to the Regal cinema for a film, before going back to the Civic for some tea. She'd offer them comics or sweets each weekend and they'd usually go for the comics. Despite the cleaning work and Ken's small allowance, Joyce had to go on the social.

There were never any new 'boyfriends' in her life – 'I've had enough of 'em,' she'd say whenever friends asked if she didn't miss having someone to warm her feet on in the winter months. 'A hot-water bottle's a lot less bother!'

One expense Joyce always did her best to be able to afford was an annual holiday. Depending on how much she'd been able to save, she would book one or two weeks at Butlin's in Skegness or Bognor Regis with her friends, who happened to also be mums to her boys' pals. There'd be three mums and five or six boys in two or three chalets (the dads having to stay at home and work), with a mum taking it in turns every night to cook the evening meal for everyone. The mums would leave the oldest two boys in charge and go dancing. Joyce accepted invitations from blokes to dance if she'd seen that they were any good, but she'd just as often stick with her pals. On one holiday in the late 1960s, Joyce came second in a glamorous mum contest in Bognor. She looked like Princess Margaret in her two-piece suit, matching hat and handbag, a string of pearls round her neck. Blimey, she thought, I'm nearly forty and winning a beauty contest! Plenty of blokes wanted to dance with her that night, but she stayed seated, looking at her trophy, drinking Babycham.

Celia passed away when the boys were in secondary school. She ended her days in a care home not far from Joyce, who used to visit every Saturday (her sons were both in the army at the time, stationed overseas). It was a quiet end, not unexpected and she didn't suffer. For that, Joyce was grateful. Not long after, and with no need to be home for the boys' sake at lunchtime, Joyce went back into the college as a bedder. This time, though, she wasn't on a students and fellows' staircase, but instead went to work at the master's lodge. She'd heard that one of the two bedders who worked there were leaving, and despite it being almost twenty-five years after Joyce had first done the job, the same housekeeper at the college was still in place. Mrs Atkins remembered Joyce as a discreet, hard worker, so the job was hers as soon as she applied for it.

The work was different and required less carrying (no coal fires on in the bedrooms to set and clean), only one set of stairs to the first floor, far fewer bedrooms and no kitchen work at all. There was a fairly new vacuum cleaner that wasn't too heavy and it had an attachment for doing stairs, which were wooden and so didn't require washing down.

The master and his wife were lovely and treated her as if she was one of the family rather than a bedder. They called her by her first name and insisted that she did likewise to them both. The master would defer to Joyce's judgement on what tie to wear if his wife was not available for consultation, and his wife would ask after Joyce's family with genuine interest. The couple were in their early sixties and, although the wife had recently retired, that was because she wanted to assist with as many duties of the master as she was able to, and both seemed to have boundless reserves of energy. The lodge was usually set for parties, events and various gatherings on most weekends, some of which Joyce attended and helped carry trays around to guests, to earn a little extra money. They had four grown-up children, so the bedrooms in the lodge were either empty or occupied for a few nights by visiting guests – some of them VIPs.

One of their most important VIP guests was Prince Philip, who first visited when his eldest son was a student, and had struck up a friendship with the master of the college. Joyce soon discovered that the Duke of Edinburgh had a great sense of humour and he liked to joke with her and other staff at the lodge. They got on so well with the duke that it became expected for them to play tricks on him during visits. Joyce's favourite became the apple pie bed – with Mrs Atkins's encouragement and assistance, they'd make his bed up with a tightly shortened sheet so that he could only get halfway into the bed, and under the bottom sheet she'd lay a few apples and a couple of books, making lumps and bumps.

The morning after the first time they did it, Prince Philip

marched into the kitchen before breakfast, wagged a finger at Joyce and the housekeeper, and smiling broadly called them 'naughty little girls', and made them 'promise' not to do it again. Naturally, the next time he was an overnight visitor the bed was again made up with apples. Joyce loved to see the master and duke all dressed up and parading their way to the Senate House or Guildhall for ceremonies. She felt proud to have been a small part of the ceremony, because she'd made sure the master's tie was straight.

The experience of working at the master's lodge was one of the happiest of her life. She got to know the master's children and their families when they visited for Christmas, which was always her favourite time of year. The tree at the lodge was huge and always beautifully dressed. On Christmas Eve she'd set a big fire in the main reception area and enjoy a glass of wine and mince pies with the master, staff and various fellows and choice students, as the college choir sang carols on the lawn (unless it was too wet or cold, when they'd sing in the entrance hall). She was encouraged to bring her sons to the lodge whenever it was convenient, and both Trevor and Kevin loved to go if they could.

Joyce was saddened that she had to take time off during the summer when the lodge was empty. The master and his wife often travelled in the summer break, and unless there was a special conference set to be hosted at the college and the lodge occupied by VIP speakers, she had nothing to do for at least six weeks. She'd discovered that some of the bedders at different colleges had begun to organize travel and accommodation in Kent in the summer weeks, in order to pick hops, and she was asked along more than once. Because her job was considered among the best of them for bedders, Joyce quickly made a lot of new friends at the college, all of them eager to hear stories about the master and his VIPs. They were all just as eager to be put in the frame for any job that might come up, Joyce understood that, and they knew a word from her to the housekeeper and master could get them in.

Life in the college had changed a lot since Joyce last worked there, she realized, and much of what she heard from the bedders made her glad that she was at the lodge and not on a staircase. For a start there were now female students at the college and in rooms that were on the same staircase as the boys, too. More than one bedder told Joyce about arriving at work and finding a girl in a boy's room and vice versa. One woman told her that she was always finding condoms lying about in the rooms of girls. 'The boys always hide them, but the girls have no shame,' she'd said indignantly. The same bedder was adamant that at least one of the fellows in residence had a different female student in his room every night. 'He's a right Errol Flynn, he is,' she'd said almost admiringly, although naturally she disapproved.

The morning after the May Ball of 1979, Joyce was in the master's bedroom making the bed when she looked out of the window to the great spreading chestnut tree below, and was amazed to see what looked like a pile of bodies under it. After opening the window and leaning out to get a better view, she realized that there were three women, all of them in various states of undress, fast asleep on the grass. She was about to go down to see if they were alright when she spotted the porter and two of the proctor's men half-running across the lawn towards them, carrying blankets. She watched as the men lay the blankets over the women while trying to keep their heads turned away so as not to see anything they shouldn't (they knew people were watching them, she thought).

The girls were students who'd drunk too much at the ball, decided to go paddling in Jesus Ditch and left most of their clothes on Jesus Green. The door to their staircase was locked when they got back, so they'd all sat under the tree to wait for the morning, fell asleep and even the sun coming up hadn't woken them. Lucky it was so warm, Joyce thought. She'd heard of boys getting drunk and falling asleep on the common, unable to find their way back to their college, who then died of cold and exposure.

The same morning, Joyce learned later from a friend at another college that an Austin 1100 car had been discovered in one of the courts, where no cars were allowed (and it seemed impossible to drive into). Apparently a lord's son had organized the prank, but he was so well liked that no one told him off. The car had to be taken apart in order to get it out. It wasn't exactly a repeat of what happened in 1958 when the university woke up one June morning to find a complete Austin 7 car on the roof of the Senate House, but it was definitely a reminder of how smart the boys could be when they put their minds to it.

Joyce heard about how one student proved very smart, and forgiving, during her time at the master's lodge. The master's wife told her how a bedder at the college had been caught trying to spend a stolen pound note at a shop in town, but the student from whom she'd taken it didn't want her to be prosecuted. Talking to other bedders about it later, Joyce was told that the woman in question 'was my neighbour, and I felt awful for her – she's alright, but in a rough marriage. She's had loads of jobs and it's no wonder, I reckon. The boy planted a pound note and 'cos she smoked she got copped in Woolworths on the cigarette counter as she handed it over. She had done it before – not every day, not every week, but he noticed money going missing, so he marked the pound note. She was followed to the shop and stopped before she handed it over. She was always borrowing money, or trying to from us, an' all.' The other bedders agreed with nods and 'me too', so the tale teller continued. 'She came round and told me when I got home. They must have taken her to the police station – she said, "I got caught, Edna." I don't think the boy wanted her to go, but 'course she was sacked. Anyway, they cover things like that up, the colleges.'

In 1981 Joyce's father died. At the time Kevin was stationed at the Old Park Barracks in Dover, serving in the Army Junior Leaders' Regiment. He was given compassionate leave and both he and Trevor, who was in the TA, obtained permission to wear their uniform at the funeral (the permission was necessary because the IRA was very active and soldiers were high risk targets). Although deeply saddened by the passing of her father, Joyce was made to feel immensely proud as her two big sons walked behind and saluted the coffin as it was unloaded.

After the funeral and when left alone, Joyce had time to consider all that her father had achieved in his life, how he had won medals in the war but never boasted about it – he'd left them to Trevor and Kevin, who treasured the gift enormously – and how he had taught her sons how to be men. Her dad had more than taken the place of their absent father, he'd improved on what Ken might have done with them, she believed. Trevor was now happily married, Kevin making great progress towards a career in the army. They'd be alright. As would her brother Douglas. After he'd suffered so much through his service, he was now relatively contented and still working for Sainsbury's, close by and always in easy contact with her.

Joyce was grateful to work with so many nice people. In the years that followed her father's death she continued as the favoured bedder at the lodge, and couldn't see any reason to leave. That was until the master told her that he was moving on. Unable to imagine what working for a new master might be like, Joyce resigned and left the lodge even before the master and his family. She applied for and got a position at the lovely Eaden Lilley department store in town just as the summer term came to an end. As the May Balls began, Joyce was at work helping to open a new restaurant at the store called The Green House. It was named for the fact that the entrance stood on Green Street, but there were plenty of flowers around the place, too. Funny, she thought, that a flower bulb led me to bedding and, now I've left, flowers are all about me again.

Although Joyce never again worked as a bedder nor at a college, after retiring she spent thirteen very happy years as a volunteer at the world-famous Fitzwilliam Museum on Trumpington Street, the building surrounded by university houses, rooms and faculties. More than once over the years, while sitting quietly in a room at the museum, someone would approach her and ask if she was, by any chance, Joyce, who used to be a bedder . . .

AUDREY

With two children under the age of three, Audrey had to cut down on the number of customers she could do at home, and the family needed another way to make extra cash. They weren't the only ones having money trouble at the time, of course. It was 1974 and the coal miners were striking. The Tory government introduced a three-day working week in January, in order to save what little coal the country's industry had until the prime minister Ted Heath could get the miners to accept his terms (which they never did). With reduced working hours came reduced wages, especially in the nationalized industries like the Post Office.

That summer, after the three-day week had ended, a few of Barry's mates discovered that if they had a spare room there was money to be had from the growing number of language schools springing up around the place. Since most of them had no 'spare' room, strictly speaking, they were renting their children's bedrooms, dining or living rooms for cash, cramming everyone else into other rooms. Barry suggested to Audrey that if they had a spare room they could do likewise next year, and she agreed. She was all in favour if it meant that she could have the new Indesit front loader washing machine she had her eye on. That would make her job a lot easier with the amount of towels from hairdressing she had to wash, as well as the kids' nappies. Barry would never buy anything 'on the knock', so she needed the cash that a lodger would bring in.

Their second child was also a girl, who they'd named Paula. Barry continued to drink heavily, but a little surprisingly he proved to be a 'fantastic father' to their two daughters, as Audrey told her regulars when they came for highlights or a perm. 'He reads to Nadine and Paula every night and makes them laugh,' she said almost proudly. 'He's brilliant, and they love him.' It was a reminder of why she had fallen in love with him. 'He's got a good sense of fun has my Barry, and is quite intelligent really. It's just the drink that spoils him.'

Barry's caring for the girls allowed Audrey time in the evenings of that winter to do extra work, but because of the babies she couldn't have customers round to the house for hairdos. Instead, she found work at the colleges doing silver service waitressing. Barry didn't object, telling her that as long as she was bringing money in and it didn't interfere with his life, he didn't mind. When he began shift work, which included nights, he didn't want women coming in for hairdos when he was trying to sleep during the day, either, nor when it was teatime. So Audrey worked her appointments around him and the children's naps, mostly in the mid-afternoons, and went out in the evenings when she had work at a college.

College waitressing sometimes involved serving between eight and ten courses in an evening, and it was hard work, but she usually found it interesting, especially when weird food was being served.

'The food is amazing,' she told Barry, 'the money that they must spend! They had quails' eggs tonight and I didn't even know what the tiny little things were. I'd never seen them before, have you?'

Audrey worked a lot of large reception dinners at colleges, many of them medieval-style banquets. She noticed that there were rarely any students present, though, which she thought was odd, until she realized that the guests were paying a lot of money to be in the big halls, eating at long refectory tables surrounded by oil paintings of important people from history, and wouldn't have appreciated the company of students.

The waitressing sometimes left scars on her, though. 'Oh Audrey, what have you done?' one of her hairdressing customers asked one afternoon, pointing to her forearms.

'It's nothing,' she replied matter-of-factly, 'just burns from carrying ten plates that were hot the other night. The heat goes straight through the napkins, especially from the great big silver trays, but it's not too bad.'

Work wasn't the only source of painful incident at the time, which proved to be the most trying period of her marriage.

Despite Audrey's extra earnings (she even made some money in tips) and Barry's shift work paying better, prices seemed to be going up daily, even food was costing more and more. There never seemed to be enough money at the end of the week for anything but the basics – which included Barry's beer, naturally. Despite being a wonderful dad, he was still sometimes an abusive husband, but Audrey wouldn't take a slap or two without retaliation. They tried to keep their rows away from the kids, which they managed to do since most happened when he came back from the pub late at night. Their set-tos never roused the kids from their sleep even though they'd shout, swear and hit each other. Neither ever caused any more than superficial damage to the other either, and Audrey was used to passing off her scratches and bruises as accidents, if the kids asked – although she always told friends and family the truth about their cause.

The family struggled through into the autumn with a slight lessening of tension between them. With money tight Barry drank a little less, and the arguments became fewer as the nights got longer until, one winter's evening in late 1974, Barry was shaken by an experience he wouldn't ever forget.

It was the usual mayhem in their house at bedtime, and he was trying to read the girls a story before they went to sleep, when Nadine grabbed the book and ripped it up in a fit of anger. Barry blew up and took every one of her books out of her room, shouting at her that she wasn't going to get any of them back until she'd learned to look after them. They were yelling at each other as Audrey tidied the kitchen when she heard a knock at the front door.

Audrey wasn't sure at first whether to console Nadine or see who was calling, but knowing that Barry wouldn't have wanted her to get involved in their spat, she answered the door. She was slightly surprised to find two policemen outside, and asked immediately if the neighbours had complained about the noise, and if so she was sorry, but their daughter was having a tizzy.

'No madam, it's not that,' one of them interrupted her. 'We all have problems at bedtime with kiddies, don't we? Actually it's a lot more serious than that.'

Audrey folded her arms and stood in the doorway, denying them entry or much of a view past her, trying to work out what Barry had done that might be classed as 'serious'.

'Well?' she asked, hardening her voice.

'Well, we've had an anonymous call to say that your husband, Barry Woolard, could be the Cambridge Rapist.'

Audrey felt a sense of relief wash over her.

'Your husband is described as being about five feet six, with dark hair. Is that correct?' The officer continued in a deep, serious voice without waiting for a response. 'He is often seen out and about at odd hours, and in areas of previous attacks. All of which matches with our descriptions and sightings of the sex attacker.'

Audrey was aware that behind her an unusual hush had fallen in the house and that the eyes of Barry and Nadine were trained on her back. She opened her mouth to speak, but then threw her head back and howled with laughter. She couldn't stop and was soon gasping for breath, leaning against the door frame for support. The policemen looked on in astonishment.

'Madam,' the deep-voiced copper half-shouted, 'we have had all sorts of reaction to this sort of inquiry, but we have never had anyone laugh.' Audrey was doubled up in pain from laughing so hard, but struggled to say, 'You haven't met him yet!' After another spluttering laugh, she tried to calm herself, took a deep breath and continued. 'Please, my husband is not the Cambridge Rapist.'

Once she'd managed to control her hysteria, Barry came downstairs, got his jacket and obligingly accompanied the officers to the station for questioning. Audrey managed to settle the children, who had become infected by their mother's hysterical laughter, and sat down to wait for Barry's return. While she was convinced, like the police, that the rapist – who the papers called the 'Beast of Bedsit Land' after carrying out horrific rapes on women living alone – had to be a local man, she knew it was not her husband. When Barry eventually returned from the station, it was clear that he'd stopped at the pub on the way home, but he was still very shaken by the incident.

Not long after that night, just before Christmas, Barry suggested that perhaps they should move house, and try to get a place with three bedrooms so that they could let one in the summer. Audrey readily agreed since she still wanted that Indesit, and was able to arrange a transfer to a recently built three-bedroomed place on Wycliffe Road quite quickly. They moved into the brand new house, and on an estate that had many young families among its residents, in March 1975.

The only downside of the move for Audrey was that it meant that she lost her regular customers. The older ones were not going to travel to her, and it was going to be too much to start a mobile hairdressing business with two small children to look after, she thought. So she carried on with the waitressing and got to know her new neighbours and, three months later, rented out the third bedroom to a German student. This embarrassed Barry, who didn't know how to behave around her because of her nationality. But it went so well that when she moved out in July, they took on another student named Witty, who was originally from Venezuela.

Witty had intended to stay for at most three months, but decided to stay indefinitely, partly because of how much she liked being with the Woolards. She quickly became practically a member of the family, and the regular money she paid them meant that they could start to think about saving for a deposit on a house of their own. They'd be able to buy somewhere once Audrey found some more work – any work – Barry suggested. Nadine was at school and Witty could collect her and pick up Paula from the childminder, feed them and even bath and put them to bed some days, although she had to get a job as the autumn began in order to pay her rent.

Audrey couldn't face traipsing around the town's hairdressing salons looking for work, she'd been her own boss for too long and would need training to work with the new dryers and equipment that was being used. She needed a job that would have regular hours, preferably allow her to be home for the kids' dinner, and be relatively secure.

Which is why she went to visit Bertha Mizen. She'd felt vaguely guilty that she hadn't since Aunty Maud's funeral, as she tried to explain when she and Bertha were seated in the gyp room at the college where Audrey had spent Saturdays helping Maud.

Despite feeling the shock of the familiar, she wasn't exactly eager to be there, especially since the reason for her visit was to ask about a job as a bedder. It wasn't her idea, but Barry's. 'I ain't being rude, my mum did it, Aunty Maud did it, but I never thought it would be my calling, you know,' she had told him when he suggested it. But when his basic wage was cut, Barry had to work seventy hours a week to bring in a wage that was anywhere near adequate.

Audrey explained to Bertha, 'The thing is, Barry's working all hours, we've got a lodger but we want to save, you know, for our future. I can't do the hairdressing from home. I would only have time to do a couple of haircuts and that wouldn't earn me enough.'

Bertha told her that she knew one of the small colleges needed a bedder, but there weren't any jobs going at hers. 'Leave it with me though,' she promised, 'I'll get you sorted, don't you worry.'

Bertha would help if she could, even though she was worried that Audrey wouldn't like being told what to do by the housekeeper at the smaller college, who had a reputation for not taking any nonsense from the young 'uns – she was well known to not like employing young bedders and Audrey was still not yet thirty years old.

As it turned out, Audrey was seen by the housekeeper only a few weeks after she'd asked about a job. One of the older women had fallen and broken her hip, which meant they needed someone urgently. Although the housekeeper told Audrey that it was against her better judgement to hire her, she had little choice and Bertha had given her a very strong reference, so she was hired. But just as Bertha feared, within a few weeks Audrey was finding it difficult working her staircase under the watchful eye of the housekeeper.

'Bloody hell, Bertha, she's bleeding crazy,' Audrey told her when she popped in to see the old woman on her way home. 'She's always turning up when I'm trying to clean. I'll turn round and she's there, like a bloody ghost. I don't hear her coming. I reckon she creeps on tip-toe, trying to catch me doing I don't know what.'

'That's 'cos you're not much older than the boys,' Bertha told her, 'she don't like it. She's lost a lot of bedders during her time there and I was worried that you might tell her where to go.'

'It's alright, Bertha,' Audrey reassured her, 'I need the work. It's not like I'm fraternizing with the students. I just like talking to them and they like talking to me. It's dull otherwise.'

Bertha laughed, 'Your Aunt Maud liked it too. Well, in the beginning, at least.'

'It was different for Maud, though, she didn't really have anything else, did she?' Audrey knew that wasn't strictly true, because she had her and they had each other. And then she realized in that moment how much she missed Maud, and that she hadn't stopped to think about her for too long now. In fact, she hadn't the time for anything other than the children and working, it seemed. When Barry was on night shifts she was able to do some hairdressing after teatime, and she'd made a few friends around Wycliffe Road, but that gave her even less time to think about anything other than working and the children.

Audrey kept her temper and tongue in check at college when around the housekeeper, and as long as she worked hard and no students complained about her, she knew that the job would provide a steady and predictable income for them. She always got on well with her students and, like Maud had taught her, only talked to those who made the effort to engage her in conversation first.

At home she found a rhythm to their week that allowed her Saturday afternoons to herself. She didn't have any hairdressing customers, Barry would take the girls out all over Cambridge if the weather was good, and occasionally to the ex-servicemen's club if it wasn't, and the housework was all done. That was when she began to experiment with cooking, creating unusual meals that were inspired at least in part by the dishes that she'd seen while waitressing (which she still did a bit of, during term times). Her cooking became a subject of conversation with some of her friendlier students.

'So Audrey, what are you making this weekend?' one of her favourite students asked her one Friday.

'I've been learning how to make a curry from scratch,' she told him. 'My friend Mary's married to an Asian chap and he's been teaching me. We've got friends coming over this Saturday for dinner, and it's going to take me all day, I reckon.'

The student asked her to, 'Bring some of that curry in for us, if there's any left over,' and Audrey promised she would. She had grown fond of these three particular young men on her staircase. They seemed like ordinary boys, not too dissimilar to the Cambridge town boys she'd known when younger.

She'd been working at the college for two years when the boys who loved her curry began to play a record that she liked hearing, by Steve Forbert. She'd ask them to leave their door open so that she could hear it while working on the stairs or in nearby rooms, which they did. It became a regular thing for them to turn it up as she worked her way along the hall, and no one objected. However, one day the housekeeper happened along the hallway, holding her hands to her ears. She slammed the boys' door closed and approached Audrey with a furious look on her face. 'What do you think you're doing? You are here to work, not have a good time!'

Audrey stopped vacuuming and looked the older woman in the eye. 'There's nothing wrong with a bit of music while you work, you know,' she said with barely concealed anger.

'There is when you work here, missy, so I'll have no more of it, do you hear?'

'You're right.' Audrey stood the vacuum cleaner against the wall and began to undo her pinafore. 'You'll have no more of it from me, 'cos I'm leaving. Find another slave, why doncha.' With that she left, with the housekeeper staring after her, angry, mute and confused, as Audrey walked out of the college.

Two days after she had walked out, there was a knock at Audrey's front door. When she answered it she found the three students from her staircase, one holding the Steve Forbert LP and the others a case of wine.

'How ever did you find me?' she asked.

'We just asked "Where's Audrey?" and demanded to know what she had done to you. She had to tell us where you lived otherwise, well . . . she knows she was out of turn.'

'That's lovely, but . . . I can't ask you in, my husband's upstairs, sleeping. He's been on a night shift. But I am really touched. Thank you.'

'No problem, we just wanted you to know that we're sorry if we caused you to have to leave. We liked having you around. You're a damn sight better than that angry housekeeper.'

'Don't be daft, it was a pleasure.'

Audrey was genuinely touched by their visit and generosity. She thanked them, wished them luck and closed the door, wondering how she was going to keep this from Barry. He would be furious if he knew three young men had paid her a visit and come bearing gifts. He'd question their intentions and probably try to raise a hand to her. Best if he doesn't find out, she thought, and so put the LP in among their own and hid the crate of wine at the back of the pantry.

Much to Audrey's surprise, three weeks later the housekeeper rang her to ask if she could clean one of the college houses for her, and take it on as a permanent job. The old woman told her that she could have the children at work with her if she needed to during the holidays, because the job wouldn't only be in term time. Audrey was so surprised that she said yes without asking any questions, not least of which would have been why her – the housekeeper didn't seem to like her at all. Audrey could only think that she appreciated her hard work.

The house was close to the Catholic Church on Hills Road and was a huge Edwardian place that housed half a dozen or so third-year students. Audrey started that week, and was delighted to discover that she'd be alone. She was the only cleaner in the house and didn't have to worry about the housekeeper (or anyone else from the college) turning up to see what she was up to. The hours were perfect, too. She could start after 9 a.m. and finish just after 1 p.m., which allowed her enough time to take the children to school and pick them up.

Barry was so pleased that she was back at work and happy that he saved up secretly and bought a new bike for her birthday that year. Just like her mum had, Audrey cycled everywhere on her Raleigh with its big basket. For a couple of weeks, that is, until it was stolen.

Barry was furious when she told him it had gone. 'Well, you'll have to get the bus, 'cos I'm not getting you another one,' he told her before slamming the door behind him on his way to the pub.

That isn't a problem, she thought, I'll just get the 102 or 133 again. Which she did, for a month, until she was forced to give the job up.

Audrey collapsed while at work one morning, and fainted clean away. A couple of students took her to hospital.

'She's exhausted,' the doctor told Barry when he arrived an hour later. The doctor pointed out to her husband that Audrey had been running their home, hairdressing whenever she could, working evenings in the colleges doing silver service and bedding every day – cleaning the equivalent of six or seven flats. The doctor warned that Audrey – indeed any woman – couldn't be expected to do as much and continue to be healthy. He suggested that the pair of them rethink their lives, and quickly.

When the doctor asked Barry how his health was, because he looked tired and slightly yellow, Barry became worried. After a lecture on the perils of drinking too much, a shaken Barry realized that while Audrey had been working all the hours God sent, he was drinking their money away and it wasn't doing anyone any good, not least himself.

When she was strong enough to hear it, the doctor strongly warned Audrey about doing too much and what the consequences of carrying on as she had would be. 'Think of your children if not yourself,' he told her, which really hit home.

When she was allowed home after several days of rest and recuperation, the first thing Audrey did was to ring the college housekeeper and quit her job as a bedder for the second and – she hoped – final time.

Feeling determined, but also a little sad as she put the phone down, Audrey had a sudden, vivid memory of her mother and Maud, laughing their heads off as they cycled side by side to work at the college – the sky was clear, the air cold and she could feel frost on her cheek as she pressed against the window, wanting to see them for as long as she could before they turned the corner and disappeared. They seemed, in that far away time, to be so happy together, to have found something in their job that they couldn't find at home, something that was so very different from their otherwise normal day-to-day existence. Back then, Audrey recalled, she had wanted whatever they had, which was why she had loved going with them to work as a bedder when she was a child.

Happy times, she thought, so long gone.

Acknowledgements

While the stories in this book are all true, some of the extraordinary women who shared their memories of life as a bedder asked to remain anonymous, and so we have changed names and in some instances dates in order to honour their wishes.

The greatest thanks go to all of them, and to the following Barnwell bedders: Joyce, Audrey, Doreen, Brenda, Jane and Gladys. A huge gratitude also has to go to the following women who started this journey with me in 2008: Margaret Granger, then a housekeeper, provided me with access into her college so I could see first-hand again the world of the bedder, and to Maggie Brown and Christine Snare for allowing me to follow them during their bedmaking routines for my 2008 film *The Bedders*. The help from Cambridgeshire Collection was integral in the early stages of research. In a small room in their temporary home at Milton Road Library, I was provided with absolutely everything that had ever been reported or written about bedmakers and landladies. Thank you also goes to Malcolm Underwood, the (now retired) archivist of St John's, who in 2008 provided me with access to servant records and also put me in contact with the late Rachel Wroth, who kindly shared with me her fascinating research on college servants. More recently, along with St John's, the Trinity archives have also been a great source of research: from servants' pay records of the nineteenth and twentieth century to minutes of meetings, they gave me a greater insight into the history of the bedder.

Thank you must also go to the Sidney Sussex chaplain who, on the day of my Aunt Shirley's funeral, told me that the stories about bedders like her and other extraordinary women should be told in a documentary, which was where the journey began. An even bigger thank you goes to all of my family and friends who have supported me, among them Marc Atkinson and Katie Barlow, who helped me with the filming and editing of my film.

It was no easy feat putting on *The Bedders* at the Cambridge colleges, where I wanted the gown to meet the town. After it was seen only by the Cambridge community of bedders during the 800th anniversary celebrations of the university, I approached The Museum of Cambridge and asked if they would hold an event, to which they agreed. It was a great success, and I have to thank Tamsin Wimhurst and her colleagues for providing me with a forum for people to share their experiences of working as a bedder and having a bedder work for them. Mal also has to thank Tamsin and Mike for the loan of their writer's retreat in Norfolk, while thanks are due from me to the Venables, the Millers and Debbie for a summer spent writing at their homes in Devon and Cornwall.

Thank you to the staff at the East Barnwell Community Centre for providing us with the space to hold an afternoon tea for the retired bedders of Barnwell, so that they could reconnect and reminisce.

In this book, Rose Hobbs and Maud Cooper are created from various tales told to me about bedders and their lives, by women who knew people like them. There was a wonderful neighbour of my nana's named Ruby, and stories of her and my nana's friendship were told to me by my mum. Audrey also had an 'aunty'. But Maud and Rose's lives, as portrayed here, are only representative of the experiences of several women who lived in Cambridge and worked as bedders during the period of 1940 to 1980.

In the early 1990s I interviewed my late Nana Adams for an A-level English project, and it was then that I started writing a play based on her life and her work. I thankfully kept the transcript of this interview, so the life of Ann 'Nance' Adams née Pilcher is more or less true to the memory and knowledge of her time, as it was told to me by her and by different members of my immediate and extended family, to whom I am eternally grateful. Similarly, Audrey and Joyce's stories reflect to the greater part the reminiscences of both women, although they include aspects of reimagined conversation and situations. Enormous gratitude goes to the women who shared their memories with us, and I hope that in reading this book you get an idea of how these remarkable people lived, loved, suffered and enjoyed their time working at one of the world's most famous educational institutions.

Thanks to Ingrid Connell at Pan Macmillan for recognizing the potential in relating the stories of what is an almost criminally neglected group of working-class women, who spent their lives making sure that the ruling classes of England got their beds made, their fireplaces cleaned and their gyp rooms tidied. Thanks also to Zennor Compton at Pan Macmillan for her help in shaping the book.

Bibliography

Elliott, Chris and *Cambridge Evening News*, *Cambridge: The Story of a City* (Breedon Books, 2001)

Hayman, Ronald (ed.), *My Cambridge* (Robson Books, 1977)

Holbrook, Margot, *Where Do You Keep? Lodging the Cambridge University Undergraduate* (Capella Archive, 2006)

Parker, Rowland, *Town and Gown: The 700 Year War in Cambridge* (Patrick Stephens, 1983)

Payne, Sara, *Down Your Street: Cambridge Past and Present* (The Pevensey Press, 1983)

Petty, Mike and *Cambridge Evening News*, *Memory Lane Cambridge* (Breedon Books, 1999)

Stubbings, Frank, *Bedders, Bulldogs & Bedells: A Cambridge Glossary* (Cambridge University Press, reprint, 2001)

Zanders, Rosemary, *The Cambridge Book of Days* (The History Press, 2011)

extracts reading groups
competitions books new
discounts extracts
competitions
books new
events books
extracts
new reading groups
interviews
discounts
new books events
events new
discounts extracts discounts
www.panmacmillan.com
extracts events reading groups
competitions books extracts new